"OLD WADDY'S COMING!"

The Military Career of Brigadier General James S. Wadsworth

by
John F. Krumwiede

Wadsworth's Gettysburg Monument at Dawn

(Personal photograph)

"OLD WADDY'S COMING!"

The Military Career of Brigadier General James S. Wadsworth

[signature: JF Krumwiede]

by
John F. Krumwiede

February 2, 2003

First Edition
Butternut and Blue
2002

Copyright 2002 by John F. Krumwiede

No part of this book may be reproduced in any form or by any means without the written consent of the publisher

ISBN 0-935523-86-3

Printed in the United States of America on acid-free paper.

Published in 2002
as the thirty-first volume of
the *Army of the Potomac Series*

by

Butternut and Blue
3411 Northwind Road
Baltimore, MD 21234
410-256-9220

Dedication

For Doris, my number one fan

CONTENTS

List of Illustrations i

List of Maps ii

Acknowledgments iii

    Prologue iv

    1. The War Begins 1

    2. Military Governor 12

    3. The Chancellorsville Campaign 19

    4. The Gettysburg Campaign 34

    5. Between Battles 83

    6. The Wilderness Campaign 88

    Epilogue 119

    James Wadsworth Remembered 122

A. Commands of James S. Wadsworth 125

B. Wadsworth and Doubleday at the Railroad Cut 130

C. Burial in the Wilderness 136

D. Wadsworth, NV 89442 140

Endnotes 145

Bibliography 171

Index 185

ILLUSTRATIONS

Wadsworth's Gettysburg Monument at Dawn .... Frontispiece

Official Party at Gettysburg Monument Dedication vi

James S. Wadsworth Wearing Grandfather's Sword 5

Wadsworth and Staff at Brigade Headquarters, Upton's Hill 9

Major General Abner Doubleday 20

Major General John F. Reynolds Congratulates Wadsworth 29

Wadsworth's Gettysburg Monument 47

Major Andrew Jackson Grover 50

14th Brooklyn's Gettysburg Monument 53

Lieutenant Colonel F. C. Miller and Major George Harney 54

Captain W. P. Carter's Battery on Oak Hill 64

Colonel Charles S. Wainwright 76

Major General John Newton 78

First Lieutenant Clayton E. Rogers 82

Wadsworth Portrait Taken in Louisville 84

Brigadier General Lysander Cutler 105

James Wadsworth's Wilderness Monument 111

Plague on Wadsworth's Wilderness Monument 112

Wadsworth's Geneseo Gravesite 117

Colonel Rufus R. Dawes 133

MAPS

First Corps's march to U. S. Ford, May 2, 1863 32

The 76th New York refuses its right flank, July 1, 1863 49

Meredith attacks Archer along McPherson Ridge 57

Attack on Davis's Brigade at the Middle Cut 58

Baxter and Cutler repel O'Neal and Iverson on Oak Ridge 66

Pettigrew's and Brockenbrough's attack 68

Pender's brigades assault the First Corps's Seminary line 70

Griffin's and Wadsworth's Divisions collide with Ewell's Corps,
  May 5, 1864 93

Wadsworth's Division strikes Heth's left, May 6, 1864 99

Longstreet assaults Hancock's columns 102

Longstreet assaults Birney's left 109

ACKNOWLEDGMENTS

I wish to express my appreciation to Richard E. Matthews for his initial guidance and support and to Wayne E. Motts for the FNMPG's Research Seminar. Eric J. Mink, NPS; Natalie J. Siembor and the Oswego County Historical Society; Eric N. Moody, Nevada Historical Society; plus John Heiser and Darrell L. Smoker, GNMP Library, provided critical information. During the past three years valuable assistance was also received from Dr. Richard J. Sommers, David H. Keough and the Military History Institute's Library, Photographic and Manuscript Archives. The State Historical Society of Wisconsin; Linda Showalter, Marietta College; and Carol Krogan, Vernon County Historical Society proved to be excellent sources of information on Wisconsin's regiments and personalities. Lawrence Turner, Kalina K. Anderson, Daniel D. Lorello, Judith A. Bushnell, and Donald C. Pfanz were kind enough to answer requests for help.

PROLOGUE

Gettysburg, October 6, 1914

Monday, October 5, 1914, veterans from New York began arriving in Gettysburg by train. Wearing regulation blue and Grand Army caps, they represented the four infantry regiments and Battery L, First New York Light Artillery that served under Brigadier General James S. Wadsworth during the Battle of Gettysburg. Members of the 102nd and 104th New York, associated with Wadsworth before 1863, were also coming. With rail transportation furnished by the State, these survivors were invited to the dedication of their general's monument. Events leading up to the next day's ceremony began four years earlier when $10,000 was appropriated to procure and erect a bronze statue.[1]

The New York Monuments Commission and Gettysburg National Park Commission agreed October 27, 1911, on a site east of Reynolds Avenue and north of the 147th New York's monument. The Monuments Commission accepted a full-size, plaster model of the statue April 16, 1913, and awarded a contract to the Gorham Company for a bronze casting. A contract to fabricate the granite pedestal was issued May 19 and the completed work accepted July 3. After reviewing and approving site drawings, the Monuments Commission authorized Colonel Lewis R. Stegman to proceed with erection. A February 2, 1914, letter to Colonel John P. Nicholson formally requested the Park Commission and Secretary of War to approve the site, monument design, and drum inscription. The parties ultimately reached agreement. Charles Lady of Gettysburg constructed the foundation upon which the pedestal and statue were put in place August 4 for a fall dedication.[2]

Tuesday proved to be a typical Indian summer day. Led by the Grand Marshall, General John A. Reynolds, First New York Light, and Troops L and M, Fifth U. S. Cavalry, the column departed the Gettysburg Square at 2:00 PM. Continuing down Springs Road, the veterans followed in wagons flying divisional and brigade flags along with regimental and battery pennants. They were greeted at the monument with a salute fired by the York Provisional Battery. A crowd of approximately 2,000 watched the general's great grandchildren, Jeremiah and Evelin Wadsworth, unveil the statue. Sitting in the front row were son, James W., and grandson, James W., Jr., United States Senator elect from New York. The

5th Cavalry's Band and a local citizen's ensemble provided appropriate music.³

Albert M. Mills gave the oration. He had fought at Gettysburg as a captain, 8th New York Cavalry, Colonel William Gamble's Brigade, Brigadier General John Buford's First Cavalry Division. Mills's speech can be summarized in one sentence.

> From the beginning of the Civil War until mortally wounded in the Wilderness, James S. Wadsworth was continuously engaged in rendering valuable, varied, and courageous service to the Union cause.⁴

Official Party at Gettysburg Monument Dedication, October 6, 1914

Son, James W. (sixth from the right), and grandson, James W. Jr., U.S. Senator elect from New York (third from the right) are in the front row. (*In Memoriam*, courtesy, Daniel D. Lorello, New York State Archives)

CHAPTER 1

THE WAR BEGINS

"...Sorrow that he died, pride that he lived...."
Albert M. Mills[1]

In 1790 William and James Wadsworth left Connecticut and after several arduous weeks reached the Genesee River in Western New York. With commissions from the Federal Government, they divided and sold extensive land tracts. Settlers arrived and the brothers prospered, investing their earnings in the best tracts. The Wadsworth Farms soon became famous throughout the Genesee Valley and later the entire state.[2]

James married and established a family home in Geneseo, where his wife gave birth to two sons and three daughters. James Samuel, the second child and first son, arrived in 1807. His uncle William fought in the War of 1812 but remained a bachelor. Before dying in 1833, he bequeathed his share of the estate to brother James and the children. The Wadsworth fortunes continued to thrive and the family took several trips to Europe. Substantial funds were donated to Livingston County common or public schools and libraries. "Few country gentlemen in the United States...were better or more favorably known (than James Senior)."[3]

After attending Harvard for two years, James S. went on to Yale Law School for a year (1829-30) then worked briefly in the Boston office of Daniel Webster. Because of James Senior's declining health and the 1831 death of his mother and a sister, the eldest son came home "and gradually assumed the chief supervision of the family estates." He married Mary Craig Wharton May 11, 1834, and started a family: Charles F. 1836, Cornelia 1839, Craig 1841, Nancy 1843, James W. 1846, and Elizabeth 1848. Becoming quite skilled and knowledgeable, James S. was elected President of the State Agricultural Society in 1842.[4]

Two years later James Senior died at age 76. The eldest son now managed three-fourths of the estate, the portion belonging to him and his sisters. William, the younger brother, owned and controlled the remainder. "According to the standards of that time, he (James S.) would be regarded as a man of wealth." Like his father, the son gave considerable attention "to the welfare of others," gaining him the reputation of being a philanthropist. Learning of the 1847 Irish Famine, James sent a ship load of corn for distribution to the victims.[5]

At first a Democrat, anti-slavery feelings forced a change in his political loyalties. Unable to accept the views of Southern Democrats, Wadsworth helped to precipitate a split among New York Democrats and joined the 'Barnburner' Wing. The most progressive or liberal party members, who opposed the extension of slavery, became "Barnburners." Wadsworth served as a delegate to the 1848 state convention. Here, they voted to join the abolitionist Free-Soil movement. The nomination for Governor was offered by the Free-Soilers but he quickly declined. As word of his uncompromising views on slavery spread, Wadsworth became a popular target of those who either supported the institution or favored leaving it alone.[6]

Efforts to reunite the New York Democratic Party failed. An invitation to join the Republicans in 1856 was accepted by the 'Barnburners.' Nominated for Governor, Wadsworth lost at the convention but later ran as a presidential elector for Fremont. Friction now openly developed between the Republican Party's two blocs: Whigs and Democrats. The former favored William Seward for President in 1860; the latter, which included Horace Greeley and Wadsworth, ultimately supported Lincoln. Declining the nomination for governor, Wadsworth's name appeared on the ballot as a presidential elector. After Lincoln's victory, the "Van Buren Democratic, Buffalo Free-soil wing of the Republican Party" supported Horace Greeley and James Wadsworth as candidates to represent New York in Lincoln's cabinet. Seward swallowed his pride, however, and became Secretary of State. Greeley tried but failed to succeed him as United States Senator.[7]

Looking for a way to avoid war, Wadsworth agreed to serve as one of the eleven commissioners representing New York at the Washington Peace Convention. After nineteen days of debate, the convention failed and he returned to New York City. At this time, Wadsworth "was in the prime of his life" and had every reason "to remain at home and live his life in dignity and peace."[8]

Volunteer Aide-de-Camp

...and on the 16th (May 16, 1861) I appointed James S. Wadsworth, of Livingston County, to the other major-generalship, and immediately advised the Secretary of State of such selection....
Governor E. D. Morgan[9]

When Rebel guns fired on Fort Sumter, James Wadsworth was at his temporary residence in New York City. As a founding member of the city's Union Defense Committee, he became aware of a new problem facing the Federal Government. Destruction of railroad bridges and track north of Baltimore had isolated Washington. Chartered boats, using a water route to Annapolis, were now required to supply the Capital with troops and provisions. On April 20, 1861, Wadsworth hired the *Kill von Kull*, a side-wheel, ferry boat, in Elizabethport and brought it to New York City. After being loaded with tools, horses, supplies, and one hundred railway workers, the steamer departed April 25 and arrived safely in Annapolis two days later. The men finished track repairs started by Massachusetts troops and reestablished rail service between Annapolis and Washington. Provisions soon reached the Capitol lifting the 'siege'. At this time Wadsworth delegated personal affairs to others and offered his services to the Federal Government in any capacity deemed useful.[10]

Wadsworth's quick and effective action was soon rewarded. On May 17, 1861, Governor E. D. Morgan informed General in Chief of the Army Winfield Scott that New York had completed organizing twenty-five, two year regiments and steps were being taken to enroll an additional thirteen. The Governor assigned eight regiments to the Second Division whose commanding officer would be Major General James S. Wadsworth. On May 28 Morgan informed Secretary of War Simon Cameron of Wadsworth's appointment and requested his endorsement. The Secretary of War politely responded June 3 that appointments of this nature were reserved for the President and required Senate confirmation. Wadsworth refused Morgan's offer of a major general's commission. Nathaniel Banks, Republican governor of Massachusetts and Benjamin Butler, a Democrat and Massachusetts state senator, however, accepted Lincoln's offer. Both were appointed major general of volunteers May 16, 1861.[11]

Possessing a more realistic view of his qualifications, Wadsworth asked Brigadier General Irwin McDowell for an appointment as aide-de-camp. At this time McDowell, with headquarters at Arlington, commanded Federal forces south of the Potomac. Surprised that someone, ten years his senior, wanted to serve as an aide, the general reluctantly agreed. On July 8, the white-haired, gentleman-farmer joined his staff. The new aide, lean and active with side-whiskers framing a narrow face, reported for duty wearing a sword that his grandfather had carried in the Revolutionary War. As events later unfolded, McDowell never regretted this decision. The war's first major battle was less than two weeks away.[12]

First Bull Run

> *My volunteer aide-de-camp, Major Wadsworth, staid at Fairfax Court-House till late in the morning (July 22), to see that the stragglers and weary and worn-out soldiers were not left behind... Maj. James S. Wadsworth [who does me the honor to be on my personal staff] had a horse shot under him in the hottest of the fight.*
>
> Brigadier General Irvin McDowell[13]

In early July, twenty miles separated McDowell's command of 30,000 from a Confederate force of 22,000, camped near Manassas and led by Brigadier General Pierre G. T. Beauregard. General Scott requested and later approved McDowell's "plan of operations against Manassas," an important railroad junction. Scott promised that Brigadier General Joseph E. Johnston's 11,000 enemy troops in the Shenandoah Valley would be "kept off McDowell's flank." A combination of newspapers crying "On to Richmond" and an inexperienced president bowing to public opinion forced McDowell to depart Arlington and advance into Virginia.[14]

The plan McDowell developed was simple and almost succeeded. While feinting an attack on the Confederate center, a second column would march north, swing around, and strike Beauregard's left flank. To accomplish this McDowell organized the army, largely three month militia, into five divisions. No one, neither the commanding general nor any of his five subordinates, had ever commanded a division before. Daniel Tyler led one of them. Sixty-two years old and a West Point graduate, Class of 1819, he had previously left the army in 1834. Now a brigadier general of Connecticut volunteers, Tyler did not accept either directions or orders well. The coming campaign would be his first experience in the field.[15]

Saturday evening, July 20, McDowell called the division commanders together at Centreville, Virginia, gave them orders for the next day, and

Brigadier General James S. Wadsworth

General Wadsworth is seen here wearing his grandfather's sword from the Revolutionary War. (Courtesy, Mass. Commandery, MOLLUS; Copy from U.S. Army Military History Institute)

emphasized the need to move units as scheduled. The advance would begin promptly at 2:00 AM. Two days earlier, a brigade from Tyler's Division launched an unauthorized attack at Blackburn's Ford. Brigadier General James Longstreet's Virginians pushed them back and Richmond claimed a Confederate success. McDowell later criticized Tyler for having precipitated this action.[16]

After the meeting, Major Wadsworth returned to his tent. Hearing the sound of an approaching horse, he stepped out and walked over to where the rider had halted. Not recognizing the officer, Wadsworth asked, "Who do you wish to see?" "I am the bearer of dispatches from General Scott to General McDowell," the rider replied. Seeing the stranger's hesitation to hand them over, Wadsworth introduced himself and learned that the courier was Lieutenant George A. Custer. After giving the documents to McDowell, Wadsworth returned and asked Custer for the latest Washington gossip. Hearing that everyone looked to the army for good news, the major said, "Well, I guess they will not have to wait much longer. The entire army is under arms and moving to attack the enemy today." Wadsworth invited Custer to dismount and have breakfast with him.[17]

Execution of the Federal plan did not go well Sunday morning. McDowell's plea for promptness seemed to be either ignored or forgotten. Daniel Tyler, possibly still smarting from the commanding general's rebuke, advanced his command so slowly down the Warrenton Turnpike that the two divisions behind him were delayed for over three hours. A victim of circumstances, McDowell narrowed his focus to the turning column and units engaged on the Turnpike. As a result, the army lost its commander. To speed up Tyler's three brigades – Colonel Erasmus D. Keyes's, Brigadier General Robert D. Schenck's, and Colonel William T. Sherman's – McDowell sent Wadsworth, who rode from bottleneck to bottleneck trying to untangle the congestion. Finally, the road was cleared. Colonel David Hunter's Second Division belatedly began its march toward the Sudley Spring Ford to turn the enemy's left, followed by Colonel Samuel P. Heintzelman's Third Division. McDowell and Wadsworth accompanied Hunter on his northward march.[18]

Tyler did not complete deployment across the Warrenton Turnpike until 6:30 AM. His batteries now opened fire on the Rebel lines. Initially, there was no reply, raising concerns about a Confederate attack at Blackburn's Ford. As Hunter's Division crossed Sudley Spring Ford, Mc-

Dowell observed Rebel troops moving north to attack them. He dispatched Wadsworth to Tyler with orders to press forward. Colonel Fitz John Porter's Brigade and one of Heintzelman's regiments engaged the enemy on Matthew's Hill. After several Federal assaults the Confederate line broke around noon. Hunter's and Heintzelman's men pushed across Young's Branch and drove the enemy south toward the Warrenton Turnpike. Sherman's and Keyes's commands forded Bull Run north of the Stone Bridge and followed the advance.[19]

On a range of hills immediately south of the Turnpike, the Confederates had posted several batteries with supporting infantry partially concealed in nearby woods. Forming line of battle across the foot of Henry House Hill, the Federals charged. Heintzelman's Division struck the Rebel center about 2:00 PM, forcing a retreat across the plateau. Wadsworth watched a brigade from Hunter's Division move forward. Seeing the 8th New York take a wrong turn, he rode to its head and corrected the mistake. No longer exposed to a flank fire, several companies charged toward the woods on their right. Unfortunately, Brigadier General Thomas J. Jackson's Brigade, positioned in a belt of trees to the southeast, opened fire on the advancing New Yorkers. The resulting panic ended the 8th New York's effectiveness as a fighting unit that day. The division's remaining eight regiments stood firm, however, and continued their drive toward the Henry House. Wadsworth brought orders from McDowell for Sherman's Brigade to leave the Turnpike and join Hunter's advance.[20]

One of Sherman's regiments, the 2nd Wisconsin, recorded that Major Wadsworth led them in a charge "to support a line closely engaged with the enemy." Hunter's Division now reached what became the Federal 'high water mark' for this battle. Confederate forces had been driven back over a mile and a half and appeared to be in complete disarray. The Warrenton Turnpike, west of the Stone Bridge, was under Union control. Steps were being taken to bring across additional troops and artillery. Shortly after 2:00 PM, Wadsworth felt that they "had won the field." He did not know, however, that the remainder of General Joseph E. Johnston's Valley Army had just arrived by rail at Manassas.[21]

McDowell ordered Captain James B. Rickett's and Charles Griffin's Batteries across Warrenton Turnpike to the top of Henry House Hill. After executing the order, they became the target of enemy artillery and rifle fire. Without warning, musketry suddenly opened at close range from the left. This fire came from a Confederate regiment mistakenly identified as a Federal unit. Hunter's troops guarding the battery's flanks began to waiver. Some regiments stood and fought while others started falling back down the hill. In spite of Wadsworth's efforts to secure additional infantry support, the Federal guns were captured. While guiding unsuccessful attempts to recapture them, he had his first horse shot from under him. Subjected to frontal and flank attacks, the Union center collapsed around 3:00 PM An organized retreat down the hillside degenerated into complete disorder that swept away three Federal divisions.[22]

Efforts to rally the troops failed. The resulting panic also ruled out any chance of taking a stand at Centreville. Wadsworth joined the army's retreat to Washington. Reaching Fairfax Court House after midnight, he had been in the saddle over eighteen hours. While assisting the wounded here, Wadsworth tried to secure a flag of truce with Confederate General Johnston. It would have permitted the removal of Federal wounded and burial of the dead. Unable to do so, the major rode on to Arlington. He reached McDowell's headquarters the afternoon of July 24. Impressed with his aide's service and performance at Bull Run, the general recommended to Lincoln that Wadsworth be promoted to brigadier general of volunteers.[23]

Upton's Hill

When he (Wadsworth) finally turned to depart, they bade him good bye in a melodious recall of "the days of auld lang syne," which brought "auld acquaintance" to the mind; and tears to the eyes of more than one.
John Harrison Mills, 21st New York[24]

James Wadsworth was appointed brigadier general of volunteers August 9. After receiving assurance from friends on McDowell's staff that a West Point graduate would be assigned as adjutant-general, he accepted the commission August 23. Craig, the second eldest son joined his father, serving as an aide. Four days later, Major General George B. McClellan assigned the new brigadier to the Department of the Potomac, commanding a brigade comprised of the 12th, 21st, 23rd, and 35th New York Volunteers with its headquarters at Arlington. October 3, this unit became the Second Brigade in McDowell's Division. The 20th New York State Militia, reorganized as the 80th New York Volunteers, joined the brigade in early November. Wadsworth never received a 'West Point adjutant.'[25]

THE WAR BEGINS

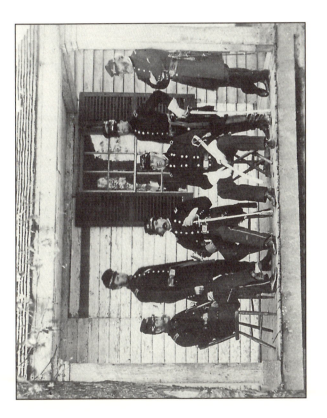

**Brigadier General James S. Wadsworth and Staff
at Second Brigade Headquarters on Upton's Hill, Late 1861**

Lieutenant Colonel John M. Sanderson (standing far right) and son, Captain Craig W. (standing second from right), were members of John F. Reynolds's Gettysburg staff. Lieutenant Colonel John Kress (standing second from left) served on Wadsworth's Gettysburg Staff. (Courtesy, Wayne Mahood and Wayne E. Motts, National Archives)

September 28, Federal pickets reported the withdrawal of enemy troops from Munson's and Upton's Hills. McDowell ordered Wadsworth's and Keyes's Brigades forward that evening to occupy Upton's Hill, a north-south ridge about one mile in length and four miles west of Arlington, Virginia. On the ridge's crest, they proceeded to strengthen abandoned fortifications and to establish picket lines three miles in advance. Approximately five miles farther west were the Confederate lines at Fairfax Court House. Brigadier General James E. B. Stuart's cavalry roamed at will in the intervening woodlands and became a serious threat to Federal outposts. Wadsworth made frequent trips to Falls Church, Virginia, a half mile west of Upton's Hill, to consult the regimental commander currently in charge of picket duty and to reconnoiter the unfriendly 'no man's land' between lines. He made personal reconnaissances not only to gain information regarding the enemy but to also locate forage at nearby farms. One such expedition almost became the last.[26]

November 8 Wadsworth, accompanied by two privates, rode down the road leading to Fairfax Court House. About three miles past Falls Church, the party stopped at the Brush farm to find forage. While eating lunch near the house, the general saw a squad of Confederate cavalry rapidly approaching. He quickly mounted his horse and escaped but the two soldiers, eating inside, were captured. This turned out to be the first and only time that Wadsworth "showed a clean pair of heels to the enemy."[27]

Using his own intelligence sources, which included scouts and fugitive slaves, Wadsworth projected enemy strength at Manassas and Centreville to be between forty and fifty thousand. Becoming more confident, he communicated his estimate to Generals McDowell and McClellan, and to Secretary of War Stanton. The New Yorker also urged McClellan to attack the enemy that winter. McClellan reported March 8, 1862, that Confederates forces in the Manassas-Centreville area numbered 80,000 men with three hundred field guns and twenty-six to thirty siege guns. Even though later evidence supported Wadsworth's estimate, McClellan did not appreciate either conflicting projections or advice from a 'Republican brigadier.'[28]

As 1862 began, Second Brigade mustered 3,504 men and their divisional commander considered them to be "well disciplined for volunteers." Sunday, March 9, 'all's quiet on the Potomac' abruptly ended. Near sunset, Wadsworth's outposts discovered the withdrawal of enemy pickets. At 5:00 AM the next day, the New Yorkers advanced through Fairfax Court House and established new camps two miles east of Centreville. While positioned here, word arrived that the Army of the Potomac had adopted a corps organization. On March 12, Second Brigade became part of Brigadier General Rufus King's Third Division, Major General Irvin McDowell's First Army Corps. A second order announcing that Brigadier General Marsena Patrick would replace Wadsworth had a greater impact on the men. The brigade assembled informally that afternoon to say good-bye. As the general mounted and moved into the road, he was surrounded by men trying to reach his hand. With tears in his eyes and a farewell speech of "Good bye, boys," Wadsworth departed to the strains of "Auld Lang Syne."[29]

CHAPTER 2

MILITARY GOVERNOR

He (Wadsworth) did not expect such a greeting (April 27), and indeed such a greeting is vouchsafed to but few men in the army.
William P. Maxon, 23rd New York[1]

In addition to creating five army corps, President Lincoln's General War Order No. 2 of March 8, 1862, appointed Brigadier General James S. Wadsworth Military Governor of the District of Columbia. The appointment caught many by surprise; some considered it rash. George McClellan preferred his friend, Brigadier General William Franklin, for the position. There is no evidence that Wadsworth wanted to leave the field but politics prevailed. In December 1861, Congress appointed a "committee on the conduct of the war with powers for gaining information first hand." December 26, James Wadsworth appeared before the new committee. The subsequent testimony and correspondence with its members strengthened his standing with the Radical Republicans. Stanton later told McClellan, "It (Wadsworth's appointment) was necessary, for political reasons, to conciliate the agricultural interests of New York."[2]

All forces left behind for the capital's defense would be under his command. To compensate for Wadsworth's lack of military experience, Stanton intended to bring Major General E. A. Hitchcock to Washington. Ethan Allen Hitchcock graduated from West Point in 1817, two years before Daniel Tyler. He resigned from the service in 1855 due to poor health. Winfield Scott insisted that Hitchcock be called back and the grandson of Ethan Allen was appointed major general of volunteers in February 1862. He went on to become an intimate of both Lincoln and Stanton. George McClellan relieved Wadsworth "from duty with his brigade" March 12, 1862, and told him to "report in person to the Hon. Sect. of War."[3]

The Military Governor's position was quasi-civil requiring an individual who would establish and maintain an acceptable balance between civil and military authorities. To clarify military responsibilities, General McClellan issued special and general orders. In addition to Washington, Wadsworth's military command included nearby defenses north and south of the Potomac, the District of Columbia, Alexandria, and Fort

Washington. The Military Governor also assumed care of all railways, canals, depots, bridges, and ferries within the specified limits.[4]

Responsibility for recruits arriving in the Capital plus all forces temporarily assigned there fell on Wadsworth. Soldiers not needed for either the city police or garrisons north of the Potomac were moved to the river's south side. This order reflected an assignment Wadsworth shared with Major General N. P. Banks, commander Fifth Corps. George McClellan vaguely defined it as covering the line of the Potomac and Washington. He also assigned top priority to rebuilding the railway from Washington to Bank's Headquarters at Manassas Junction. Like Wadsworth, Banks had no military experience and this would be his first field command. Unfortunately, Stonewall Jackson would lead the opposition.[5]

Wadsworth soon found that his duties covered a wide spectrum. On March 17 Stanton told him to seize the *Sunday Chronicle* because it published information about troop movements. Two weeks later Commissioner John A. Dix requested that Mrs. Rose O'Neal Greenhow and other prisoners be escorted into Virginia beyond Federal lines and released. What appeared to be a straight forward and reasonable order from the commanding general arrived April 1. McClellan directed Wadsworth to send at once four thousand troops from Washington to relieve Second Corps units at Manassas and Warrenton. An additional four regiments were removed from the District and assigned elsewhere. Subsequent events would show that McClellan's communiqué from the Steamer *Commodore* ignited a controversy that followed Wadsworth for the rest of his life.[6]

From a logistical standpoint, the most critical issue was getting relief troops to Manassas. After reviewing his forces, Wadsworth sent an April 2 telegram to Brigadier General Edwin 'Bull' Sumner, Second Corps commander, reporting that no regiments "really fit to move or go into the field" could be found. Sumner had been commissioned directly into the army the same year that Tyler graduated from West Point, 1819. He gained the nickname "Bull" when a musket ball supposedly bounced off his head. Seniority earned him a corps command. Recognizing its implications, Sumner immediately forwarded Wadsworth's telegram to McClellan while the Military Governor explained his action to Stanton.[7]

Wadsworth counted 19,000 men present and ready to defend Washington. Two days before McClellan reported 20,800 within the Military

District. Even though the totals were reasonably close, the interpretations that each general gave them were far apart. From Wadsworth's viewpoint, the Army's departing brigades left their worst regiments behind. These troops required training and discipline before they could effectively replace the units vacating the Capital's defenses. At that time General Banks was west of the Bull Run Mountains. This required Wadsworth's command to also defend the front from Manassas to Aquia Creek. Regardless of their qualifications, McClellan felt that sufficient troops and artillery had been left behind to secure both Washington and Manassas, thereby, fulfilling his commitment to Lincoln. To test the validity of Wadsworth's concerns, Stanton ordered a general alarm sounded. "It took three hours for 4,000 men to assemble, a good half of them without am-munition."[8]

Stanton instructed E. A. Hitchcock and Adjutant General Lorenzo Thomas to investigate the situation. They concluded that the forces left behind appeared to be "entirely inadequate" to carry out the President's March 13 directive to McClellan to leave Washington and Manassas secure. Recognizing the seriousness of the situation, Wadsworth went out April 4 and again inspected the forces under his command. He informed Stanton that there were no regiments "fit to take the field." The President reacted immediately. That afternoon he created the Departments of the Shenandoah and Rappahannock with Major Generals Banks and McDowell in command respectively. April 6 the Secretary of War telegraphed a belated explanation to the army commander saying that to secure the Capital, McDowell's First Corps must be held back. McClellan and his supporters later claimed that this act doomed the Peninsula Campaign to failure. Justified or not, many officers found Wadsworth's behavior unacceptable.[9]

Before departing, George McClellan had assured Stanton that 50,000 men would be "left around Washington." The actual total was less than 26,000, most of them untrained and ill-equipped recruits. Wadsworth did not have sufficient forces to defend the Capital. The evening of April 5 McClellan telegraphed Lincoln that "the loss of the First Corps imperiled his entire campaign." Historian Stephen Sears concluded that there was no "substance to McClellan's claim that holding back McDowell to guard Washington dislocated all his plans for getting the Peninsula campaign off to a fast start." James Wadsworth demonstrated both courage and intelligence when he took this controversial position.[10]

A more rewarding experience occurred Sunday, April 27. Not having seen his old command since March 12, Wadsworth decided to visit General Patrick at Falmouth. Brigade pickets recognized their white-haired general and raised the cry "Waddy's coming! Old Waddy's coming!" As general and staff galloped into camp, they were surrounded by officers and men swinging their caps and shouting, "Hurrah for General Wadsworth!" While a band played "Hail to the Chief," he leaned down and shook hands. As before, Wadsworth's efforts to hide his tears were unsuccessful. The participants never forgot that emotional afternoon.[11]

In late May Stonewall Jackson began his campaign to rid the Shenandoah of Federal forces. He drove Bank's army out of the valley and across the Potomac River. The resulting "great scare" ended Wadsworth's dual responsibilities of defending Washington while serving as its Military Governor. On June 18, the army was reorganized again. Stanton placed all forces in and around the Capital in a separate corps commanded by Brigadier General S. D. Sturgis. An 1846 graduate of West Point, Samuel Davis Sturgis fought in the Mexican War and several Indian campaigns. Recently appointed general, he strongly supported George McClellan. Wadsworth retained control of only those troops required to carry out his duties as Military Governor of Alexandria and the District of Columbia. At the end of June 1862, they numbered just under five thousand declining to four thousand in September.[12]

James Wadsworth openly favored the abolition of slavery throughout the nation. At this time, Lincoln sought to confine the institution by preventing its expansion into the western territories. This difference obviously affected their relationship. The Military-Governor provided quarters for escaped slaves or 'contrabands' from Virginia. The treatment of similar fugitives from Maryland, a Border State, proved to be more difficult. It was necessary to first determine whether a specific slave had escaped from a 'loyal' or 'disloyal master.' Wadsworth refused to return those belonging to owners with "secession sympathies." His behavior upset many slave-holders, particularly now that Congress had abolished slavery in the District of Columbia. The creation of a nearby 'safe haven' and repeated failures to recover 'lost property' drove them to the President's office.[13]

On May 19, 1862, a delegation of Maryland farmers and a few Congressmen met with Lincoln. They complained about Wadsworth establishing a rule that no Negro should be taken out of the District as stipulated by the Fugitive Slave Law. At this time the President wanted the

Border States to begin a policy of compensated emancipation. He made a commitment to the group that Marshal Ward H. Lamon would enforce the Fugitive Slave Law. Wadsworth became aware of the situation when Lamon's deputies began seizing run away slaves, many under the Military Governor's protection. Lamon took them before court-appointed commissioners who quickly returned the fugitives to their masters.[14]

Wadsworth had seen enough. Soldiers led by Lieutenant John A. Kress, an aide, seized the jail or 'slave-pen,' arrested the jailer and deputy marshal, and freed the captives. Lamon ran to the White House but Lincoln was out of town. He retaliated by recapturing the jail that night. On June 11, the President discussed the problem with Wadsworth and Lamon. Unable to reach agreement, the conflict between military and civil authority continued.[15]

In spite of the disagreement over slavery, both Lincoln and Stanton sought Wadsworth's advice on military and political issues. Eager to rejoin his brigade, the general reluctantly accepted their request to remain in Washington. By now Lincoln was considering emancipation in some form and would need Wadsworth's help in shaping public opinion. The Military Governor became concerned about Lincoln's personal safety and detailed a squad of cavalry to escort the President on his rides to and from the Soldier's Home. Lincoln later complained that the soldiers made such a clatter with their sabers and spurs that he and Mary "couldn't hear themselves talk." Popular or not, the escort continued.[16]

Concern over the coming fall elections brought politics to the forefront. With Governor Morgan finishing a second term, Secretary of State Seward and Thurlow Weed, the Republican's skillful and astute political manager, wanted to broaden the party's appeal in New York. To accomplish this, they proposed that Major General John Dix, a War Democrat and commandant of Fort Monroe, be a joint, Republican and Democratic nominee for governor. He would run as the new Union Party's candidate. The Democrats rejected both Dix and the idea of a temporary alliance. Instead they nominated Horatio Seymour who disliked Lincoln and emancipation. Representing the radical wing, Horace Greeley now forced Weed to reconsider and finally accept James Wadsworth as the nominee.[17]

Two years earlier, the general had declined the party's nomination in favor of Morgan. Now, a desire for field command and discouragement over Pope's defeat at Second Bull Run combined to make refusing to run the most attractive choice. In addition to Seymour's nomination, three events ultimately changed Wadsworth's mind. First, Lincoln's decision to proceed with emancipation was a pleasant surprise. Second, Stanton refused to release Wadsworth from his current assignment. Third, Thurlow Weed guaranteed an unanimous nomination. The Military Governor decided to reenter Empire State politics. Stanton favored a candidate that "stood foursquare against slavery." By refusing to give Wadsworth a field command, the Secretary of War most likely forced him to accept the nomination.[18]

At first, the Republican choice for governor was received with enthusiasm throughout New York. The political climate soon changed. George McClellan, a Democrat, strongly disliked Wadsworth for his abolitionist beliefs. He also remembered quite well how the general's actions that spring had upset his plans for the Peninsula Campaign. The army commander not only supported Seymour but openly attacked his opponent.

> I (George McClellan) must confess a double motive for desiring the defeat of Wadsworth. I have so thorough a contempt for the man & regard him as such a vile traitorous miscreant that I do not wish to see the great State of N. Y. disgraced by having such a thing at its head.[19]

George McClellan also weakened Wadsworth's Republican support. After Antietam, the Army of the Potomac slowly pursued Lee through Virginia with no apparent plans to fight before winter. Radical Republicans, upset with the army's inactivity, held Lincoln responsible because he retained McClellan in command. Retaining 'Little Mac' not only risked a low turnout among Republicans but could also induce protest votes against the Administration. The President realized that removing the general before election day, however, would aid the opposition by generating an outpouring of protest votes. Lincoln concluded that doing nothing was the lesser of two evils.[20]

Except for an October speech in New York City, Wadsworth remained on military duty. Under attack for his rigid stand on emancipation, lack of a military record, and support of the current administration, the general failed to generate enthusiasm anywhere. Seymour easily won November 4 with a majority of 10,752 votes. The next day Lincoln replaced McClellan with Ambrose Burnside. Anxiety then arose in some quarters that emancipation combined with McClellan's removal would lead to an army revolt, particularly among the officers. The President gambled and won that his deposed general would not attempt a coup d'état. Colonel Charles S. Wainwright, First Corps's Chief of Artillery, observed that "all the loose talk and threats came to nothing."[21]

After the election, Wadsworth requested a release from his current assignment and expressed a desire for active duty. Stanton agreed but could not find an opening for the general. A leave of absence was granted and on November 19, 1862, Brigadier General John H. Martindale became the District's new Military Governor. Unlike his predecessor, Martindale had a military education, graduating from West Point in 1835. Commissioned brigadier general of volunteers the same day as Wadsworth, he commanded a brigade throughout the Peninsula Campaign. After visiting his family, Wadsworth returned to the Capital and waited. News of the Fredericksburg defeat arrived and he went immediately to the front. Fortunately, his son Craig, now serving as an aide to Major General John F. Reynolds, commander First Corps, was not injured. Finding no need for his services, James Wadsworth returned to Washington.[22]

CHAPTER 3

THE CHANCELLORSVILLE CAMPAIGN

Second Bull Run became a disaster for both John Pope and Irvin McDowell. Disappointed by the battle's outcome, civilians and soldiers began to dislike McDowell as much as they did Pope. A target of recrimination, McDowell's personal valor and loyalty on the battlefield came under attack. He demanded a court of inquiry that convened in November 1862. Even though it ultimately ruled "the accusations of betrayal false," McDowell never received another field command and disappeared from the war. After two years of inactivity, he was assigned to the Department of the Pacific in July 1864 and departed for the Presidio. In time he became a close friend of Leland Stanford, a founder and later President of the Central Pacific Railroad.[1]

While testifying at McDowell's Court of Inquiry, Wadsworth received a December 16 order from Major General Burnside assigning him to the Left Grand Division, commanded by Major General William Franklin. On December 23 John Reynolds selected Wadsworth to succeed fellow New Yorker, Brigadier General Abner Doubleday, as First Division commander. Colonel Wainwright recorded his caustic reaction to the news.

> I know nothing of his (Wadsworth's) natural ability, but it ought to be very great, as he knew nothing of military matters before the war, is not a young man, and has had no experience in battle to entitle him to so high a position.

Thirteen years younger than his new division commander, John Reynolds never discussed Wadsworth in family correspondence. Reynolds's subsequent decisions at Chancellorsville and Gettysburg indicate an effective relationship between them. At the same time, things had not gone well for Abner Doubleday.[2]

Doubleday departed First Division Headquarters December 22 and returned to an earlier posting of brigade command in the same division. This was the second time in less than two months that Abner Doubleday had been removed from First Division leadership. The first, ordered by George McClellan, took affect November 7, 1862. Three days later Ambrose Burnside granted Doubleday an unexpected reprieve by transferring

Major General Abner Doublday

On December 22, 1862, Wadsworth replaced Abner Doubleday as commander of the First Division, John Reynolds's First Corps. (Courtesy, USAMHI)

his replacement, Brigadier General C. C. Augur, to General Bank's Army. Doubleday's second removal was evidently initiated by John Reynolds. In late December, Major General George Meade departed Third Division for the Fifth Corps. Three weeks passed before Reynolds announced January 18, 1863, that Doubleday would replace Meade. An explanation by either major general for their treatment of Doubleday could not be found.[3]

Containing seventeen regiments in four brigades, Wadsworth's Division was the Corps's largest, but numbers were deceiving. Three out of four regiments in Colonel Walter Phelps's First Brigade had enlisted for two years and were scheduled to be mustered out in June 1863. Brigadier General Gabriel R. Paul faced a similar problem in his Third Brigade. Nine month enlistment terms for one Pennsylvania and four New Jersey regiments expired in late June. The two remaining brigades plus Phelps's 14th Brooklyn reflected experience and strength. The Second Brigade, led by Colonel James Gavin, included the 7th Indiana, 76th and 95th New York, and 56th Pennsylvania. The four regiments of General John Gibbon's 'Iron Brigade', plus the 24th Michigan comprised Fourth Brigade, now commanded by Brigadier General Solomon Meredith.[4]

In spite of his initial setback, Ambrose Burnside remained fixed on capturing Fredericksburg. In late December he proposed to march up the Rappahannock, cross at Bank's Ford above the town, swing to the left, and attack "the rear of an unsuspecting enemy." At first Lincoln hesitated, then reluctantly approved the plan. Wadsworth's Division left Belle Plain about noon January 19, 1863, and marched toward Falmouth. The weather was fine until 3:00 PM when a cold, driving rain began. "The rain poured down in torrents and the air was very cold." Stopping at sunset they passed the night "in water, mud, and wretchedness." The next day brought no relief. "Rain continued to pour down, washing out every attempt to kindle a fire." Cannons, caissons, and wagons sank down to the axles; horses and mules "to their bellies." After gaining less than five miles, the division halted and made camp in a pine forest.[5]

On January 21, a large sign could be seen posted across the river, "Burnside stuck in the mud." With the enemy obviously aware of Burnside's intentions, there was no choice but to turn back. During its return, the division was forced to stop at "a deep ditch, now running swiftly with rushing water." Wadsworth rode back and gave the leading regiment a choice: detour around the problem or build a foot bridge. The 7th Indiana chose the latter and watched as the general dismounted, removed his sword, and waded into the muddy water to help "the Hoosier privates." Afterward, the regiment "christened him Old Corduroy," a nickname he carried into the Wilderness. That day, they marched fifteen miserable miles, reaching Belle Plain after dark.[6]

The 'Mud March' turned out to be Burnside's last straw and Lincoln appointed Major General Joseph Hooker army commander. The First Corps took position on the army's extreme left at Belle Plain. Wadsworth focused on corduroying roads that ran from the Aquia Creek landing to divisional supply depots. The general then turned to foraging with the same dedication and tenacity shown at Upton's Hill. For these assignments he favored Meredith's Brigade. On February 12, the 2nd and 6th Wisconsin Infantry occupied Heathsville, Virginia where they seized horses, mules, bacon, and a few smugglers. Six weeks later, Colonel Lucius Fairchild led the 2nd Wisconsin to Westmoreland County, Virginia and achieved similar success. To some extent, John Reynolds shared his divisional commander's enthusiasm for these expeditions. The First Division reported being fully supplied with horses and mules.[7]

Foraging also brought back a large number of slaves or contrabands. Wadsworth enjoyed seeing them liberated but Colonel Wainwright, a Democrat and McClellan supporter, recorded a different reaction. "Wadsworth is one of the nervous sort, who must be doing something all the time which will show. Quiet, unostentatious preparation he does not appreciate."[8]

Lieutenant Colonel Rufus R. Dawes, 6th Wisconsin, was more charitable toward his new division commander. He later wrote:

> General Wadsworth was a strong character, and his command of our division left a deep impression upon its history. He was an intensely practical commander, indefatigable as a worker, and looking closely after details. No commander could do more for the personal comfort of his men.

The coming Chancellorsville campaign brought foraging to a halt.[9]

The Chancellorsville Campaign

Major General Joseph Hooker

From that time on, the order (Hooker's) was a dead letter, and General Wadsworth's rule to "first protect your men" prevailed instead.

Henry H. Lyman, 147th New York[10]

After the 'Mud March', the two opposing armies retired again to winter quarters. On January 25, 1863, the day Joseph Hooker took command of the Army of the Potomac, Robert E. Lee had reached a decision. With twenty-five miles of river frontage to defend, the Confederates would strengthen their river line to the point "that the enemy would think twice before attacking him (Lee) anywhere." From Bank's Ford to Port Royal, fieldworks occupied the high ground. Artillery redoubts appeared on hilltops and infantry trenches at the bottoms. Lee's offensive options, however, were severely limited by shortages of food and forage. Manpower also became a problem that winter.[11]

In January Robert E. Lee lost Brigadier General Robert Ranson's First Corps Division which departed for Charleston, South Carolina and the North Carolina coast. About a month later, Ambrose Burnside's Ninth Corps left Hooker's army, boarded ships at Aquia Creek, and set off for Newport News near Fort Monroe. Richmond became concerned that Burnside's movement to the Virginia Peninsula signaled the start of a new campaign against the Confederate capital. Under pressure to help, Lee sent two more divisions from Lieutenant General James Longstreet's Corps. Accompanied by "Old Pete," Major General John Bell Hood's and George Pickett's commands moved to southeastern Virginia. This combined loss of over 20,000 men further weakened the Rappahannock line but it also reduced the demands for food and fodder. Lieutenant General Thomas Jackson's Second Corps remained in place and Lee took direct command of the two remaining First Corps divisions, Major General Lafayette McLaws's and Richard Anderson's.[12]

Across the river, the Army of the Potomac suffered through its own version of Valley Forge. Spirit of the officers and enlisted men reached bottom during the Winter of 1862-3. Under the new commander, several effective steps were quickly taken to improve morale and reduce desertions, including the institution of a distinctive badge for each corps. As a result of these moves, the 'winter of discontent' ended. Soldierly pride and confidence in the commanding general returned. Organizational changes included the abolishment of Burnside's grand divisions and appointment of Major General Daniel Sickles and Oliver O. Howard to corps command. Hooker now concentrated on planning a spring campaign against the Army of Northern Virginia.[13]

One of Hooker's tactical objectives was to make the army more mobile by making it less dependent on a fixed base of supply. Increasing the load carried by each soldier and employing pack animals for what remained substantially reduced the number of wagons required. Consequently, Army Headquarters issued an order to all commands that no teams should be employed and that each man should:

> carry ten day's rations (thirty pounds), one hundred rounds of cartridges (twelve pounds), extra shoes, overcoat, blanket, poncha tent, canteen and clothing (forty-five pounds), and musket (eight pounds) in all ninety-five pounds.[14]

After receiving this order, Wadsworth called his orderly and told him:

> to pack a knapsack, canteen, haversack, and cartridge-box, and roll the tent and overcoat, and place them upon the knapsack, according to orders, and put the rig on me, and hand me a gun. I am going to see if this order can be obeyed by the men.

While carrying the entire load, the general paced back and forth in his tent for almost an hour. He stopped, called the orderly, and with perspiration running down his face said, "No man can carry such a load and live. It is preposterous." There was no choice but to pass on the mandate to his brigade commanders. Wadsworth did not enforce it and his infantry did not carry ninety-five pound loads to Chancellorsville.[15]

February 27, 1863, Wadsworth sent a note to Adjutant General Thomas. "I beg have to request that my son, 1st Lt. Charles F. Wadsworth, 116th N. York Vol, now serving in Brig Gen. Emory Div. under Major Genl Banks be assigned to duty on my staff as ADC." Major General Henry Halleck, Army Chief of Staff, decided March 3 that "an officer cannot be moved from one army to another for this purpose." Three weeks later, Wadsworth tendered his request again, this time to the President. Lincoln in turn, "submitted (it) to the Sec. of War April 1." Stanton supported Halleck's decision and Wadsworth's oldest son remained with Banks.[16]

In spite of his efforts to improve mobility, Joe Hooker's star continued to rise among the enlisted men. He, in turn, felt that the army "was in condition to inspire the highest expectations." One challenge remained; defeat Robert E. Lee. To cross the Rappahannock and attack the Army of Northern Virginia in its fortifications would repeat December's disaster at Fredericksburg. With the armies in open view of each other, he had to find a way to move his command to a more promising battlefield; one that would force Lee to abandon the river and fight on ground of Hooker's choosing. Attacking anywhere between Bank's Ford and Port Royal was ruled out. The receipt of accurate military intelligence helped Hooker select an option that avoided a frontal assault. Federal cavalry would cut the single Confederate supply line. With no stockpiles, Lee would be forced to fall back toward Richmond, pursued by Federal infantry. This approach failed, however, forcing Hooker to consider alternatives.[17]

He ultimately implemented the plan that turned out to be the most radical, innovative, and daring of the three seriously considered. A flanking column consisting of three corps would march north, cross the Rappahannock at Kelly's and Ely's Fords, turn south, cross the Rapidan River, then march down river to Chancellorsville. If successful, the Confederates would find Joe Hooker in their left rear. Two other Federal corps, serving as a diversion, would cross the Rappahannock below Fredericksburg. One serious limitation was that the commanding general could not pick the best suited command for each assignment. Secrecy could not be maintained if large bodies of troops were seen marching back and forth. Consequently, the three corps farthest from the river would comprise the turning column – Meade's Fifth, Howard's Eleventh, and Henry Slocum's Twelfth. The two corps farthest left, Reynolds's First and Sedgwick's Sixth would implement the downstream diversion. Darius Couch's Second and Dan Sickle's Third would initially serve as a reserve, crossing over later. As future events unfolded, Hooker's ablest corps commanders – Meade, Reynolds, and Slocum – found themselves relegated to secondary roles at Chancellorsville.[18]

On April 20, Hooker directed that a 'spirited' regiment from First Corps be sent down river to create a diversion. The objective was to convince Robert E. Lee that the Federal's main attack would be made in this area. Reynolds selected two regiments from Wadsworth's Division, the 24th Michigan and 14th Brooklyn. Their orders were to cross the Rappahannock using a canvas pontoon train and capture enemy troops stationed at Port Royal. The regiments set out April 22, crossed over the next morning, and found Port Royal deserted. After capturing a wagon train and some prisoners, they returned to Belle Plain in continuous rain, their mission accomplished. John Reynolds commended the effort and expressed his appreciation to Colonel Henry A. Morrow, 24th Michigan, who led the expedition and to Colonel E. B. Fowler, 14th Brooklyn. In spite of this success, James Wadsworth was one week away from facing his first crisis as a divisional commander.[19]

First Brigade's 24th New York Infantry volunteered for two years of duty in April 1861 and was subsequently mustered into Federal service May 17. The troops felt that their coming discharge should be based on the April date of state acceptance. The Adjutant General's office in Washington, however, ruled that the enlistment period did not begin until the day of muster as United States volunteers. When Company A received orders April 20 to be ready to march, they concluded that another battle would have to be fought before discharge. As April 24 approached, the second anniversary of the 24th's enlistment, Lieutenant Colonel R. Oliver, Jr., expected trouble but nothing happened.[20]

Fitzhugh's Crossing

No man ever entered the service of our union army possessed of a better heart -- truer to the principles of justice and equity -- braver, and more patriotic than James S. Wadsworth
   Captain John T. Davidson, 50th NY Engineers[21]

Led by General Hooker, the Fifth, Eleventh, and Twelfth Corps left camp April 27. Proceeding northwest they began a turning movement around the Army of Northern Virginia's left flank. The First Corps prepared to march toward its selected location a few miles south of Fredericksburg. That afternoon, Company A, 24th New York turned in a petition refusing to march. When orders came to move out at noon, April 28, twelve members of Company A carried out their threat. Retaining Meredith's Fourth Brigade, Wadsworth told his other brigades to go on to White Oak Creek near Pollock's Mill. He then marched the 6th and 7th Wisconsin plus an artillery battery to the 24th New York's camp and formed a battle line. After giving orders to load and come to the ready, General Wadsworth rode to the front, removed his cap, and addressed the twelve mutineers. "Take two steps to the front as your willingness to obey the command to march. Unless you do, by the Almighty, I will bury you here." The command was given and every man moved forward. The Wisconsin regiments covered arms and loudly cheered their division commander as he rode past. The subject was closed.[22]

Hooker now set in motion his feint on the left. After marching down the Rappahannock's north bank, the First and Sixth Corps would each put across one division. This might convince Lee that the main Federal attack would be at Fredericksburg. Hooker charged Brigadier General Henry W. Benham, Commanding Engineering Brigade, with the responsibility of having two pontoon bridges in place by 3:30 AM, April 29; one at Franklin's Crossing and the second down river at Fitzhugh's. Benham reviewed his plan with Major General John Sedgwick and John Reynolds the evening of April 28.[23]

Before launching his December assault on Marye's Heights, Ambrose Burnside had to seize the town of Fredericksburg. To accomplish this, a pontoon bridge had to be constructed from the Rappahannock's north bank. At first everything went well. During the night of December 10, engineers laid two-thirds of the pontoons. Finishing the bridge became a nightmare. With daylight the Engineers and supporting infantry came under heavy enemy fire from town. Brigadier General William Barksdale's Mississippi Brigade occupied the river front. High casualties forced the builders to reform, race to the end, push out another boat, lay a few planks, then run back for cover. Finally the losses became so high that construction was halted. Later that afternoon, Federal Infantry rowed across and drove out the Mississippians. After suffering severe losses, the 7th Michigan, 19th and 20th Massachusetts finally occupied the river front.[24]

To minimize casualties this time, the opposite bank was to be seized before beginning bridge construction. With engineers at the oars, pontoon boats would carry the infantry, sixty men per boat, across the river and then return for a second load. Benham requested that one hundred boats be available at each crossing. A single trip would transport a full division. To maintain secrecy and minimize noise, the pontoon boats would be carried manually about two-thirds of a mile through broken woods. Unfortunately, Benham's view that seventy-two men per boat in double reliefs could easily carry out the plan soon proved to be wrong.[25]

Reynolds selected his First Division to cross at Fitzhugh's or Deep Run. Evidently, he had more confidence in his division commander than

Colonel Wainwright who observed at this time, "Wadsworth is active, always busy at something and with a good allowance of common sense, but knows nothing of military matters." In any case, the assignment stood. At Deep Run, four miles below Sedgwick's Sixth Corps, the river was about three hundred feet wide and varied in depth from five to eight feet. Steep banks rose two feet or more at water's edge. On the enemy's side, the land extended back almost two hundred feet like a table top, then abruptly climbed twenty-five feet forming a second plateau. Rebel rifle pits were dug along the brow of these heights.[26]

Wadsworth gave Phelps's Brigade the task of moving the flat-bottomed pontoons to the Rappahannock's edge. The New Yorkers – 22nd, 24th, 30th, and 84th (14th Brooklyn) – would have to carry the 1500 pound boats over a half mile in total darkness through scattered woods and wet fields. After several frustrating hours, it became obvious that Benham's plan was not the answer. Wadsworth concluded not only had the element of surprise been lost, but bridge assembly would be completed long after sunrise. He ordered the pontoons and timbers reloaded and the wagons driven to the river. Heavy fog, turned into a ghostly white by early daylight, initially shielded the 2nd Wisconsin and 24th New York as they unloaded the wagons. Sunrise found only twenty boats in the water. Rebel musketry soon drove back the engineers and their working parties. The 14th Brooklyn's right wing reacted to Wadsworth's urging and rushed the remaining boats forward. Reynolds and Wadsworth watched as the fog lifted and saw that the opposing enemy forces were limited to those manning the rifle-pits.[27]

About this time General Benham returned from the upper crossing and discussed lower crossing problems with Reynolds. After correcting some misunderstandings regarding his plan, Benham encouraged the corps commander to move ahead. Reflecting for a few moments, Reynolds rode over to Wadsworth and gave the order to move two regiments across and clear the Rebel entrenchments. Wadsworth turned to his Inspector General, Lieutenant Colonel John A. Kress, and said, "Colonel Kress, you will go down to General Meredith's Brigade and give proper instructions for crossing the river at once at all hazards." Meredith formed two lines facing the river; 6th Wisconsin and 24th Michigan in front; 2nd Wisconsin, 19th Indiana, and 7th Wisconsin in the rear. The First Brigade right faced, marched upstream until opposite the pontoons then faced left. In front, the 56th Pennsylvania deployed along the river's edge to provide cover for the storming party.[28]

The Chancellorsville Campaign

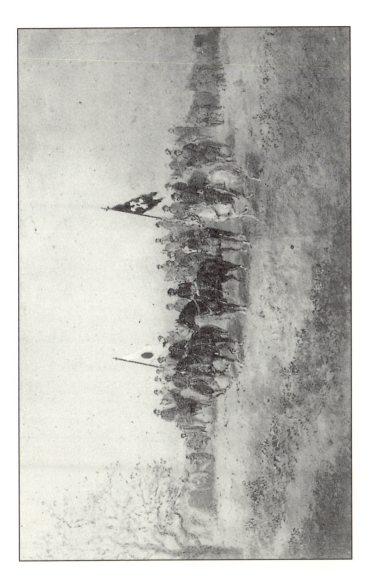

Major General John F. Reynolds Congratulates Brigadier General James S. Wadsworth

John Reynolds congradulates James Wadsworth after the successful crossing at Fitzhugh's Crossing. (Photocopy, Vernon County Historical Society)

With Reynolds and Wadsworth riding behind them, the 6th Wisconsin and 24th Michigan double-quicked down the embankment, filled the assigned boats, and pushed off. Companies C and H, 50th New York Engineers manned the oars. Coming up behind them, the 2nd and 7th Wisconsin returned Rebel fire as the pontoons embarked. After the first group had departed, they launched the remaining boats and followed the two leading regiments. Leaving Reynolds, Wadsworth rode up, yelled, "Hold on" and leaped into the last boat, pulling his reluctant horse with him. Poles, oars, and muskets propelled them across the Rappahannock while batteries opened up on both sides. Holding the bridle in his left hand, Wadsworth remained standing, ignoring the musketry and shell fire. Those left behind watched as the boats landed and small groups, accompanied by "their white-headed general," climbed the bank and ran toward the heights. After a few minutes men from the 6th Louisiana and 13th Georgia, Major General Jubal A. Early's Division, Jackson's Corps, were driven from the pits. Wadsworth rode ahead to observe the retreating enemy. In less than ten minutes the fight was over and a hundred prisoners taken. The General returned and stopped in front of Colonel Henry Morrow's regiment which was formed in line. Taking off his cap, which now contained two bullet holes, he shouted, "God bless the gallant 24th Michigan. God bless you all."[29]

The boats returned for a second trip and brought back the remaining Fourth Brigade troops. Bridge construction advanced quickly with both spans completed well before noon. To strengthen the bridgehead, the First Division's three other brigades crossed over and started constructing entrenchments. The Corps's Second and Third Divisions remained in support on the north bank. April 30 found the First Division's four brigades throwing up breastworks for protection against Rebel fire. Next morning, the fortifications were finished. Ordered by Reynolds "to feel out the enemy," Wadsworth pushed his pickets ahead to the Massaponax River but learned little about Confederate strength.[30]

March to U.S. Ford

At 1:30 AM, Saturday, May 2, General Hooker decided to close the gap between Oliver Howard's Eleventh Corps and the Rapidan River with the First Corps. Orders for it to withdraw from the Rappahannock and march by way of United States Ford to Howard's right were issued. They did not reach John Reynolds until 7:00 AM. Hooker had intended for Wadsworth's retrograde movement to be done under the cover of darkness. The delay in receiving these instructions forced the movement to be made in daylight. While Reynolds and Wadsworth conferred about withdrawing from the bridgehead, the Second and Third Divisions set out immediately for the Federal's right flank, twenty-six miles away. "The pontoon bridges were covered with straw and the artillery first crossed and the infantry last." When the withdrawal began, a Confederate battery started shelling the bridges. Captain John A. Reynolds's First New York Light Battery returned fire and ultimately silenced the Rebel artillery. Wadsworth had his entire command on the north shore by 10:00 AM. Taking up the march, they soon passed through Brigadier General John Gibbon's Second Corps Division, left behind to support Sedgwick. After covering twenty miles in eleven hours, the four brigades halted at 9:00 PM, two miles short of the ford.[31]

Wadsworth rode ahead and learned of the Eleventh Corps's rout by Stonewall Jackson's men. Finding Reynolds, he received orders to form a second line behind the Second and Third Divisions posted along Hunting Creek. About 1:00 AM Wadsworth recrossed United States Ford on the pontoon bridge and led his men to new positions near Ely's Ford Road. By 6:00 AM, three brigades were constructing rifle pits and breastworks. Cutler's Brigade, which included the 76th New York, was positioned in support of Brigadier General Romeyn B. Ayres's Regular Infantry Brigade, Major General George Sykes's Division, Meade's Corps. Later that morning heavy musketry rolled up and down the line. Wadsworth came over and spoke with the 76th. "If those Regulars should break and run, you brave fellows must open ranks and let them through. Take the front but then stand the ground like men." Sykes's men never ran. After dark the New Yorkers marched back to U. S. Ford and helped stop a Confederate cavalry probe along the Rappahannock's eastern bank.[32]

Wadsworth's men remained in reserve until early morning May 6 when orders came to retreat. After waiting for the bridges to clear, the First Division marched across and camped that night on the Warrenton Road. The next day they bivouacked at Pollock's Mill where Hooker's Campaign had begun so favorably a week before. Both armies returned to the same positions held prior to the battle. After the fighting had ended, Longstreet and his two divisions rejoined the Army of Northern Virginia.[33]

On the evening of May 2, 'friendly fire' shattered Stonewall Jackson's left arm. Complications followed its amputation and Jackson died May

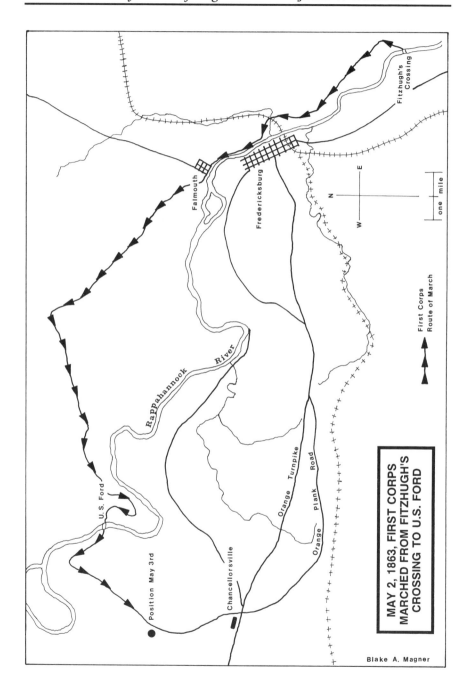

10. His death forced Robert E, Lee to reorganize the Army of Northern Virginia. It now consisted of three corps commanded by Lieutenant General James Longstreet, Richard S. Ewell, and Ambrose P. Hill. Each corps contained three divisions. Lee also developed plans for a June invasion of the North and presented them to Jefferson Davis May 15. In spite of serious problems at Vicksburg and in Tennessee, the president approved. General Lee returned to Fredericksburg and started writing orders. Meanwhile, on May 15, Wadsworth requested and received from John Reynolds a ten day leave of absence "to attend to important private business and visit my family."[34]

CHAPTER 4

THE GETTYSBURG CAMPAIGN

> *He [Wadsworth] ordered the seizure of every pair of boots or shoes suitable to our needs, as we could obtain along the road. Some were taken from the feet of civilians and transferred immediately to those of soldiers in great need of them.*
> Lieutenant Colonel John Kress[1]

Lee's campaign plan called for Ewell's Corps to lead the advance toward Maryland, driving off any Federals found in the Shenandoah Valley. Longstreet would move along the Blue Ridge with Jeb Stuart's Cavalry on his right flank, protecting the passes against enemy probes. After A. P. Hill's Corps, last to withdraw from the Rappahannock, had passed behind them, Longstreet and Stuart would follow the general advance. On June 3 Longstreet's and Ewell's Corps began pulling back from the river line and moving northwest toward Culpeper Court House. Back at Fredericksburg, Hill actively demonstrated to hold the Army of the Potomac in place. Hooker, unsure of what Lee was up to, ordered Major General Alfred Pleasonton's three cavalry divisions to cross the Rappahannock and find Stuart, a reconnaissance in force. Union infantry, including detachments from Wadsworth's Division, defended Beverly and Kelly's Fords as Pleasonton's columns crossed over the morning of June 9. The resulting Battle of Brandy Station, largest cavalry fight of the war, ended as a stand off. In spite of having a day that "made the Federal Cavalry," little was learned about Lee's plans. Ewell resumed his march toward the Shenandoah Valley.[2]

By June 11 evidence clearly indicated that at least part of the Army of Northern Virginia was on the move but no one knew where or why. One result of this uncertainty was Washington telling Hooker to do what he considered to be impossible; cover the Capital and Harper's Ferry while holding the Fredericksburg line. Accepting the need to keep all options open, the general decided to move part of his army north. Hooker selected Bealeton, Virginia as a central point for supplies and issued orders that evening "to move before daybreak." Corps commanders received instructions directing all civilians to leave at once and extra baggage sent to the rear.[3]

Next morning, the First Division left Camp Wadsworth near White Oak Church and set out for Bealeton. Around noon they stopped at Berea Church. Here, the entire division was drawn up into a hollow square to watch the execution of Private John P. Woods, 19th Indiana. After deserting at Chancellorsville, Woods obtained a Confederate uniform. He returned to the First Corps and attempted to pass himself off as a Rebel deserter. Unfortunately, someone at headquarters recognized the ruse. It was Woods's third attempt to desert. This time the court found him guilty. Reynolds sent Captain Stephen Weld, acting Aide-de-Camp, to Wadsworth with orders "to have the affair hurried up." The firing party selected to carry out the court's sentence consisted of two officers and twenty enlisted men from the 6th Wisconsin. The final detail of twelve formed in line and listened to a few remarks from General Wadsworth. Blindfolded and handcuffed, Woods sat on his crude coffin placed next to an open grave. Lieutenant Clayton Rogers, divisional provost, shouted the commands. The detail fired, and Private Woods fell dead. After a hasty internment, the column moved out with the brigade band playing a quick step. Weld later wrote:

> It seemed rather hard to march a man all the morning and then shoot him at noon, but this was one of the hardships of war. Although I have seen lots of men killed, I could not wait to see this affair come off, – it was too sickening.[4]

Having covered over twenty miles since morning, the First Division halted at 6:00 PM near Deep Run, Virginia. Shortly after sunrise June 13, they marched up the Warrenton Road and after fifteen miles stopped at Bealeton Station. Here, a reunion of sorts took place. Details, sent out earlier to provide infantry support for Pleasanton's cavalry movement across Beverly Ford, rejoined the 56th Pennsylvania and 7th Wisconsin. Late evening, John Reynolds received word that Hooker had decided to transfer his entire army to the line of the Orange and Alexandria Railroad. News that Ewell's Corps was in the Shenandoah Valley created an immediate need to swing the Army of the Potomac northward and cover Washington. Given right wing command by Hooker, Reynolds would coordinate withdrawal of the First, Third, Fifth, and Eleventh Corps from the Rappahannock line and their movement by forced marches to Centreville, Virginia.[5]

The advance resumed at 6:00 AM Sunday, June 14 along the Orange and Alexandria. First Corps, Abner Doubleday commanding, found itself in a race to reach Centreville before the enemy. At dusk the column stopped for one hour at Kettle Run and the men made coffee. They marched all night, using torches and bonfires to cross Broad Run after midnight. The corps pushed ahead in some confusion through Bristoe's Station but reached Manassas Junction just before sunrise. Halting here, the regiments formed line of battle and stacked arms. After four hours of rest, they moved across the plains of Manassas, crossing at Blackburn's Ford. In spite of extreme heat, dusty roads, and a lack of good drinking water, Wadsworth's Division reached Centreville around 3:00 PM, June 15. The Army of the Potomac, now concentrated at Centreville and Fairfax, had won the race. Unfortunately, the Army of Northern Virginia was never a participant. Lee's objective was neither Washington nor Baltimore but Pennsylvania.[6]

After marching sixty-four miles in seventy-eight hours, the First Division spent June 16 at Centreville, washing bodies as well as clothes. General Hooker arrived at Fairfax Station and Reynolds returned to corps command. Since June 1, expiration of service for two years' and nine months' men had shrunk the First Corps from 16,000 to 9,000 effectives. Two entire brigades in Wadsworth's Division ceased to exist. Reynolds ordered a reorganization. Only Brigadier General Lysander Cutler's and Meredith's units survived. The latter became First Brigade and carried the Divisional Flag. Gabriel Paul transferred to John Robinson's Second Division and commanded the First Brigade. After two years service, Walter Phelps returned home and mustered out. Meanwhile, word came that Ewell's men had driven the Federal garrison under Major General Robert H. Milroy out of Winchester, Virginia. Lee now had an open road to Pennsylvania. By 8:00 PM, Hooker decided to shift the army from Centreville to Leesburg and suggested that marching be limited to early morning and late at night.[7]

Reveille sounded about 2:00 AM, June 17, and Wadsworth's men marched north toward Leesburg. This seemed to be the hottest day so far and hundreds fell out as a result of either heat stroke or exhaustion. Sunstroke claimed at least three lives. Wadsworth reacted to their suffering. Valises belonging to his staff officers filled one of the ambulances. He ordered all of the baggage, including his own, thrown out and replaced with knapsacks and muskets belonging to exhausted soldiers. In spite of having to make a countermarch, over twenty miles were covered that day. The corps passed through Frying Pan and bivouacked at Herndon Station on the Loudoun and Hampshire Railroad which ran to Leesburg. The worst was over. Rest and rain with cooler temperatures gave the men an opportunity to recuperate. They advanced four miles northeast to Guilford Station June 19 and camped along Broad Run.[8]

Heavy cannonading heard June 22 came from a cavalry encounter at Snicker's Gap. Reynolds received word that Ewell occupied Chambersburg, Pennsylvania June 22 and that Robert E. Lee's two other corps had crossed the Potomac June 24. Hooker reacted by giving John Reynolds command of the Army's left wing, First, Third, and Eleventh Corps. His instructions to Reynolds were to cross the Potomac and seize the National Road passes, Crampton's and Turner's Gap, as quickly as possible. This would shield both Washington and Baltimore from a potential breakout by Lee's Army of Northern Virginia. Additional cavalry and artillery units were also assigned to Reynolds.[9]

Thursday morning, June 25, the First Corps marched to Young's Ford. Finding the water too deep for infantry, they moved on to Edward's Ferry and crossed the Potomac on a pontoon bridge. In steady rain the march continued over eighteen miles to Barnesville, Maryland. Here, Wadsworth bought a stack of straw, which was distributed for bedding. In spite of muddy roads and miserable weather, Reynolds's men crossed Sugar Loaf Mountain, the Monocacy River, then Catoctin Mountain June 26 and camped just south of Jefferson, having advanced about fifteen miles. Saturday, June 27, the First Division moved northwest toward Middletown. A few regiments brought their drum corps to the front and entertained the local citizens as they paraded through Jefferson with flags flying and drums beating. Wadsworth's command bivouacked at the foot of South Mountain near last September's battlefields. Howard's Eleventh Corps occupied the mountain passes. Earlier that day, President Lincoln removed Joseph Hooker from command and appointed George C. Meade to lead the Army of the Potomac. More changes were coming.[10]

Ringing church bells in Middletown greeted the men Sunday morning. The 11th Pennsylvania, Brigadier General Henry Baxter's Brigade, Robinson's Division, was preparing to hold afternoon religious services when the 'long roll' sounded. Unfortunately, orders arrived from their new army commander. Concluding that Lee must be followed north, Meade instructed Reynolds to immediately turn east, recross the mountains, and bring the three corps back to Frederick, Maryland. The march began at 3:00 PM and First Corps reached its goal by 9:00 PM. Meade's instructions for the next day called for an advance by Reynolds and Howard to Emmitsburg, Maryland.[11]

The First Division halted that night in a damp clover meadow of about twelve acres surrounded by a rail fence. Existing General Orders of June 28 stated "that troops should not forage or burn the fences of the citizens." Wadsworth did not want his men spending the night in wet clothes without coffee. He sent for the owner, William Dipon, and asked, "How much was the value of the rails around that field?" The farmer didn't want to sell them at any price. An angry Wadsworth replied:

> I am a farmer myself; your fence won't be needed to protect the clover which is already flat and ruined; my men are tired, wet and hungry and must have coffee; your rails will be burned by either Union or Rebel soldiers in the next ten days; they're worth about $250; here it is; take it or take your chances.

Dipon took the money. His fences quickly disappeared replaced by several hundred campfires and cheers for General Wadsworth. Not everyone shared the good feeling. Next day, Doubleday ordered Wadsworth to pay Mr. Dipon an additional $35 for wood and rails taken the previous night.[12]

Before resuming the march that morning, officers informed the men that Joseph Hooker no longer led the army. With Reynolds back in command, First Corps continued north June 29. Heavy rain turned the roads into quagmires. The resulting mixture of mud and stones quickly wore out the men's shoes. There were no replacements. To Wadsworth the problem became an "increasing evil." The column passed a large, stone flour mill with several employees sitting in front. Riding over, Wadsworth asked if they knew of any shoes for sale. In a "surly and ungracious" tone, the owner said no. His temper up, the general remarked, "You have a good pair of boots on your feet, give them to one of my soldiers." The owner said no a second time. Turning, Wadsworth told a nearby orderly to dismount and take the man's shoes.[13]

Two miles south of Emmitsburg, Mount St. Mary's College for men came into view. Within town, the Sisters of Charity watched as Wadsworth's Division marched by the extensive grounds and buildings of St. Joseph Convent House. Over twenty-five miles were traveled before halting that evening. Divisional wagon trains and the rear guard, 56th Pennsylvania, did not arrive until after 9:00 PM. Reynolds informed Major

General Daniel Butterfield, Meade's Chief of Staff, that Jubal Early's Division was approaching York, Pennsylvania; Major General Robert E. Rodes's Division Carlisle; and A. P. Hill's Third Corps moving through Greencastle toward Chambersburg. Closer yet, John Buford's troopers found one of Hill's brigades at Fairfield, Pennsylvania, five miles to the northwest.[14]

Tuesday morning, June 30, Wadsworth's and Doubleday's Divisions advanced to Marsh Creek, a branch of the Monocacy, five miles south of Gettysburg. This ended a one hundred and sixty mile journey from the Rappahannock. Cutler's Brigade, stopping short of Marsh Creek, bivouacked in cultivated fields. Meredith's Brigade camped north of the creek in line of battle. Pickets from the 19th Indiana pushed north about two and a half miles. They deployed left and right covering a front three miles across. Captain James A. Hall's Second Maine Battery, now assigned to Wadsworth, commanded the Gettysburg Pike bridge over Marsh Creek. Wadsworth sent Kress to find a good map of Adams County, Pennsylvania. Expecting an attack from either Cashtown or Fairfield, both brigades stood at arms. During afternoon 'musters for pay', officers read Meade's first message to his army. Robinson's Second Division and Wainwright's Artillery Brigade remained near Emmitsburg.[15]

From his Taneytown Headquarters, nine miles to the south, Meade reassigned John Reynolds to command the left wing, First, Third and Eleventh Corps. With a new army commander, no one was sure what this meant. General Howard and the Eleventh Corps, south at Emmitsburg, had previously accepted Reynolds's leadership but Daniel Sickles, having returned to command the Third Corps, might resist the change. Sickles, once a Democratic Congressman, was also a political general. Like Wadsworth, he made up "for his lack of military training by acting on the battlefield with reckless courage, and was much admired for it by his men." Unlike Wadsworth, however, many considered Sickles to be "notorious" with lofty plans and ambitions for the future. Attention also focused on First Corps changes. Doubleday commanded the Corps with John Reynolds close by. Brigadier General Thomas A. Rowley once again took over the Third Division and Colonel Chapman Biddle, 121st Pennsylvania, the division's First Brigade. Both were untested in the new assignments and generally unknown outside their division.[16]

Before leaving the Rappahannock, James Longstreet dispatched his favorite scout or spy with orders and told him not to return until "he could bring information of importance." Harrison caught up with Longstreet the night of June 29 and told him the approximate location of five Federal corps and that George Meade had replaced Hooker. At first reluctant to accept this news, Lee countermanded orders issued the night before. The Army of Northern Virginia would now concentrate "east of the mountains at Cashtown."[17]

Earlier that day, George Meade informed his corps commanders that Longstreet's and Hill's corps were near Chambersburg, and Ewell's scattered between Carlisle and York. With pressure on Philadelphia and Harrisburg relieved, Meade expressed a desire to optimize the army's position for either offensive or defensive operations. In a later circular, the army commander discussed information that the enemy was now advancing in strong force on Gettysburg. There would be no major changes regarding Corps dispositions, however, until Lee's plans were better understood.[18]

If necessary, the First Corps would defend its June 30 position. Reynolds had posted the First and Third Divisions to guard against attack from either north or west. While Wadsworth and Hall covered the Gettysburg road, Doubleday and Rowley watched the approaches from Fairfield. Two, parallel, farm roads, separated by Middle Creek, ran southeasterly to the Pike. Colonel Roy Stone's Second Brigade covered both roads, connecting with Chapman Biddle's Brigade at a nearby intersection. Biddle's command extended the Corps's picket line eastward to Meredith's 19th Indiana. General Reynolds and his staff were headquartered on the pike at Moritz's Tavern, south of Wadsworth and southeast of Doubleday and Rowley. The First Corps was the extreme left of Meade's line which extended that night over thirty miles east to John Sedgwick's Sixth Corps at Manchester, Maryland.[19]

Around noon June 30, Buford's cavalry column passed through Gettysburg and stopped just outside the town at a Lutheran Seminary. To the northwest, they observed Brigadier General J. J. Pettigrew's North Carolina Brigade, Major General Henry Heth's Division, Hill's Corps, withdrawing along the Chambersburg Pike. Federal cavalry cautiously followed Pettigrew. That evening, Buford positioned his troopers to monitor all roads coming into Gettysburg from the west, north, and east. Colonel William Gamble's Brigade would observe the roads from Fairfield and Cashtown; Colonel Thomas C. Devin's the ones from Carlisle, York, and Harrisburg. Buford knew that Hill's Corps was camped to the northwest and that Ewell's Corps was approaching from the northeast. He expected trouble the next day.[20]

James Wadsworth possibly enjoyed an evening reunion with one of his old brigade regiments. Two days earlier, Reynolds ordered Colonel Theodore B. Gates and the 20th New York State Militia to join the First Corps. On June 30, they marched from Lewiston, halting in front of Mount St. Mary's College. Later that day, the 20th NYSM marched north through Emmitsburg and before sunset became part of Biddle's Brigade, Rowley's Division. Gates's Regiment spent the night watching one of the roads from Fairfield.[21]

July 1, 1863 — Morning

No one now living will ever again see those two brigades of Wadsworth's Division file by as they did that morning. The little creek made a depression in the road, with a gentle ascent on either side, so that from our point of view the column, as it came down one slope and up the other, had the effect of huge blue billows of men topped with a spray of shining steel, and the whole spectacle was calculated to give nerve to a man who had none before.
                                                            Augustus Buell[22]

The previous day, Wadsworth's First Division had led the march north followed by Rowley's Third and Robinson's Second. Observing army practice or custom, Doubleday sent his divisional commanders a marching order for July 1 that established this sequence: Rowley, Robinson, and Wadsworth. Marching first was the favored position; fresh road and minimal dust or mud. There was a complication this morning, however. The Third Division was nearby but the Second Division was a few miles south at Emmitsburg. As the order stood, Wadsworth would be forced to wait until Robinson's command had cleared Marsh Creek.[23]

The long roll sounded from division headquarters then was repeated by brigade, waking the men to a blood-red sunrise. Shortly before 7:00 AM, John Reynolds rode up to Wadsworth's tent and asked what orders had been received from Doubleday. Wadsworth gave him the day's order of march. The Wing Commander disagreed and ordered First Division to move out immediately. Their objective was to support John Buford as he pushed out from Gettysburg. Reynolds did not expect any trouble and, possibly for that reason, issued only verbal orders. Wadsworth immediately sent orderlies to inform Cutler and Meredith of the change in march order. He then told Lieutenant Clayton E. Rogers to move the command toward Gettysburg. "It happened to be the turn of Cutler's Brigade to lead the column on the morning of July 1."[24]

Reynolds returned to Moritz Tavern and summoned Abner Doubleday for a briefing. Arriving around 7:30, the First Corps commander listened as Reynolds read the latest dispatches from Meade and Buford and summarized the tactical situation The wing commander would accompany Wadsworth's Division and Hall's Battery who were moving out immediately.

> He (Reynolds) then instructed me (Doubleday) to draw in my pickets, assemble the artillery, and the remainder of the corps, and join him as soon as possible. Having given these orders he rode off at the head of the column and I never saw him again.

Doubleday amended the marching orders and began readying the Second and Third Divisions. Over an hour passed before they were moving toward Gettysburg.[25]

Bugles sounded to pack up and soon Cutler's Brigade headed north in this sequence: eighteen men from the 147th New York serving as headquarters guard; 76th New York under Major Andrew J. Grover; 56th Pennsylvania, Colonel J. W. Hofmann; 147th New York, Lieutenant Colonel F. C. Miller; 14th Brooklyn, Colonel E. B. Fowler; and 95th New York, Colonel George H. Biddle. Detached for special duty by John Reynolds, the 7th Indiana remained at Marsh Creek. Passing by Hall's Battery, Meredith's Iron Brigade camps, and the 19th Indiana's pickets, the men found road conditions to be excellent with no encumbrances. The morning sun highlighted South Mountain to the west. Trouble was coming from 'Bobby Lee' but not today.[26]

Initially, Wadsworth and Cutler led the column. This morning, James Wadsworth "wore the full dress coat of his rank, a cap of the U. S. Cavalry pattern, and rode a sorrel horse," followed by the divisional flag; white square field with a red disc in the center. John Reynolds, accompanied by his aides, soon caught up and took the lead. After advancing a mile and a half, they stopped for about ten minutes. Reynolds and Wadsworth sat together in a fence corner studying a large map secured on June 30 by John Kress. After remounting, Wadsworth instructed Kress to take a small party, ride ahead to Gettysburg and seize all the boots and shoes available. The column marched two more miles then stopped briefly while Reynolds dismounted and reexamined the map.[27]

About two miles south of Gettysburg, distant reports of cannon fire could be heard. As Cutler's Brigade approached a peach orchard, smoke from bursting artillery shells became visible to the northwest. The column halted here to rest the men and let Meredith catch up. While General Reynolds was surveying the field in front, an officer came up at full gallop and handed him a message. He read it quickly then told Wadsworth that enemy infantry was driving Buford back. The generals briefly conferred about whether to march through or around Gettysburg. Reynolds picked the latter. After giving instructions to close up the division, he rode off with his aides. The first refuges from Gettysburg, old men, women, and children, passed by heading south with terror and fear on their faces. This exodus, however, did not discourage the 76th New York from enjoying nearby trees loaded with ripe cherries.[28]

John Reynolds galloped into Gettysburg, passed through town, and found John Buford near the Lutheran Seminary. After studying Confederate infantry and artillery going into line farther west and discussing the situation with Buford, he sent aides to bring up Cutler's Brigade. Reynolds also dispatched Captain Weld with a verbal message to George Meade. Weld's diary entry for July 1 contains this communiqué:

> The enemy are coming on in strong force and could secure the heights on the other side of town before he [Reynolds] could. he would fight them all through the town, barricade the streets, and keep them back as long as possible.

James Wadsworth later learned of this message, mostly likely from Reynolds. Its contents would influence his decisions that morning.[29]

With the First Brigade over a mile behind, Wadsworth dispatched Lieutenant Clayton Rodgers with orders to close up. Buford's situation ruled out waiting for Meredith. Cutler's men moved down the hill at a double-quick and halted opposite a farm on the right. Reynolds's aides could be seen riding from the northwest toward Wadsworth and Cutler. They met, talked briefly, then Wadsworth issued orders. Pioneers from the 76th New York came forward, and tore down fencing on the west side. Cutler's column swung left and began marching north across open fields. The order resounded, "Forward! Double quick!, Load at will!" Kress, returning from Gettysburg without shoes, joined Wadsworth at the head.

While crossing a rocky stream bed, Stevens Run, Hall's Battery dashed past the infantry. Up ahead, fences running along both sides of the Fairfield Road stopped the battery. While the 76th's pioneers tore down boards and chopped off posts, the infantry climbed over. Crossing the road, the brigade filed into a narrow lane leading north. Before reaching the brick seminary building, they were forced to the side as Hall's Battery double-quicked to the front.[30]

A mile back, Colonel Henry Morrow received Wadsworth's message to hurry up. This ended First Brigade's "route step and merriment." All non-combatants and pack mules went to the rear. Stripped for action, the column moved off at a double quick. Their order of advance was 2nd Wisconsin, 7th Wisconsin, 19th Indiana, 24th Michigan, 6th Wisconsin and the brigade guard. In anticipation of marching through Gettysburg, the 6th Wisconsin closed ranks, unfurled colors, and moved their drum corps to the front.[31]

Wadsworth, Kress, and Captain Thomas E. Ellsworth, Acting Assistant Adjutant General, rode ahead to find Reynolds and get instructions for posting the division. A Confederate battery stationed on Herr Ridge opened fire as they descended Seminary Ridge and rode northwest toward a house and farm buildings. Up ahead, Reynolds was waiting on the Chambersburg Pike, north of a large stone and wood barn. Captain Hall and Lieutenant Colonel John Sanderson of Reynolds's staff joined the group on McPherson Ridge. Looking at Hall, John Reynolds pointed to where he wanted the battery positioned on the ridge's crest north of the Pike.[32]

Reynolds then turned to Wadsworth and said, "General, move a strong infantry support immediately to Hall's right for he is my defender until I can get the troops now coming up into line." He quickly positioned Cutler's five regiments: first three to the right and last two to the left saying, "I will look out for the left." Wadsworth and Cutler took the 76th and 147 New York and 56th Pennsylvania. North of the Pike, they would form a battle line facing west, their right thrown out toward Devin's Cavalry Brigade. Reynolds would position Hall's Battery, the 14th Brooklyn and 95th New York. Returning to Hall, the corps commander added, "I desire you to damage the artillery to the greatest possible extent, and keep their fire from our infantry until they are deployed, when I will retire you somewhat as you are too far advanced for the general line." Reynolds rode off to Herbst's woodlot while Wadsworth's aides carried orders to Cutler.[33]

As Cutler's Brigade advanced in columns of four through yards and gardens, the 76th New York's pioneers continued removing obstacles. The men halted at the foot of Seminary Ridge while fences on the crest were torn down. Two women near a house gate offered them a hurried drink of water. The column turned left, marched west past the seminary, and halted briefly on the crest of Seminary Ridge. After receiving Wadsworth's orders, Cutler and his staff surveyed the field.[34]

A quarter mile behind them was Gettysburg. In front, three ridges, roughly parallel, ran north to south. The first, Seminary, was highest in elevation and longest in length with open woods covering its top in both directions. Moving west, the ground fell away, leveled off, then rose forming Middle Ridge. It was lower in elevation and the smallest of the three. Less than a quarter mile west of Middle Ridge stood the third, McPherson. Similar in elevation to the second, it seemed to be the widest. Running northwest from Gettysburg, the Chambersburg Pike followed the land's contours. South of where the Pike intersected McPherson Ridge stood a house, large barn, and smaller out buildings with an orchard and woods on one side and a lane running from house to road on the other. This was the farm of Edward McPherson. A hundred and fifty yards north and running almost parallel to the Pike was an unfinished railroad bed having neither ties nor rails. In the valleys, the bed's surface was close to ground level but deep cuts marked its passage through the three ridges. North of the first or East Cut, Seminary Ridge became Oak Ridge which continued on to Oak Hill. About 250 yards north of the railroad bed, the second and third ridges merged, forming a plateau.[35]

Accompanied by Wadsworth, John Reynolds met Cutler's Brigade at the crest and escorted it down Seminary Ridge. The column headed northwest passing through the retreating 8th Illinois Cavalry. Wadsworth told Colonel Fowler "to deploy his regiment (14th Brooklyn) and the 95th New York to the left." There wasn't time to put out skirmishers. The five regiments moved onto the field with no knowledge of either the terrain or enemy disposition. Led by Lysander Cutler, the 56th Pennsylvania and 76th New York turned half-right and marched north. For some reason, the 147th New York did not follow the 56th but marched northwest toward the farm buildings. As instructed by Wadsworth, the last two regiments moved in the same direction. Reynolds rode up and hurriedly gave final directions to Fowler. The 147th New York, Cutler's largest regiment, halted at a white-washed fence east of the farm house and stonebasement barn. Lieutenant Colonel Miller told his men to lie down and waited for orders. As enemy artillery shells passed overhead, the 14th Brooklyn and 95th New York continued on until west of the McPherson buildings. With Herbst's woodlot to the left and Hall's Battery unlimbering on the right, they formed a battle line here facing northwest. To the south, Buford's dismounted troopers continued falling back through the trees, pursued by Rebel infantry who now opened fire on Fowler's men.[36]

As Cutler's infantry moved onto the field, the 2nd Maine Battery came over Seminary Ridge and galloped down the pike drawing enemy fire. Captain Hall rejoined his unit near Middle Ridge. After tearing down a section of fence, the artillery column turned right and moved ahead using McPherson Ridge for protection from Confederate artillery. When east of Reynolds's designated position, Hall ordered "to the left into battery" and the guns were unlimbered. Soon a cannonade began with Rebel artillery outnumbering the Federals by at least five to three.[37]

James Wadsworth watched from the Pike as Cutler's Brigade executed his orders and Hall's Battery took position. Seated next to him, Colonel Kress scanned the front. On the left, he saw enemy infantry approaching Herbst's woodlot. It was Brigadier General James A. Archer's Brigade, Heth's Division. Recognizing the threat to Cutler's flank and rear, Wadsworth sent Kress with instructions for Meredith to come up and attack the enemy. Colonel Kress met the brigade as it descended Seminary Ridge and passed through the 8th New York Cavalry. With Solomon Meredith riding at the rear, Wadsworth's order was first given to Colonel Fairchild, 2nd Wisconsin, then to successive regimental commanders. As they formed *en echelon*, prolonging the Union line westward, the Iron Brigade came under the personal supervision of John Reynolds.[38]

Captain William Bloodgood, Cutler's acting aide, rode up to the 147th at McPherson's Farm and spoke with Lieutenant Colonel Miller. Bloodgood left and pioneers quickly tore down fences next to the Chambersburg Pike. The 147th moved forward into the road, turned right then left, passing along low ground in Hall's rear. As soon as the left company had cleared the railroad bed, Miller shouted, "By the left flank; guide center!" In line of battle, they headed northwest through a wheat field and started climbing the eastern slope of McPherson Ridge; the West Cut

Wadsworth's Gettysburg Memorial

General James S. Wadsworth's Gettysburg statue appears to be warning of the coming flank attack by General Joseph Davis's Brigade. (Personal photograph)

on their left and a rail fence on the right. In several places, dense bushes hid the fence. West of the farm, Archer's left regiment, the 7th Tennessee, spilled out of the woods and engaged the 14th Brooklyn and 95th New York.[39]

North of the Pike, Colonel Joseph R. Davis's Infantry Brigade, Heth's Division continued marching southeast toward Middle Ridge. Earlier that morning, this brigade had followed Archer's down the Chambersburg Pike. On Herr Ridge Davis swung his three regiments to the left, put out skirmishers and advanced. After crossing Willoughby Run and driving Federal cavalry from McPherson Ridge, the command started drifting northeast away from Archer. This was particularly true for Davis's left regiment, the 55th North Carolina. Even though Davis and Buford had been engaged for over an hour, it appears that Wadsworth received little information regarding this enemy force. Unseen from Middle Ridge, the three Confederate regiments quietly approached Cutler's right flank and center.[40]

The headquarters guard, 76th New York, and 56th Pennsylvania moved north in column along Middle Ridge's eastern face. Two hundred yards past the railroad bed, they executed a left flank and began forming line of battle. With no warning, two lines of Rebel infantry – the 55th North Carolina – appeared on the right, less than two hundred feet away. First into line, the 56th Pennsylvania executed Hofmann's command, "Ready, Right-oblique, Aim, Fire." The North Carolinians immediately replied, halting Cutler's advance. Now, the 2nd Mississippi came up on the left front and fired into both Federal regiments, hitting the New Yorkers hardest. Using an east-west ravine for cover, the North Carolinians wheeled right, charged, and struck the 76th New York's right rear. Outflanked and caught in a cross fire, Major Grover ordered the 76th's right wing to change front to the rear. Before it could be executed, Grover fell mortally wounded. With two regiments in position, the Rebel assault intensified.[41]

Sergeant Edgar Haviland, Company E, 76th New York, later described his company's destruction in an August 1863 letter home.

> We was on the head of the column that day and our Regiment was on the lead of all of the troops which caused us to get in the battle the first day[.] We had a great many killed and wounded from the cannons before we got into the musketry[.] After we got into the musketry[,] the men fell like sheep on all

THE GETTYSBURG CAMPAIGN 49

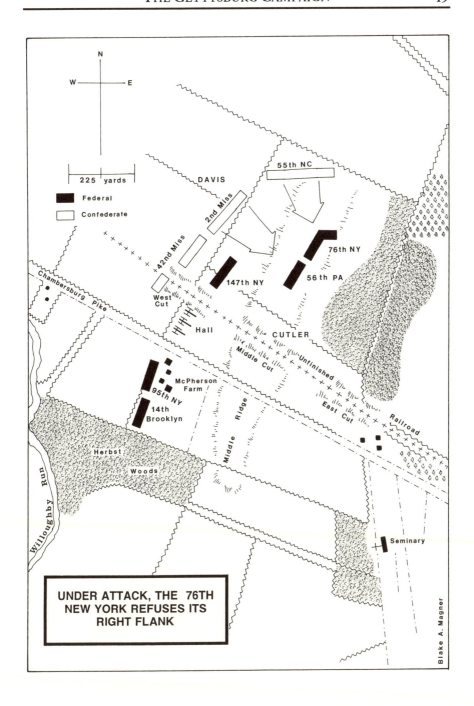

UNDER ATTACK, THE 76TH NEW YORK REFUSES ITS RIGHT FLANK

Major Andrew Jackson Grover, 76th New York

Major A. J. Grover was the only regimental commander in Wadsworth's Division killed at Gettysburg. (Courtesy, USAMHI/Author)

sides of me[.] When we first came into line, there was a corporal hit with a cannon ball and fell right back into my arms[.] In such times a man don't have much time to take care of the men so I threw him down[.] No sooner had I done that then there was another one fell by my side.

...in a few minutes our captain was killed and then the lieutenant was in command of the Company[.] It was not long before he received a wound that will make him loose his leg[.] Then we was with no commissioned officers and then I took the Company in hand myself and maid it go first best.

...Just as I took command of the company [,] Sergeant Walter B. Wood of Barrington [New York] was killed...and [in] a few minutes I heard some one say that B. F. Carpenter was killed[.] that made me feel like as if I would like to speak a word to him before he was gone fore good so I went down the line to speak a word to him but he was dead and so he could not speak to me[.]

...I hastened to my command and just then we was ordered to the rear into the woods. the Major in command of the regiment ordered me to give my gun to one of the men in the ranks...afterwards he was killed[.] He was a gentlemen and a grand officer[.] His name was A. J. Grover.[42]

Two hundred yards farther west, the 147th New York climbed McPherson Ridge, their right flank 'in the air'. While moving through a wheat field, musketry erupted to their right rear – the 55th North Carolina's opening attack. When the 147th was about opposite Hall's caissons, a line of Rebel infantry – the 42nd Mississippi – suddenly appeared in front and opened fire. The first volley killed many New Yorkers before they could fire a shot. Others dropped to a kneeling position and fired back. In spite of heavy casualties and being engaged at close quarters for the first time, they continued advancing. When just short of Hall's cannons, the order came to lie down and fire through the wheat. To find targets in the smoke, many had to stand up after loading.[43]

From Seminary Ridge, Wadsworth saw the punishment being taken by Cutler's three regiments. The Rebel sweep southward threatened his division's line of retreat. After twenty minutes of heavy fighting, he made a decision. If Meredith did not arrive soon and relieve the pressure, an order to pull back and reform east of Oak Ridge would be sent to Cutler. Captain Ellsworth rode off to give this message to John Reynolds. Colonel Kress returned and reported that Meredith's line was entering the woods under Reynolds's direction.[44]

Unable to either turn the 147th's left or break through its center, the 42nd Mississippi started shifting northeast. Their goal: the Federal's exposed right flank. This movement was initially mistaken by the New Yorkers as a retreat. When Rebel fire dropped off, the 147th's two left companies moved ahead to the crest of McPherson Ridge. On their left front, enemy troops were advancing through a field toward Hall's guns. Looking west they saw Confederate skirmishers climbing out of the West Cut. All were firing into the battery. Second Lieutenant J. V. Pierce, Company G, ordered "left oblique fire." After several volleys, the Mississippians fell back down the slope and took shelter in the cut.[45]

Ellsworth returned with news that John Reynolds was dead. Unaware that Doubleday had arrived, James Wadsworth assumed field command. He issued instructions for Cutler to withdraw his three regiments beyond Seminary Ridge, fall back into Gettysburg, and barricade the streets. Besides protecting Meredith's line of retreat, this would also fulfill Reynolds's earlier commitment to Meade. The 56th Pennsylvania and 76th New York received and executed the order. An aide from Cutler's staff waved his sword as he rode toward the 147th New York, evidently a signal to fall back. Lieutenant Colonel Miller, just wounded, placed Major George Harney in command and left the field. Harney did not see the signal to retire.[46]

When supporting infantry to the right rear started falling back, Hall took action to extract his battery. Lieutenant Ulmer withdrew the right section to Middle Ridge and attempted to provide covering fire. No longer held back by the 56th Pennsylvania and 76th New York, Confederate infantry swung south toward the Middle Cut, firing on Ulmer as they advanced. With musketry raking its position, the left section was unable to fire a shot. In spite of this setback, Hall, using smoke as a cover, directed the remaining guns to be rolled down the slope, limbered up, and started for town. Even though he was exposed to enemy fire and could pass only one gun at a time through the fence, Hall managed to save five out of six guns.[47]

Following his men up the Chambersburg Pike, Captain Hall met General Wadsworth near the East Cut. Unaware of the 147th's stand,

14th Brooklyn Gettysburg Monument

The 14th Brooklyn gazes at the ground where Joseph R. Davis's Brigade, Heth's Division, engaged the 147th New York on the morning of July 1, 1863. (Personal photograph)

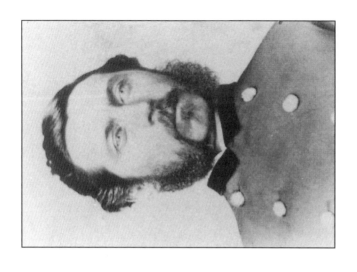

Lieutenant Colonel F. C. Miller, 147th New York

On two occasions, July 1, 1863, Lieutenant Colonel Miller failed to carry out Wadsworth's orders. (Courtesy, USAMHI, NY State Adjutant General Office)

Major George Harney, 147th New York

After thirty minutes of severe fighting, Major Harney finally received Wadsworth's order to withdraw the 147th New York. (Courtesy, USAMHI)

Hall strongly criticized Cutler's withdrawal. Wadsworth ignored the remarks and said, "Get your guns back to some point to cover the retiring of these troops." "This General is that place, right here in the road," Hall replied. "No, go beyond the town for we cannot hold this line," Wadsworth remarked as he started to leave. Hall asked for time to retrieve the lost gun. The general snapped back, "Loose no time in getting your guns into position to cover the retreat." Their conversation ended abruptly.[48]

Having driven two Federal regiments beyond Seminary Ridge, Davis's infantry concentrated their attack on the 147th New York. Rebel skirmishers quickly occupied Hall's former position. What had earlier been mistaken for a retreat turned out to be a right wheel by the 42nd Mississippi against the New Yorker's flank. As Hall's Battery dashed down the Pike, Harney was forced to refuse his right by drawing the right two companies back to the rail fence. Riding toward the Seminary with Captain Ellsworth, Wadsworth saw that instead of retiring, the 147th remained in position, fighting alone. He sent Ellsworth to bring them out. The general also dispatched Lieutenant Rogers to Meredith requesting help to stop Davis's advance before his men cut off the Iron Brigade.[49]

Earlier that morning, General Doubleday and Colonel Wainwright were riding at the head of John Robinson's Division, about three miles behind Cutler. Captain Craig Wadsworth, an aide to John Reynolds, brought news of Reynolds's death. Pushing ahead, Doubleday arrived on Seminary Ridge as Meredith's Brigade charged into the Herbst woodlot. Reacting to an earlier message from Reynolds and his own observations, Doubleday concluded that the road to Fairfield and the Herbst woodlot must be held at all costs.[50]

Instead of joining the Iron Brigade's battle line, Meredith told Colonel Dawes to stop the 6th Wisconsin and wait in a ripening wheat field just north of the Fairfield Road. He also placed the brigade guard under Dawes's command. An order to advance arrived but it was countermanded by Doubleday who now detached the regiment to serve as a divisional reserve while securing the Fairfield Road. A few minutes later three general's aides – Lieutenant Meredith Jones from Doubleday, Captain James Wood from Meredith, and Clayton Rogers from Wadsworth – came up with orders to "move your regiment at once to the right." The Colonel yelled out, "Up, Change front, By company into line, on right company, Forward!" Facing north, the regiment marched at a steady double-quick through a stubble field. With Lieutenant Rogers riding alongside, they passed behind Meredith's regiments fighting in the woods and headed north toward the Chambersburg Pike. The accompanying staff officers urged Dawes to move faster, yelling that Cutler's men were being driven. Reaching a post and rail fence, the 6th Wisconsin started filing to the right, moving past the Middle Cut and opposite the advancing enemy's left flank.[51]

From a position northwest of McPherson's farm buildings, Colonel Fowler watched the disaster unfolding to the east. Confederate forces north of the Pike were firing into his rear ranks. Before long, they would be ready to drive south and cut off his line of retreat. Meredith's charge into the adjacent woods relieved enemy pressure on the 95th New York and 14th Brooklyn. Seizing this opportunity to disengage, Fowler ordered both regiments to change front to the rear on tenth company. Retreating eastward until opposite the Middle Cut, they changed front forward on the right. Facing the Pike, Fowler's 'mini-brigade' marched toward the same fence as Dawes. While the three regiments moved into position, one Federal unit continued fighting to the north.[52]

The 42nd Mississippi pushed across the rail fence. With the 147th New York's right broken, Major Harney began polling his company commanders whether to retreat or stay, Before a decision could be reached, Ellsworth rode up with Wadsworth's order. "In retreat, double-quick run," rang out and they fell back, every man for himself. At first, those on the right retreated directly east toward Oak Ridge. Heavy fire from enemy troops advancing southward drove them toward the Pike. Many on the left jumped into the West Cut for shelter but found it already in Confederate hands. To avoid enemy fire, the New Yorkers climbed the cut's southern face and ran back through a meadow between the Pike and railroad bed. Pursued by yelling Rebels to the Middle Cut, the survivors crossed the Chambersburg Pike and gathered in a small peach orchard. Captain John A. Kellogg, Second Brigade's Acting Assistant Adjutant General, informed Wadsworth that enemy troops now held the Middle Cut.[53]

The complete collapse of organized resistance north of the Pike opened a direct path to Meredith's rear. Wadsworth's Division now faced the threat of being cut off and defeated before Rowley and Robinson reached the field. After crossing a second rail fence, Confederate forces on Middle Ridge realigned themselves then started moving southeast toward the Seminary. Fowler's and Dawes's efforts to form a battle line south of the Pike caught the attention of Joseph Davis's men. They

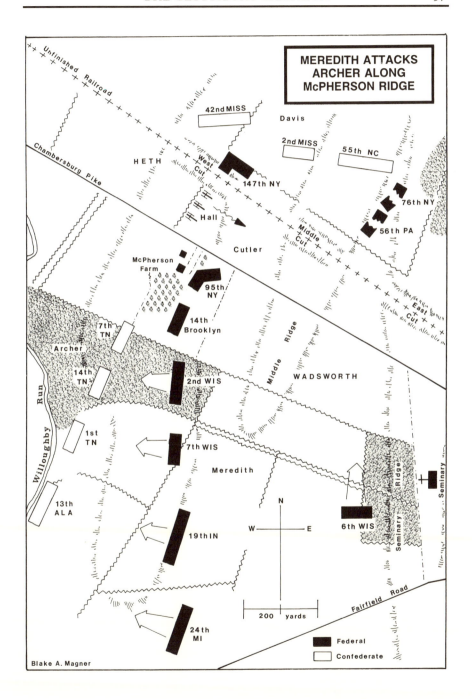

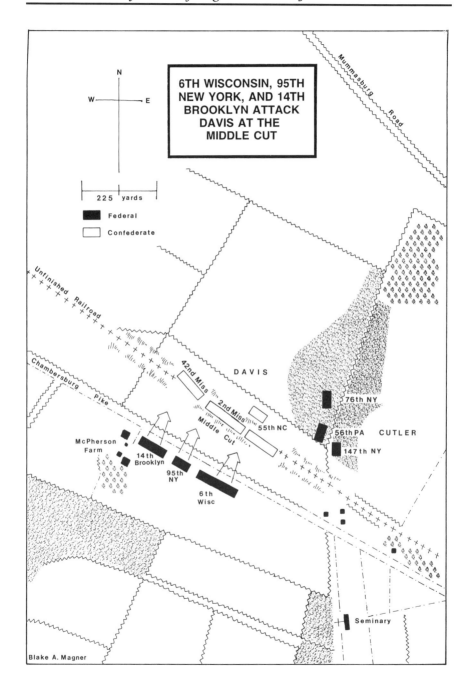

began firing at the Federals, only three hundred feet away. A return volley struck the Confederate right flank. This unexpected fire not only stopped Davis's advance but many from the 2nd and 42nd Mississippi ran into the Middle Cut.[54]

Under Dawes's orders, the 6th Wisconsin moved forward and climbed the first fence. Followed by the 95th New York, they ran across the Chambersburg Pike, scaled a ditch, and started climbing the second fence. At this point, Davis's Mississippians, protected by the cut, let loose a devastating volley that staggered both Federal regiments. Many were left hanging on the fence. In spite of this, Dawes's men advanced through a meadow, loading and firing at will. Rising casualty rates were offset by support from the 14th Brooklyn. Several times the 6th's regimental colors dropped out of sight then reappeared. A Confederate flag continued flying above the cut's western edge. Finally, the Federal right reached its goal and hand to hand fighting ensued.[55]

Prior to the charge, Lieutenant Rogers joined Wadsworth on Seminary Ridge. They watched the 'V-shaped,' blue mass surge forward, the flag at its center. Many fell to the ground while others limped back to the Pike. At the cut, it became impossible to see what was happening. Yells and shouts rose above the musketry as savage fighting continued. After a few minutes, musket firing fell off and the Confederate flag dropped out of sight. Enemy troops began surrendering but many avoided capture by running out the cut's western end. The cloud of smoke began to break up. When the 6th Wisconsin's national flag became visible, Wadsworth turned to Rogers, twirled his hat, and shouted, "My God, the 6th has conquered them." They rode down to the Middle Cut. A cavalry guard, brought up by Wadsworth, started moving the prisoners toward Gettysburg. The three Federal regiments withdrew to Seminary Ridge for rest and refitting. The 147th's solitary stand north of the Pike had not been in vain. Harney's New Yorkers gave Dawes and Fowler the time they needed to organize a counterattack.[56]

Captured prisoners confirmed that in less than two hours, First Division had fought and defeated two brigades from Heth's Division: Davis's north of the pike and James Archer's in Herbst Woods. As desultory cannon fire and musketry continued, Robinson's and Rowley's Divisions neared Gettysburg. A. P. Hill's failure to mount a second attack before noon gave Doubleday and Wadsworth an opportunity to strengthen and improve the Federal line.[57]

With the fortunes of war suddenly reversed, Wadsworth concluded that the Seminary Line could be held. This made it necessary to cancel previous withdrawal orders to Cutler and Hall. A countermand reached the 56th, 76th, and 147th regiments east of Oak Ridge. Colonel Kress set out to find and bring back the Second Maine Battery. Executing Wadsworth's earlier order, Captain Hall withdrew his guns through Gettysburg and took a new position south of town on Cemetery Hill. Kress found him there and offered to lead the battery back to Oak Ridge. Following the Colonel's suggestion, Hall used the railroad grading to return north but came under enemy fire for over 1200 yards. Meeting again on the ridge, the captain received instructions from Kress to "go into battery on the open ground" beyond the woods. As it turned out, both Captain Hall and advanced elements of Richard Ewell's Corps were moving toward the same location, the northern end of Oak Ridge.[58]

The Iron Brigade formed a new battle line east of Willoughby Run and about halfway through Herbst Woods. Meredith ordered the troops to lie down and rest. Cutler's three regiments that had fought north of the pike reformed in meadows east of Oak Ridge. The 147th New York mustered only seventy-five effectives. In less than thirty minutes, the 76th New York had lost a total killed and wounded of eighteen officers and one hundred and fifty-one men. After filling canteens in Steven's Run, the 56th Pennsylvania, 76th and 147th New York, under Colonel Hoffman, climbed the ridge and headed northwest through a corn field. As ordered by General Doubleday, they reoccupied the exposed position on Middle Ridge, where dead and wounded marked their first battle line. Casualties left behind also defined the 147th's stand on McPherson Ridge. Joined by the 14th Brooklyn and 95th New York, the five regiments soon became the target of enemy artillery. With no Federal batteries to oppose them, A. P. Hill's cannoneers concentrated their fire on Cutler's Brigade, now at less than half its original strength.[59]

As casualties rose on Middle Ridge, Wadsworth concluded that Hall's missing guns must be replaced. Since Wainwright had not responded to his earlier request for a battery, the general went looking for an answer. Caissons belonging to Horse Battery A, 2nd U. S., stood near the Seminary; the men engaged in refilling ammunition chests. Wadsworth ordered the battery commander, Lieutenant John H. Calef, to replace Hall. Calef's reply that he was under Buford's control and McPherson Ridge "was not a proper place for a battery" was unacceptable. Angered by Cutler's mounting casualties and Wainwright's lack of support, the general placed Calef under arrest and sent him to the rear. Finding no other officers present, Wadsworth repeated his order to First Sergeant Joseph Newman, commanding the left section. The general rode off to find infantry support for the guns.[60]

Threading their way through the dead and wounded, Sergeant Newman and Charles Pergel, commanding the center section, reached McPherson Ridge in "column of pieces". Approaching the crest, they came under heavy musketry from Rebel skirmishers. Battery A's left and center sections unlimbered in the same position previously occupied that morning by Lieutenant John W. Roder, commanding Calef's right section, and James Hall. Outnumbered six to one, Newman and Pergel engaged enemy artillery to the front and right, and waited for infantry support.[61]

Relieved of their prisoners, Wadsworth ordered the 6th Wisconsin to retire to the woods on Oak Ridge. While reorganizing his regiment, Dawes received instructions to move forward and support Battery A's two sections. Advancing with the 14th Brooklyn to McPherson Ridge, they drove a line of Rebel skirmishers beyond Willoughby Run. In spite of this support, Calef's men continued to suffer casualties from enemy musket fire. Responding to a request from General Buford, Colonel Wainwright took steps to relieve Newman and Pergel with Captain Gilbert Reynolds's Battery L, First New York Light. To ensure that the battery would not report to Wadsworth, Wainwright personally accompanied it to McPherson Ridge.[62]

Shortly before noon, Rowley's Third Division reached the field. Doubleday positioned Biddle's First Brigade to cover the Fairfield Road on Meredith's left and Colonel Roy Stone's Second Brigade to fill the gap between Meredith and Cutler. His battle line strengthened, Wadsworth rode south to Biddle's Brigade on the far left. Here, he found Colonel Gates who complained about enemy sharpshooters located in a farm house and stone barn, Harmon's, across Willoughby Run. They were firing on his men and into Captain James H. Cooper's Battery. At this time Doubleday commanded the field which elevated Wadsworth to corps commander. The general promptly told his former subordinate to seize the buildings. Two companies from the 20th New York State Militia drove off the rebels and held the farm for over two hours, safeguarding the left flank. Around 12:00 PM, Major General O. O. Howard arrived and being senior, took command of the field. This returned Doubleday and Wadsworth to corps and divisional responsibilities but elevated Major General Carl Schurz to Eleventh Corps command.[63]

July 1, 1863 — Afternoon and Evening

The activity, efficiency, and, if I may so express it, ubiquity, of General James S. Wadsworth in the battle was remarkable. He was of venerable and commanding appearance, and was absolutely fearless in exposing himself to danger.
Colonel Rufus R. Dawes[64]

Henry Heth broke off the fighting and reformed on Herr Ridge. He brought two fresh brigades, Pettigrew's and Colonel J. M. Brockenbrough's, forward in the center, and placed Archer's and Davis's on the two flanks. Major General Dorsey Pender's Division went into reserve immediately behind Heth. Robert E. Lee, who did not want a general engagement this early, arrived on the field, discussed the situation with Heth, and restrained him from further attack. About this time Richard Ewell and Robert Rodes's Division were approaching Gettysburg from the northeast. Ewell later reported:

> I notified the general commanding of my movements, and was informed by him that, in case we found the enemy's force very large, he did not want a general engagement brought on till the rest of the army came up.
>
> By the time this message reached me, General A. P. Hill had already been warmly engaged with a large body of the enemy in his front, and Carter's artillery battalion, of Rodes' division, had opened with fine effect on the flank of the same body, which was rapidly preparing to attack me, while fresh masses were moving into position in my front. It was too late to avoid an engagement without abandoning the position already taken up, and I determined to push the attack vigorously.

Rodes positioned two brigades to open the assault on Doubleday's right.[65]

Several regimental bands had assembled in Gettysburg's town square. As the fighting died down, their playing of military music could be faintly heard on Seminary Ridge. The noon respite gave Federal commanders an excellent opportunity to withdraw Wadsworth's battered brigades to Seminary Ridge. Aware that reinforcements were at hand, Abner Doubleday, however, decided to continue the fight where John Reynolds had started it. Oliver Howard, now field commander, confirmed this decision. Both generals failed to properly heed John Buford's warnings that a second enemy corps was approaching from the northeast. Its subsequent appearance should not have been a surprise but neither Doubleday nor Howard made any preparations on Oak Ridge. The latter left the field to bring his Eleventh Corps forward. Robert Rodes's infantry now entered the battle. For the second time today, Cutler endured a surprise attack on his right flank.[66]

Earlier, Wadsworth had misread the realignment of Heth's troops as a retreat and suggested an advance to Howard and Doubleday. They ignored his recommendation. Developing a more realistic view about a possible threat on the right, Wadsworth sent John Kress north to reconnoiter. While studying Oak Hill, covered with trees and higher in elevation than Oak Ridge, he saw Confederate officers placing artillery. When ready, these guns would enfilade three Federal brigades, Cutler's, Stone's, and Biddle's, and three batteries, Calef's, Reynolds's, and Cooper's. Kress discussed this with Wadsworth who immediately sent him to Doubleday. The general also forwarded a warning to Eleventh Corps commander Carl Schurz that "the enemy was making a movement toward his (Wadsworth's) right."[67]

Just as Captain Gilbert Reynolds's first section came into position behind Battery A, Confederate batteries on Oak Hill opened fire with case and solid shot, enfilading Federal units on both McPherson and Middle Ridges. The artillery crossfire plus arrival of Rodes's infantry forced Stone's Brigade to change front immediately. Wadsworth gave Cutler the option of selecting a "proper position." Leaving the 6th Wisconsin and 14th Brooklyn for artillery support, he ordered the remaining four regiments to change front to the right. Advancing to a zig-zag, rail fence, they faced north and opened fire on enemy skirmishers approaching a stone wall and embankment along the Mummasburg Road.[68]

Finding McPherson Ridge untenable, both Federal batteries limbered up and withdrew. Reynolds went into position on Middle Ridge, south of McPherson's barn which sheltered his left. After the batteries had left, the 6th Wisconsin and 14th Brooklyn retreated to Oak Ridge, using the Middle Cut for cover. Wadsworth later ordered Dawes to take a position supporting Lieutenant James Stewart's Battery B, 4th U. S., at the East Cut. North of Gettysburg, Colonel Thomas C. Devin's remaining cavalry

Captain W. P. Cater's Battery

From this site, Captain Carter's Battery directed an enfilading fire against Cutler's and Roy Stone's First Corps brigades on the afternoon of July 1, 1863. (Personal photograph)

was driven off. A retreating cavalryman's warning provided sufficient time for Captain James Hall to countermarch his battery and avoid Rodes's skirmishers.[69]

Informed by Kress that enemy artillery and infantry units were arriving from the northeast and that lead elements of Howard's Eleventh Corps were just coming into line, Doubleday belatedly decided to strengthen his right. He ordered Kress to accompany two regiments, the 97th New York and 11th Pennsylvania from Brigadier General Henry Baxter's Brigade, John Robinson's Division, up Oak Ridge beyond Cutler. Baxter's remaining regiments soon followed. Their purpose was to prevent Ewell's fresh troops from 'rolling up' the First Corps's right flank.[70]

Around 2:00 PM, General Howard inspected the First Corps's position. Riding south along the ridge's eastern slope, he probably missed both Cutler's and Baxter's positions. The field commander met Wadsworth near Stewart's Battery and told him to hold Seminary/Oak Ridge as long as possible then withdraw to Cemetery Hill. They may have watched James Hall's small party struggle and finally succeed in removing an abandoned cannon from Middle Ridge. Howard rode off to find General Doubleday. Contrary to Wadsworth's orders, Colonel Wainwright now instructed Hall to retire south of town and refit the battery.[71]

To gain better protection for his men, Cutler refused the brigade's left. Sheltered by a strip of woods, the 56th Pennsylvania and 147th New York continued to face north behind the rail fence. Within the woods, the 14th Brooklyn, 95th and 76th New York formed a battle line looking west. Baxter's 11th Pennsylvania shifted left to close the gap between brigades. Shortly after 2:00 PM, Brigadier General Alfred Iverson's four North Carolina regiments launched an oblique attack against Baxter's line. Skirmishers from the 56th Pennsylvania and 147th New York began firing from behind trees. Executing a right-wheel, Cutler's three left regiments charged out of the woods into an open field and fired on the enemy's right flank. This, combined with a successful frontal and opposite flank attack by Baxter, resulted in the capture of many prisoners and two regimental flags. Returning to its original battle line, Cutler's infantry and Stewart's Battery B helped Roy Stone's men stop Brigadier General Junius Daniel's North Carolinians from seizing the Chambersburg Pike.[72]

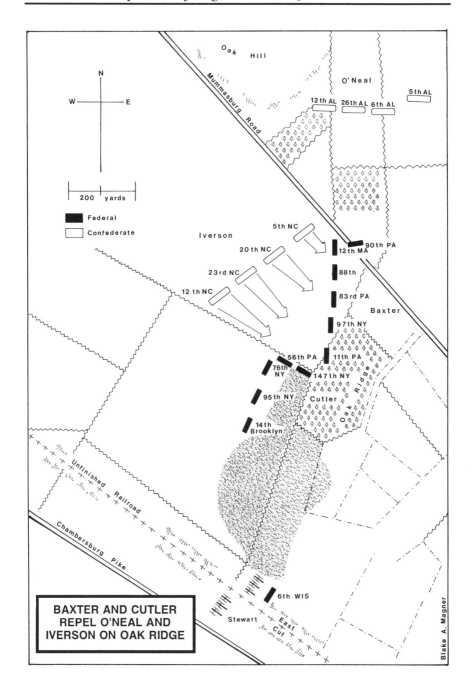

While Robert Rodes's infantry made preparations for a third assault against Oak Ridge, Doubleday reluctantly sent Brigadier General Gabriel R. Paul's Brigade accompanied by General John Robinson to reinforce Baxter and relieve Cutler. Except for one regiment, the 151st Pennsylvania, the First Corps had no reserves left. With most of its ammunition consumed and the men exhausted, Cutler's Brigade withdrew from the line. They retired down the eastern slope of Oak Ridge and initially took a position behind the 94th New York. Here, they waited to be resupplied with ammunition. To avoid fire from Carter's batteries on Oak Hill, the battered regiments moved farther south toward the East Cut.[73]

At mid-afternoon, Doubleday's line extended from Fairfield Road on the left to Mummasburg Road on the right, about a mile and a half in length. Since noon, the Confederate's inability to coordinate attacks had provided the Federals with opportunities to shift units and stop isolated assaults north of the Pike. In addition to a lack of reserves, other problems confronted the First Corps. To the north, Brigadier General Alexander Schimmelfennig's Eleventh Corps Division failed to connect with John Robinson, leaving his right flank exposed to enfilading fire. South of the Pike, Biddle's left flank was 'in the air.' In Herbst Woods, Colonel Morrow, 24th Michigan, did not like his battle line and three times sent a message to brigade headquarters stating that the present position could not be held. Three times permission to withdraw was denied. Similar protests were made by Colonel Samuel J. Williams, 19th Indiana, who wanted to retire to the crest of the hill behind them. Meredith did not approve this change either. Around 2:30 PM, A. P. Hill abruptly ended the debate. After resting in line of battle for over an hour, Heth and Pender received orders to attack Doubleday's center and left. Even though Longstreet had not come up, Lee now desired a general engagement.[74]

Across Biddle's, Meredith's and Stone's front, two lines of Henry Heth's infantry emerged from the woods – Brigadier J. J. Pettigrew's North Carolinians on the Federal left and Colonel J. M. Brockenbrough's Virginians on the right. The first line, preceded by skirmishers, drove straight ahead. The second moved obliquely to the left then attacked. Conditions near the Fairfield Road rapidly deteriorated. Pettigrew over lapped Biddle's left by a quarter mile and began driving the brigade eastward toward Seminary Ridge. This exposed the entire 19th Indiana and Morrow's left wing to enemy cross fire. Meredith was wounded and departed the field. Colonel William W. Robinson, 7th Wisconsin, assumed brigade command. Outflanked on the left, the 19th Indiana

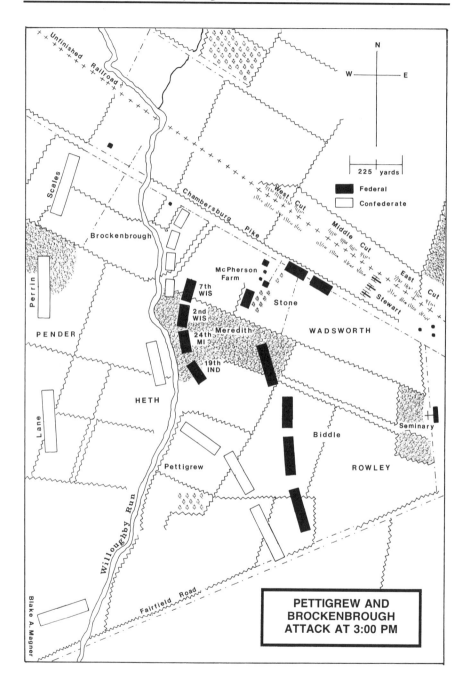

pulled back to the hill's crest and formed a new line. This exposed the 24th Michigan's right wing, then fighting the 26th North Carolina, to enfilading fire. The Rebel frontal attack pushed ahead and finally broke the Iron Brigade's battle line.[75]

Wadsworth saw Meredith's regiments pulling out of Herbst Woods. Once again he asked Wainwright for artillery support. The Colonel responded by ordering a section of Battery L, First New York under Lieutenant Benjamin Wilbur into the McPherson farm orchard between Meredith and Stone. It was too late. Brockenbrough's Virginians, advancing down both flanks, made it necessary to remove the guns before they could fire a shot. About midway between the woods and Seminary Ridge, the Iron Brigade regiments independently stopped, faced to the front and fired before resuming their retreat. Cutler received a request from Wadsworth for infantry support at the Chambersburg Pike. He sent the 14th Brooklyn, 76th, and 147th New York. They took position south of the East Cut, supporting Battery B's left section while the 6th Wisconsin remained north of the cut behind Stewart's right section.[76]

Forced to retire from exposed positions in the woodlot and farmyard, Meredith's and Stone's Brigades suffered more casualties during their withdrawal. By 3:30 PM survivors had reformed on Seminary Ridge where many found shelter behind breastworks constructed earlier by Robinson's Division. At this point Pettigrew pulled his regiments back to reorganize. This respite gave Doubleday, Wadsworth, Rowley, and Wainwright about fifteen minutes to organize their Seminary Line. Then, two brigades from Dorsey Pender's Division, Brigadier A. M. Scale's North Carolinians on the Federal right and Colonel Abner Perrin's South Carolinians on the left, moved forward from Middle Ridge. Their line extended from the Chambersburg Pike to the Fairfield Road. Wadsworth sent another request to Howard for reinforcements but never received a reply. Pender's assault struck the ridge about 4:00 PM.[77]

Standing behind Captain Greenleaf T. Stevens's 5th Maine Battery of 12 pounder Napoleons, Wadsworth watched the fighting. The 2nd Wisconsin and 150th Pennsylvania were in front of the guns. Word came that Schurz's Eleventh Corps, east of John Robinson's Division, was falling back. At the same time, Perrin's men broke Chapman Biddle's line south of the Seminary. An aide from Doubleday rode up and handed the brigadier an order to fall back to Cemetery Hill. Initially, Wadsworth hesitated because Scales had been stopped and showed no sign of renewing the

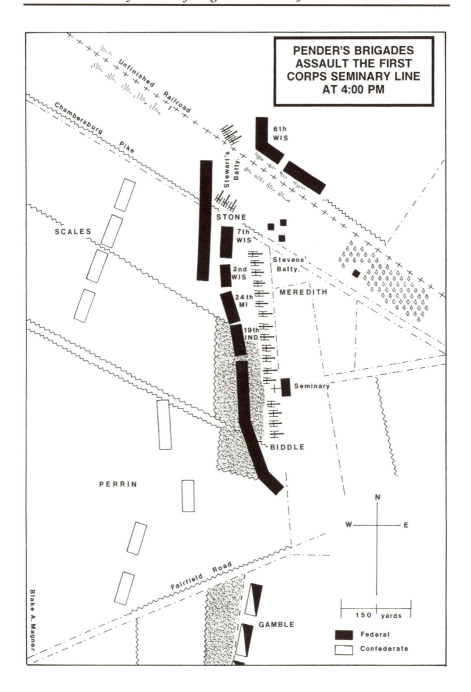

attack. The Federal line between the Seminary and railroad bed held. It was an excellent artillery platform, but Biddle's collapse forced Wadsworth to implement the order.[78]

Having decided to retreat without Howard's concurrence, Doubleday rode off to Cemetery Hill. Wadsworth instructed Cutler to retreat along the railroad embankment and ordered Captain Stevens to withdraw his battery. Lieutenant Clayton Rogers carried orders for Colonel Dawes to "retreat beyond the town." The general remained behind while the 5th Maine fired their final rounds of canister. Mounting up, Wadsworth and his staff departed the Seminary and rode into town on the Chambersburg Pike. After fifteen to twenty minutes of intense fighting, the First Corps began a nearly simultaneous but haphazard withdrawal. In some cases the infantry abandoned the artillery. Last to leave the Seminary breastworks, the 7th Wisconsin suffered their heaviest losses of July 1 while serving as the brigade's rear guard.[79]

There were two routes of retreat from Seminary Ridge to Cemetery Hill; through and around the town. In most cases, an individual's position in the line determined which one he used. Troops stationed on the left retreated across open lots, avoiding most of the congestion within Gettysburg. William Gamble's Brigade kept this route open by delaying Pender's advance beyond the Fairfield Road. North of the Pike, however, there was no choice but to escape through town. Exposed to flank and rearward fire, Cutler's Brigade withdrew down the railroad bed and into Gettysburg. Confused and terrified, they crowded through the streets and alleys and climbed fences, anything to keep moving. The 14th Brooklyn finally reached Baltimore Street only to find it filled with Eleventh Corps troops.[80]

The resulting bottleneck brought the brigade's retreat to a halt. The problem occurred because neither Howard, Doubleday, nor Schurz had made any preparations for the withdrawal. Fleeing men from both corps were drawn to Baltimore Street, the widest road. Most ignored side streets until forced to find another route of retreat. This delay exacted a high price from those units last to leave the Seminary and Oak Ridge. Stevens's and Cooper's guns passed through town mixed together. Robert Rodes's advancing skirmishers captured hundreds in Gettysburg. Confederate artillery added to the misery by firing shells into town. Several struck buildings lining Baltimore Street, spraying the Federals with brick and mortar. Soldiers who accepted offers of shelter from the residents regretted it later that evening when they were rounded up as prisoners.[81]

Pushing into Gettysburg, Perrin's 1st and 14th South Carolina along with Georgians from Brigadier General George Doles's Brigade, Rodes's Division, shot at retreating First Corps units. They fired from stoops, through windows, and down cross streets. This Rebel harassment persisted over halfway through the town. Near Cemetery Hill, part of Cutler's Brigade was stopped and given orders by an unknown, general officer who claimed First Corps command. This interference only increased the number taken prisoner. Discipline and organization broke down within town. Individual judgment and courage, not orders, drove the men to Cemetery Hill.[82]

Sitting on his horse, Wadsworth watched as First and Eleventh Corps survivors came down Baltimore Street and climbed Cemetery Hill. Except for Colonel Orlando Smith's Eleventh Corps Brigade, nothing but a mob milled around the crest. Rufus Dawes remembered seeing at first "a confused rabble of disorganized regiments of infantry and crippled batteries." Gradually, "cool, courageous, and efficient men...brought order out of chaos." Officers began yelling for the exhausted men to fall in. Sergeants waved regimental flags as rallying points. Seeing one soldier with 'Nineteenth Indiana' on his hat, Wadsworth pointed to the regimental color bearer and said, "There is your flag." A passing thunder storm lowered the temperature as organization slowly returned. With it came the awareness of what the First Corps had lost that day.[83]

About the time that Pender broke through at the Seminary, Major General Winfield Scott Hancock, Second Corps commander, arrived on Cemetery Hill. With orders from George Meade to take field command, Hancock set out to stop the Federal retreat and establish a defensive line. A ravine or saddle that separated Cemetery and Culp's Hills offered the enemy a favorable line of attack. Hancock was near the Cemetery Gate when Captain Stevens came up with part of his battery. The major general ordered Stevens "to take his battery on to that hill," pointing to Culp's, "and stop the enemy from coming up that ravine." The captain asked, "By whose order?" "General Hancock's," came the reply. Stevens yelled, "Fifth Battery Forward!" Having assigned artillery to cover this approach, Hancock now wanted a First Corps brigade to occupy the western slope of Culp's Hill. After a heated discussion with Hancock and his chief of staff, Lieutenant Colonel Charles H. Morgan, Doubleday reluctantly ordered Wadsworth to provide the infantry. "Still full of fight," Wadsworth instructed Colonel William Robinson to reform the First Brigade.[84]

After escorting an ammunition train from Emmitsburg, the 7th Indiana arrived on Cemetery Hill around 5:00 PM. Near the cemetery entrance, they found Wadsworth and Cutler sitting on a stone fence, most likely discussing Hancock's orders. Wadsworth greeted the troops warmly remarking, "I am glad you were not with us this afternoon." Cutler quickly injected, "If the Seventh had been with us we could have held our position." "Yes, and all would now be dead or prisoners," Wadsworth replied. Major Ira G. Grover received instructions to occupy the crest of Culp's Hill. Assigned to hold the extreme right with a single regiment, Grover ordered breastworks constructed on the crest and established a picket line that ran down the hill's eastern slope. With a combination of luck and bluff, the major later succeeded in capturing several from a 42nd Virginia scouting party. Those who escaped reported to Major General Jubal A. Early that Federal troops occupied Culp's Hill.[85]

About 6:00 PM Wadsworth, Colonel Robinson, and four regiments marched toward their assigned position. They passed between the 5th Maine's line of limbers and caissons, and formed a line on the western slope of Culp's Hill. Wadsworth's divisional flag was placed near Steven's right gun. Lieutenant Clayton Rogers, Colonel Dawes, and the 6th Wisconsin followed the brigade's eastward advance. Behind them the wounded and stragglers continued to pass through Orlando Smith's ranks. In spite of conflicting orders from Howard, Hancock, Doubleday, and Rowley, Lysander Cutler finally succeeded in reforming most of his brigade by sunset. Facing town, they bivouacked in a meadow opposite the cemetery's entrance, dug rifle pits, and slept on their arms. Cutler's command had fought from 10:00 AM to 4:00 PM. It was the first infantry unit engaged July 1 and among the last to leave the field.[86]

After dark Captain Craig Wadsworth joined his father on Culp's Hill. Results from regimental roll calls told James Wadsworth that he now commanded a small brigade. Out of 380 present at Marsh Creek that morning, only seventy-nine answered the 147th's evening roll call. Seventy-two New Yorkers had been killed or mortally wounded and 146 seriously wounded north of the Chambersburg Pike. For the 6th Wisconsin, sixty-five made the climb to Culp's Hill. The 24th Michigan began July 1 with 496 effectives. Twelve hours later, ninety-nine reported for duty.

General Meade reached Gettysburg about 1:00 AM, July 2. Officers awaiting his arrival at the cemetery's gate included Hancock, Howard, Schurz, Doubleday, and Wadsworth. They summarized the day's fighting for the army commander.[87]

Gettysburg, July 2 - 4, 1863

> *During the severest fighting that night (July 2) Wadsworth rode up in the rear of the writer's company, pulled his hat down as if to shelter his face from the rain of minnie balls that were coming in almost a solid sheet. He was a grand old man and brave to a fault, beloved by his command.*
>
> J. N. Hubbard, 7th Indiana[88]

Remembering the severe losses on McPherson Ridge, Iron Brigade survivors began the day by digging entrenchments and later rested behind breastworks. The woods in front were relatively free of underbrush and the hill's northern face dropped off sharply. Howard's Eleventh Corps was on their left. Around 6:00 AM, Brigadier General John W. Geary's Second Division, Twelfth Corps arrived on the crest, completing the Federal occupation of Culp's Hill. The 7th Indiana connected with the 78th New York of Brigadier General George S. Greene's Third Brigade, the brigade lines almost perpendicular to each other. Before noon, Cutler's regiments moved up to Culp's Hill, taking a reserve position behind William Robinson, who replaced Solomon Meredith, and George Greene. Although many soldiers, who were missing the previous night, rejoined their regiments, Wadsworth concluded that his division had less then 1600 effectives. Word came that George Meade had selected Major General John Newton to command the First Corps. Abner Doubleday returned to the Third Division, currently in reserve behind the Eleventh Corps. Intermittent skirmishing and artillery firing continued throughout the day.[89]

The next encounter between James Wadsworth and his 'artillery nemesis,' Colonel Charles Wainwright, took place July 2 on East Cemetery Hill, most likely near Gilbert Reynolds's First New York Battery. The general requested that artillery fire be directed against enemy forces massing in the woods east of Culp's Hill. Wainwright replied this could not be done without endangering Twelfth Corps troops. Not easily discouraged, Wadsworth pointed out where he wanted the fire. To Wainwright's comment that shells would fall within Federal lines, Wadsworth said that he had just been there and knew the enemy's position. To avoid a confrontation, the general was asked to aim one of the guns which he did. After watching one shot fired, Wadsworth returned to Culp's Hill. Wainwright claimed that he maintained a desultory fire until a Twelfth Corps officer came over and complained that the shells were dropping into his lines.[90]

Sometime that morning, Robert Lee finished his plans for July 2. Longstreet's Corps, assisted by Hill's, would make the main attack on the Federal left. When the firing commenced, Richard Ewell's Second Corps was "to make a diversion in their favor, to be converted into a real attack if an opportunity offered." Ewell's primary objective that afternoon was to prevent Meade from shifting reinforcements to the left. Around 4:00 PM, Longstreet began his assault on Sickles's Third Corps. Instead of immediately launching an infantry 'diversion' on Culp's Hill, the Confederates started an artillery duel with Federal guns on Cemetery Hill. Ewell reported "that immediately after the artillery firing ceased, which was just before sundown, General Johnson ordered forward his division to attack the wooded hill in his front, and about dusk the attack was made."[91]

As Longstreet's blows battered the Third Corps, George Meade asked the Twelfth Corps for help. Commanding the Army's Right Wing, Major General Henry Slocum immediately complied by ordering the First Division and Brigadier General Henry Lockwood's Brigade to vacate Culp's Hill and reinforce the Federal left. Half an hour later, two brigades from Geary's Division also departed. Shortly after 7:00 PM, only Greene's command remained on the eastern slope. In the lengthening shadows, Edward Johnson launched his attack. Even though it was two hours late, Johnson had picked the ideal time to strike Culp's Hill.[92]

Brigadier General George H. Steuart's Brigade struck the Federal right, Colonel J. M. Williams's the center, and Brigadier General John M. Jones's the left. Shortly after the fighting began, George Greene asked Wadsworth and Howard for help. Wadsworth sent the 6th Wisconsin, 147th New York and 14th Brooklyn, approximately 355 effectives. Taking a position on the right of the 60th New York, the 147th supported and relieved Greene's men who needed to replenish ammunition and clean their muskets. Arriving after dark, the 6th Wisconsin and 14th Brooklyn advanced down the hill and stopped a Rebel assault against Greene's exposed right. On the crest, Cutler's remaining regiments moved forward to fill first line vacancies and opened fire on Johnson's advancing troops. During this attack, Wadsworth rode up, got off his horse, and sat on a

Colonel Charles S. Wainwright

A critic of Wadsworth's performance at Gettysburg, Colonel Wainwright served with distinction throughout the war. (Courtesy, USAMHI)

rock above and behind the 7th Indiana's breastworks. He encouraged the men and refused to move until the fighting ended. Around midnight John Geary's two brigades returned to Culp's Hill and relieved the 6th Wisconsin.[93]

The 14th Brooklyn and 147th New York remained with Greene's Brigade. Fighting resumed at 3:30 AM, July 3 and continued for the next ten hours. After sunrise, the New Yorkers retired to the second line but later took another turn in the rifle pits, being relieved four times to replenish ammunition. About 4:00 PM the two regiments rejoined Cutler. The 14th Brooklyn, however, was called back to the Twelfth Corps position and remained there until evening.[94]

In a clump of trees just behind the Iron Brigade's line, Wadsworth and his staff sat down at a cracker-box table to eat lunch. Without warning the Confederates opened a cannonade. A dozen shells burst nearby covering the food with dirt. The officers abandoned lunch and ran for their horses to see what was happening. At first, enemy artillery shells seemed to strike every portion of the Federal line. Uncertainty spread "as to where the Confederate attack would occur." Several recognized the vulnerability of Cemetery Hill. To assist Wadsworth in case an attack developed on his front, George Greene detached the 102nd New York. Its colonel, Lewis R, Stegman, reported to James Wadsworth who directed the New Yorkers to the left, where they reinforced William Robinson's First Brigade.[95]

From Cemetery Hill Wadsworth watched the start of the Pickett-Pettigrew-Trimble charge. He sent Colonel Kress to Meade with an offer of help. As a precaution, Hofmann moved the 7th Indiana, 56th Pennsylvania, and 95th New York to support artillery on Cemetery Hill. The fighting ended, however, before they could reach the batteries and General Meade graciously replied that the First Division was not needed. Next morning Wadsworth and Hofmann advanced the 56th Pennsylvania and 7th Indiana through Gettysburg to bring back the July 1 wounded. Before reaching Seminary Ridge, the movement was canceled and they returned to Culp's Hill. Even though his brigade and regimental commanders had not written their after-action reports, Wadsworth submitted a brief one to General John Newton.[96]

Major General John Newton

Physically ill, Major General Newton, First Corps commander, asked Wadsworth to attend George Meade's July 12, 1863, Council of War. (Courtesy, Cumberland County Historical Society Collection, USAMHI)

Pursuit and Resignation

Sunday, July 5, most of Cutler's Brigade moved left onto Cemetery Ridge, behind the Taneytown Road, and encamped in a field full of enemy dead and wounded. Wadsworth's Division set out at 5:00 AM, Monday in pursuit of Lee's Army. They reached Emmitsburg around 10:00 AM and went into camp. Local citizens told them that Rebel cavalry had passed through the previous day. Wadsworth resumed his earlier practice of gathering shoes from homes along the march route and giving them to barefoot soldiers.[97]

Proceeding in heavy rain, the First Division crossed the Catoctin Mountains Tuesday and marched over twenty-two miles before halting outside Middletown. Roads were so rough and narrow that at times the men marched in single file. Rumors placed Confederate infantry on the other side of South Mountain. In spite of continuing rain, the column reached Middletown before noon on Wednesday and went into camp. At 2:00 PM they resumed the march, hearing distant cavalry fighting and artillery firing. The division spent the night of July 8 in Turner's Gap. Wadsworth wanted an aggressive pursuit of Lee but this view did not prevail at headquarters. He concluded that no matter what shortages the Army of Potomac experienced, the Army of Northern Virginia faced worst problems.[98]

The men remained in bivouac July 9 and received a new issue of clothing and shoes. The day was quiet, mail arrived from Middletown, and George Meade concentrated his army. Twelve miles away, a swollen Potomac River stopped Lee's retreat at Williamsport and Falling Waters. With continuous cannonading in front, the division left camp about 7:00 AM, July 10, passed through Brownsville and advanced five miles to Beaverdam where they remained for two days. The Fifth and Sixth Corps were up ahead, slowly pushing forward. Enemy infantry was seen from the picket line but there was little firing.[99]

Sunday, July 12, the division fell in at 4:00 AM during a heavy thunderstorm and moved off to the right. At Funkstown, the column crossed Antietam Creek, swollen by heavy rains, and found the enemy in front. Troops went into line of battle southwest of the creek and started building breastworks. General Newton became ill and Wadsworth assumed corps command that afternoon. After sunset General Meade called the corps commanders to his headquarters for an evening council. Wadsworth went in Newton's place.[100]

Meade began by briefly reviewing the condition of his army and available information concerning Lee's. Starting with John Sedgwick, he polled the corps commanders as to their thoughts about a morning attack. Sedgwick, Henry Slocum, George Sykes, William French, and William Hays were opposed. Only Howard, G. K. Warren, Alfred Pleasonton, and Wadsworth favored an attack as did Meade. The army commander, however, would not risk a major engagement unless a majority supported it. His most competent and aggressive corps commanders were either dead (Reynolds) or wounded (Hancock).[101]

In spite of being in a weak position, Wadsworth did not let go. He openly challenged the four ranking officers to explain their opposition. Warren, Pleasonton, and Wadsworth argued in favor of a morning attack but nothing changed. After failing to support a reconnaissance in force, the council disbanded. Wadsworth returned to his headquarters, convinced that an opportunity to severely damage the Army of Northern Virginia had been lost. Heavy skirmishing continued throughout the night. The men expected a battle to begin Monday morning but nothing happened. It rained and the enemy fired a few artillery rounds. The general's depression deepened significantly upon hearing Tuesday that Lee's army had successfully recrossed the Potomac with minimal loss.[102]

Noah Brooks, a correspondent of the *Sacramento Daily Union*, described his feelings July 14.

> Turning my horse's head in the direction of Meade's headquarters, I looked across the swollen and turbid Potomac where I could see the smoke of Rebel camps rising in the thick Virginia woods on the other side of the stream. It is impossible now to describe – almost impossible to recall – the feeling of bitterness with which we regarded the sight. Lee's army was gone. In spite of warnings, expostulations, doubts, and fears, it had escaped, and further pursuit was not even to be thought of.

Later that afternoon, Brooks met Wadsworth:

> who almost shed tears while he talked with us about the escape of the Rebel army. He said that it seemed to him that most who participated in the council of war had no stomach for the

fight. "If they had," he added, "the rebellion, as one might say, might have been ended then and there."[103]

From Wadsworth's viewpoint, results of the Gettysburg Campaign did not justify the July 1 destruction of Meredith's and Cutler's Brigades. Never reluctant to act, he submitted the following letter.

> Headquarters, First Division, First Corps
> July 14, 1863
>
> To the Adjutant General of the Army
> Sir:
>
> I beg respectfully to state that in consequence of the considerable reduction of the recruiterial strength of the army and the simultaneous increase of general officers, it appears to me that I can now leave the service without detriment to it.
>
> In the First Corps, for instance, in which I have the honor to serve there are about nine thousand muskets (the time of service of several regiments nearly expired) and eleven general officers sworn for duty.
>
> Under these circumstances, as I am constrained to think, that by continuing in the service I become a problem rather than an aid to it and I accordingly respectfully tender my resignation of the commission which I hold and ask the early action of the department there upon.
>
> I have the honor to be, General Brigadier of Volunteers,
> Brigadier General J. S. Wadsworth[104]

General Meade reluctantly approved but Secretary Stanton rejected the resignation. He relieved Wadsworth from duty, placing the general on leave of absence until further orders. Cutler took over the First Division. Before leaving the Army of the Potomac July 17, Wadsworth shook the hand of every officer and enlisted man in the 76th New York. The regiment mustered only eighty that day; a bittersweet farewell. He discussed efforts to have the regiment placed on detached duty. "Having failed in this, I cannot bear to see the small remnant of the brave old Regiment put up to be shot at any more," noted the general. Lieutenant Clayton Rogers also resigned July 14.[105]

First Lieutenant Clayton E. Rodgers

Lieutenant Clayton Rodgers, Assistant Aide-de-Camp, resigned from the army the same day as James Wadsworth, July 14, 1863. (Courtesy, Sawyer County, Wisconsin Historical Society)

CHAPTER 5

Between Battles

He set far higher store, so far as his own feelings were concerned, by the position which his valor had won for him in the national army than if he had been the successful candidate for governor....
                                                New York Times[1]

For the second time, James Wadsworth left the Army of the Potomac and stopped in the nation's capital. Evening of July 16, President Lincoln was having tea with his personal secretary John Hay, Lieutenant Colonel B. S. Alexander, an ordnance officer, and Judge William Whiting, War Department Solicitor. General David Hunter and Wadsworth joined the group. Hay remembered the conversation in his diary.[2]

Alexander asked, "Why did Lee escape?" "Because nobody stopped him," Wadsworth shot back. He then described Meade's July 12 'Council of War'. "The non-fighters thought, or seemed to think, that if we did not attack, the enemy would...." Thinking back, Wadsworth reflected that no one at the 'council' that night expected Lee to abruptly retire into Virginia. Meade favored attacking with three columns of 20,000 each but he (Wadsworth) wanted to duplicate Stonewall Jackson's move at Chancellorsville. "Double up their left and drive them down on Williamsport." Either plan would probably have succeeded. Looking at Hunter, Wadsworth said, "General, there are a good many officers of the regular army who have not entirely lost the West Point [idea] of Southern superiority. That sometimes accounts for an otherwise unaccountable slowness of attack."[3]

October 9, 1863, the War Department issued Special Orders No. 452 by which Secretary Stanton gave Brigadier General James S. Wadsworth a new task. The special duty was to review black troops currently being raised and organized in the Mississippi Valley. His assignment began at Cairo, Illinois and could extend as far south as New Orleans. Besides sending reports to Adjutant General Thomas, Wadsworth would discuss his findings in person with Stanton.[4]

Brigadier General James S. Wadsworth

This picture of General Wadsworth was taken in January 1864 while he was serving on a court of inquiry. (Courtesy, Library of Congress)

Just before departing on the inspection tour, Wadsworth spoke with the paymaster with whom he had always dealt. The general reaffirmed his desire:

> ...to have his accounts with the government kept by one and the same officer, because it was his purpose, at the close of the war, to call for an accurate statement of all the money he should have received, and then to give it, whatever might be the amount, to some permanent institution, founded for the relief of invalid soldiers.

"This is the least invidious way," he said, "in which I can refuse pay for fighting for my country in her hour of danger."[5]

Ultimately, the general and aide, Captain T. E. Ellsworth, journeyed to New Orleans and back, inspecting all principal points where black troops were being concentrated, organized, and/or drilled. In November 1863 Adjutant General Thomas accompanied them from Vicksburg to Baton Rouge. Wadsworth departed New Orleans for New York on November 18. After his return to Washington, reports were completed and a discussion held with Stanton. On December 19, E. D. Townsend, Assistant Adjutant General, granted the general a leave of absence until new orders were issued.[6]

January 9, 1864, James Wadsworth was assigned to serve on a court of inquiry investigating the conduct of Major General Alexander McCook, Thomas I. Crittenden, and James S. Negley during the Battle of Chickamauga. After twenty-one days of hearings in Nashville and Louisville, the court issued a final report exonerating all three. Wadsworth informed the Adjutant General February 23 that "my address until further advised will be 18 East 16th St., New York." War Department orders dated March 15 instructed Wadsworth to report to George Meade on or before March 25. The significance of this date became apparent with the March 24 announcement that the First Corps had been merged into the Fifth. The Third Corps experienced a similar fate when it was assimilated by the Second. Meade told Wadsworth to report to Major General G. K. Warren, commander Fifth Corps, for his next assignment. Two days later General Orders No. 21 announced that James S. Wadsworth commanded the Fourth Division. His regimental commanders received word of the assignment April 7.[7]

Wadsworth's appointment to divisional command at this time was particularly significant. The Army of the Potomac's reorganization eliminated several corps, divisions and brigades, creating a surplus of general officers. Non-military factors were secondary to Lieutenant General U. S. Grant who gave the highest priority to proven effectiveness. For a non-professional, it was an honor to even be seriously considered. The fact that all three corps commanders asked to have him assigned as a division commander was a tribute to James Wadsworth. It reflected the esteem that Major General Warren, Hancock, and Sedgwick held for him as a soldier.[8]

The new Fifth Corps contained four divisions: the First led by Brigadier General Charles Griffin; Second, John Robinson; Third, Brigadier General Samuel W. Crawford and Wadsworth's Fourth Three infantry brigades made up the Fourth Division. The First, commanded by Lysander Cutler, included the former Iron Brigade regiments plus the 7th Indiana and 1st New York Sharpshooters. Brigadier General James C. Rice's Second Brigade contained Cutler's Gettysburg regiments less the 7th Indiana. Commanding the Third Brigade, Colonel Roy Stone had not only his Gettysburg regiments but also the 121st and 142nd Pennsylvania. Sixteen regiments plus the Sharpshooters made up this division, Warren's second largest. To some extent, Wadsworth must have felt that he was returning to his June 1863 command. Unfortunately, future events would show that this was not the case.[9]

Several weeks of drilling and preparation ended May 3, 1864, when Fifth Corps received word that Grant's march south would begin at midnight. Warren held an afternoon meeting with his four division commanders and artillery brigade commander, Colonel Charles Wainwright. That evening, Wadsworth wrote what would become his last letter home.

> May 3rd., 9 P. M.
> My Dear Wife
>
> I have just received your most kind letter of April 30th (Saturday). We have just received marching orders to move at 12 tonight and all is bustle and confusion. Still I withdraw my mind from the scene and the duties of the hour a few moments, my dear wife, to tell you that we are all well (Tick* is with me) and in the best spirits. We feel sure of a victory. I wish I could tell you how much I love you and our dear children, how anxious I am that all should go well with you, that

you will all live in affection and kindness, and that none of our dear children will ever do anything to tarnish the good name which we who are here hope to maintain on the battlefield. Write a kind letter to dear Jimmie.** if he is not with you. With all the love and affection I can express. Kiss Nancy and Lizzie and believe me, my dear wife, fondly and truly yours,

Jas S. Wadsworth

*Son Craig currently on the staff of Brigadier General A. T. A. Torbert, commanding First Cavalry Division.

** Youngest son James W. enlisted in November 1864 and served on General G. K. Warren's Fifth Corps Staff. He was brevetted major for meritorious service in the Battle of Five Forks, April 1, 1865, and mustered out of service June 26, 1865.[10]

CHAPTER 6

THE WILDERNESS CAMPAIGN

How odd it would be, if every man who was to die in the days just ahead had to wear a big badge today, so that a man watching by the river could identify all of those who were never coming back.
  Lieutenant Colonel Theodore Lyman[1]

Spring arrived and U. S. Grant set out to destroy the Army of Northern Virginia. His major weapon, George Meade's Army of the Potomac, would soon cross into Virginia. It would not attack Lee's defensive line behind Mine Run, thus avoiding a second Fredericksburg. By quickly passing through the Wilderness, fifteen square miles of second-growth forest between Orange Court House and Fredericksburg, Hooker's failure at Chancellorsville would not be repeated. If the Federals moved quickly enough, they would "turn the enemy's right flank" and drive a wedge between Lee's army and Richmond.[2]

North of the Rapidan River, George Meade started the 'overland campaign' with approximately 74,000 infantry, 2,700 artillery men, and 12,500 cavalry. Burnside's Ninth Corps mustered 19,000 effectives. Together, they would cross the Rapidan in two columns, advance through the Wilderness, and draw Lee out into open country. Here, Federal superiority in manpower and artillery would dominate. To ensure no surprises, each infantry column would be preceded by a division of cavalry "that were directed to push well out to the front and flanks and feel for the enemy."[3]

Across the river, the Army of Northern Virginia occupied a strong position "well protected in front by field-works, with its left flank covered by the Rapidan and the mountains near Orange Court House, and its right flank guarded by an entrenched line extending from Morton's Ford to Mine Run." Lee's command of 64,000 men was physically split. Hill's and Ewell's Corps spent the winter near Orange Court House while Longstreet's was nine miles away at Gordonsville. Recognizing his deficiencies in numbers and firepower, Robert E. Lee decided to fight where his opponent's advantages would be minimized. The Wilderness's tangle of stunted trees, thick underbrush, ravines, and poor roads would 'level the playing field.'[4]

At midnight May 4, Warren's Fifth Corps vacated their Culpeper camps and took the Stevenson Plank Road to Germanna Ford. The Fourth Division reached the Rapidan River around 6:00 AM and waited its turn to cross. Around 11:00 AM Wadsworth's men marched past positioned artillery and descended the north bank. Blue infantry could be seen climbing the south bank's rocky heights. Lieutenant Colonel Theodore Lyman, an aide to George Meade, rode across. It was a beautiful day. Dogwood, bush honeysuckle, and violets were in full bloom. From a high bluff Lyman watched Warren's infantry, artillery, and wagons cross on two pontoon bridges:

> ...and had a curious thought: How odd it would be, if every man who was to die in the days just ahead had to wear a big badge today, so that a man watching by the river could identify all of those who were never coming back![5]

Heading southeast, Warren followed Brigadier General James H. Wilson's Third Cavalry Division down the Germanna Plank Road and entered the Wilderness. With approximately 6,500 effectives, the Fourth Division cleared the pontoon bridge by 1:00 PM. As they marched southeast, it became very quiet. Wadsworth rode among the men that afternoon, talking with several of them including the 76th New York.

> The old gentleman is as good natured as ever. He wears the regulation cap, rides a light gray horse, his gray hair cut short and side whiskers closely trimmed. The boys all like the old "Abolish."

At the Old Wilderness Tavern, a two-story stage house, the division turned right. A short time later the column "broke off by regiments on either side of the road (Orange Turnpike)" and bivouacked for the night. It was about 4:00 PM. General Grant, Meade, and Warren arrived and headquarters bands started to play. "The scene is sublime; the red sun hangs just over the woods, the trees are brilliantly green and filled with happy birds."[6]

Later that evening, Colonel Wainwright assigned Captain James Stewart's Battery B, 4th U. S., and George Breck's Battery L, 1st New York Light to Wadsworth. Wilson's cavalry continued on to Parker's Store, about four miles to the southwest. The Orange Turnpike, an east-west road running from Fredericksburg through Chancellorsville to Orange

Court House, intersected the Germanna Plank Road at the tavern. Assigned the duty of flank guard, Griffin's First Division advanced two more miles west on the Turnpike, stopped, and established a picket line. Fog appeared as the sun went down. Having marched most of the night before, the men quickly fell asleep.[7]

Sedgwick's Sixth Corps camped that night on the heights just beyond the ford and Hancock's Second Corps on the old Chancellorsville battlefield. The infantry and cavalry could have escaped the Wilderness May 4 but that would have left the army's long supply trains unprotected and vulnerable to Confederate attack.[8]

May 5, 1864

General Wadsworth seemed to possess this exalted power (of personal attraction) to an eminent degree, even to drawing men around him who had never seen or scarcely heard of him before, holding them almost in the jaws of death and impressing them with his own lofty spirit of loyalty which rose above all fear of danger.
Captain John Anderson, 57th Massachusetts[9]

Meade's marching orders for May 5 assumed that Lee would not interfere with the Federal movement. At 5:00 AM, the advance would resume: Fifth Corps to Parker's Store, Sixth to Wilderness Tavern, and Second to Shady Grove Church.[10]

"Before day(light), bugles blowed, drums beat; men get ready to march." Crawford's, Wadsworth's, and Robinson's Divisions made preparations to resume a southwesterly march. Griffin's would remain on the Turnpike serving as the rearguard. The Fifth Corps's objectives that day were to secure the Wilderness's two, east-west roads – the Orange Turnpike and Orange Plank – and screen the Second and Sixth Corps's advance toward Spotsylvania Court House. As Crawford started south from the Lacy House, Charles Griffin's pickets observed a column of enemy cavalry, followed by infantry, advancing east on the Orange Turnpike. Coming under fire, the Rebels immediately deployed in line of battle. Hearing the musketry of their skirmishers, Griffin's Division also formed a battle line and started constructing breastworks. Wilson's cavalry screen had failed to detect the approach of Ewell's Corps.[11]

Learning of Griffin's engagement, Grant and Meade concluded that it was only a small force left behind to watch the Federal advance. Completely underestimating what was out there, they ordered Warren to halt, concentrate his four divisions on the Pike, and "capture or disperse" the rebels. G. K. Warren wanted to delay the attack until Sedgwick's Corps had come up on his right but was overruled. Meade also sent word to Hancock to halt at Todd's Tavern. Grant's movement to turn Lee's right and force the Army of Northern Virginia into the open ended that day at 9:00 AM.[12]

After marching about two miles under a bright and pleasant sky, a message from Warren reached Wadsworth at 7:30 AM. "The movement toward Parker's Store is suspended for the present. You will halt, face toward Mine Run, and make your connection with General Griffin on your right." The three brigades stopped and changed from flank march into battle front. Facing northwest, they stood about two miles north of the Plank Road and a mile south of the Turnpike. Regiments in the first line threw up breastworks while those behind dug rifle pits.[13]

About 8:00 AM Major General Warren rode up and told Wadsworth "to find out what was in there," pointing to woods on the right. Before departing, Warren added that Crawford would march north from the Chewing Farm. In an update to Charles Griffin, Wadsworth described his current position.

> I find an opening and tolerable position for artillery (Jones' Farm) about 1 mile from Lacy's house. I am at that point with two batteries and one brigade (Rice's). Have a brigade (Stone's) stretched thinly through a piece of very thick woods, and one brigade (Cutler's) near you.

A new complication closed his message. "Crawford's troops in front, roar in sight." Fighting had broken out near Parker's Store on the Plank Road. Wadsworth prudently delayed an advance and waited for clarification from Fifth Corps's Headquarters.[14]

After contacting Griffin's pickets, the leading elements of Richard S. Ewell's Second Corps stopped and started constructing breastworks. Griffin pulled back his skirmishers and waited for reinforcements. Farther south, Samuel Crawford, commanding Third Division, sent a message to Warren around 8:00 AM. "I have advanced to within a mile of Parker's Store. There is brisk skirmishing at the Store between our own and the enemy's cavalry. The general's order is received, and I am halted in a good position." Wadsworth's "roar in sight" was the arrival of A. P. Hill's Corps on the Orange Plank Road. Lee pulled a second surprise on Grant and Meade.[15]

General Crawford recognized that his current position commanded the Plank Road and did not want to leave it. He told Warren at 10:15, "The enemy are working around to get upon the plank road. No firing at this moment." The Fifth Corps Commander, under pressure from Meade and Grant, replied, "You will move to the right as quickly as possible." Major Washington Roebling, serving on Warren's staff, came to Crawford's defense.

> It is of vital importance to hold the field where General Crawford is. Our whole line of battle is turned if the enemy get possession of it. There is a gap of half a mile between Wadsworth and Crawford. He cannot hold the line against an attack.

At 11:15, Samuel Crawford asked Corps's Headquarters, "Shall I abandon the position I now hold to connect with General Wadsworth, who is about a half a mile on my right; he having moved up to connect with Griffin?" Fifteen minutes later he reported, "Firing has ceased in my front, excepting occasional shots. It is reported that the enemy are passing up the plank road in my rear." Warren ended the debate. "You must connect with General Wadsworth, and cover and protect his left as he advances." At noon Crawford responded, "The connection with Wadsworth is being made. The enemy hold the plank road and are passing up."[16]

Crawford had watched as skirmishing between pickets grew into serious fighting. Henry Heth's infantry pushed Wilson's Cavalry aside and resumed their advance toward the Brock Road. If A. P. Hill captured this key intersection, Hancock's Corps would be isolated. Withdrawing Crawford's Division from Parker's Store was an unfortunate decision. Meade hurriedly dispatched George W. Getty's Sixth Corps Division down the Germanna Plank Road. Getty reached the Orange Plank Road in time to stop Hill's advance. Regardless, for the second time in less than twelve hours, Federal cavalry had failed to "push well out to the front and flanks and feel for the enemy." The Fifth Corps would now pay the price on the Turnpike.[17]

At 10:30 AM, Wadsworth received Warren's instructions. "Push forward a heavy line of skirmishers, followed by your line of battle, and at-

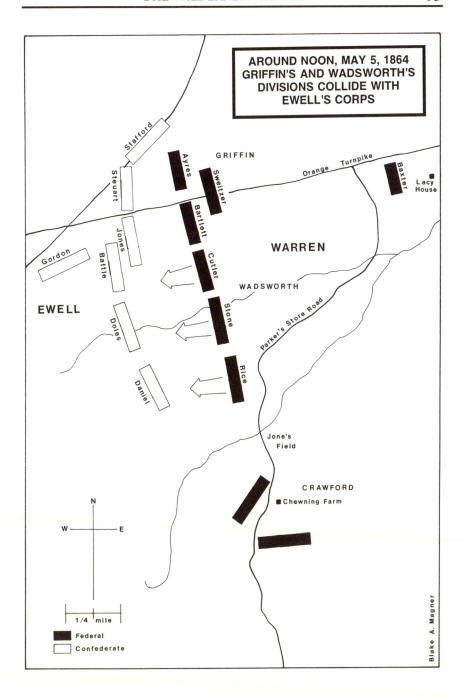

tack the enemy at once and push him. General Griffin will also attack. Do not wait for him, but look out for your own left flank." Orders went down the lines for companies, and in some cases regiments, to go forward as skirmishers. About 11:00 AM, the advance began. Word spread among the men that this would be a reconnaissance. Warren's plan, however, called for Cutler to connect with Griffin's left, followed by a westward advance of the entire Federal line. Simple in concept, its execution proved to be impossible. The Major General was still unaware that his two divisions faced Ewell's entire command. With Crawford still near the Chewing Farm, Wadsworth's left was 'in the air'.[18]

Rice, Stone, and Cutler, left to right, moved forward to find and attack the enemy. Stewart's and Breck's Batteries remained at Jones's Farm, covering the road to Parker's Store. Ahead of the advancing infantry, the sound of fighting grew louder. Dense undergrowth and thick woods limited visibility, isolating brigades and creating confusion between regiments. Pushing on with great difficulty, Cutler's right regiment, the 7th Indiana, connected with Griffin and they advanced westward The troops stumbled and hacked their way through matted underbrush, briar thickets, and dense groves of pine. Communications between brigades ceased and some regiments broke up into isolated companies. As the division struggled forward, Rice's and Stone's Brigades started drifting left. This problem grew steadily worse until they were well in front with both flanks exposed. About 1:00 PM Cutler found the enemy.[19]

The 'Iron Brigade' charged and broke through John M. Jones's Brigade, Edward Johnson's Division. The 7th Indiana captured the 50th Virginia's colors and over two hundred prisoners. Success was brief, however. Like the other brigades, Cutler's had also drifted left during the final advance, losing contact on the right with Griffin. The situation was no better on the division's far left. Expecting to be reinforced by Crawford, Rice's men continued forward, struggling through the dense woods. Without warning, heavy musketry from an unseen enemy struck the Federal line. An officer in charge of the skirmishers came running back and described an advancing line of Rebel infantry that extended far beyond the brigade's left. Samuel Crawford had failed to reach Rice's left flank in time. Trouble now occurred on Rice's right.[20]

Roy Stone moved ahead with the 150th Pennsylvania out front as skirmishers. Regimental formations became nonexistent and several commands stopped trying to advance in line of battle and resorted to flank marches. Before long, "the regiments were entirely and impossibly intermixed, confused, and lost." Battle noise from the right seemed to indicate that Griffin and Cutler were successful at the Turnpike. Stone's officers and men became complacent. Besides the thickets, vines, and stunted trees, several companies now stumbled into a swamp. At this point, a heavy volley or "sheet of flame" opened on the right. Like the volley that hit Rice, it came from an unseen enemy. While Rice and Stone had been "thrashing through the woods," two Confederate brigades, Junius Daniel's North Carolinians and John B. Gordon's Georgians, quietly moved into position. Daniel fired into Rice's front; and Gordon into his right and Stone's left. The unexpected attacks destroyed the effectiveness of both Federal brigades that afternoon.[21]

Wadsworth's Division collapsed like a stack of dominos. Cutler later reported:

> Stone's brigade gave way soon after meeting the enemy, thus letting the enemy through our line. Rice lost nearly all of his skirmish line as prisoners, and a large number of men and officers killed and wounded. The First Brigade (Cutler's) continued to drive the enemy until it was ascertained that the troops on both flanks had left, and that the enemy was closing in his rear, when he was obliged to fight his way back, losing very heavily in killed and wounded.

Officers attempted to reform the men and make a stand but the rout was complete. The three brigades fell back to where they had started that morning. Fortunately, Ewell did not pursue. For the first time, Wadsworth's Division had panicked and ran off a battlefield. The losses were heavy, many taken prisoner. The general sent Captain Frank Cowdrey, Assistant Adjutant General, to inform Warren of the disaster. Wadsworth stayed and assisted Cutler, Rice, and Stone in reforming their commands "on the crest of a hill in front of the Lacy house."[22]

By mid-afternoon, fighting at the Turnpike reached a stalemate. The Fifth Corps lost about three thousand men May 5 and accomplished nothing. Grant's and Meade's attention now focused on the Orange Plank Road. Running roughly parallel to the Turnpike and about three miles south, the road was half planking and half dirt. The key to this portion of the Federal line was its intersection with the Brock Road, less than a mile east of the current Second Corps line. Two of A. P. Hill's Divisions, Henry Heth's and Cadmus Wilcox's, were trying to cut the Army of the Potomac in two by seizing this critical junction. About 2:00 PM near the Lacy House, Grant discussed the situation with Warren and his staff. He asked, "Would it be possible to send a force straight (south) through the woods to strike Hill in the left flank." Without hesitating, Wadsworth said yes and volunteered to lead it. Possibly, he wanted to recapture for his men that which had been lost south of the Turnpike. The Lieutenant General agreed and added Henry Baxter's Brigade from John Robinson's Division to Wadsworth's force. One relatively fresh and three battered brigades would now attempt to relieve the pressure on Hancock.[23]

At 6:00 PM, Wadsworth's Division set out, their goal to support Hancock's right about three miles away. The men had been under arms for over fourteen hours. Entering dense woods "in many places impenetrable," they formed a line of battle and advanced; Stone and Baxter in front, Cutler behind, and Rice in reserve. Heavy musketry could be heard farther south. These brigades experienced the same problems in trying to reach the Plank Road that they had earlier in trying to find Griffin. Behind schedule, the division did not approach the fighting until almost sunset. Following Wadsworth's orders, they advanced quietly until skirmishers from Major General Wilcox's Division appeared and opened fire. At this point, something went amiss in Stone's Brigade.[24]

This unit entered the Wilderness short of good field officers. Its best regimental commander, Colonel Edmund L. Dana, 143rd Pennsylvania, had been captured near the Turnpike. When Baxter's and Wilcox's men started exchanging fire, a wave of emotion, panic or fear, swept through Stone's command. Men reacted by shouting, running to the rear, and firing their muskets. Other brigades, hearing the noise started firing at an invisible enemy. "Pandemonium ensued." What had been a quiet advance turned into a "howling wilderness."[25]

Wadsworth ordered a cease fire and quiet to be restored. Colonel Stone not only ignored it but "had his troops deliver a roaring cheer for Pennsylvania." For the second time today, he lost control of his men. Regimental officers and, "Cutler's bayonets behind them" finally reestablished order. Short of patience after a disastrous day, Wadsworth ordered Stone to report immediately. Instead, Roy Stone left the field and the Army of the Potomac. Rice's and Cutler's Brigades moved to the front and Stone's went into reserve. Before May 5, 1864, Roy Stone possessed an excellent record. His Gettysburg wound had not healed and he may have been taking something for the pain. Whatever the reason for Stone's breakdown, Wadsworth lost a brigade commander and probably the brigade's effectiveness.[26]

Baxter's men advanced to within a half mile of the Plank Road when darkness stopped the fighting about 8:00 PM. The brigades took position – Cutler, Baxter, and Rice, left to right – and formed a line roughly parallel to and north of the road. Pickets were advanced and the men spent a restless night sleeping on their arms. Wadsworth's command had clearly failed to match its outstanding July 1 performance at Gettysburg. That evening, the general most likely wondered why.[27]

Unlike Adams County Pennsylvania, the Wilderness was not 'beautiful ground' to fight on but both sides faced the same terrain problems. Ewell knew what was out there the morning of May 5, but Warren did not. By itself, this lack of good intelligence did not completely explain the outcome. Going into battle, Wadsworth's Division possessed good command integrity and continuity at the divisional and brigade levels. This was also true at regimental except in Stone's Third Brigade. Here, new commanders led four of his five regiments. All of the 150th Pennsylvania's original field officers had resigned because of wounds received at McPherson's Farm. The Bucktails represented only 'the tip of the iceberg'.[28]

Wadsworth's sixteen Wilderness regiments had seen 'the elephant' at Gettysburg. Their average, total loss for July 1863 – killed, wounded, missing or captured – exceeded 50%. For half of them, it surpassed 65%: 19th Indiana, 24th Michigan, 84th and 147th New York; 121st, 149th, and 150th Pennsylvania, and 2nd Wisconsin. The percentage total loss in Rowley's, Stone's, and Meredith's Brigades was surpassed only by Gabriel Paul's. Many soldiers, initially reported as missing, later returned. Still, almost half of Meredith's and Rowley's commands were either killed or wounded. The volunteers of '61 and '62 were now a minority. First Corps never recovered from Gettysburg and faded into history. Wadsworth's Division tried but failed May 5. Augustus Buell recognized what had been lost at Gettysburg when he later described that July 1 morning on the Emmitsburg Road: "No one now living will ever again see those two brigades of Wadsworth's Division file by as they did that morning." The same could have been said about Abner Doubleday's Division.[29]

May 6, 1864

He (Wadsworth) literally led his men into the battle, a thing which, as far as my own experience shows, was rare, at least on the part of Northern general officers.
                    Z. Boylston Adams, 56th Massachusetts[30]

Darkness ended the fighting May 5 shortly after A. P. Hill had committed his last reserves to stop Hancock's final attack. Fortune favored Robert E. Lee that evening. Hill's and Ewell's men held the lines from which they had fought during most of the day. Lee ordered James Longstreet to make a night march, expecting to have his First Corps in position on the right, by daylight. The entire Confederate battle line would then advance at dawn. Longstreet's men began their march at 1:00 AM. Four hours later Ewell would open the battle by attacking Warren and Sedgwick.[31]

Grant and Meade agreed that the Second, Fifth, and Sixth Corps would attack the enemy at 5:00 AM. Two of Burnside's Ninth Corps divisions, Wilcox's and Potter's were coming up. They would close the gap between Wadsworth's right and Warren's left by advancing west to Parker's Store. Initially, the remaining Ninth Corps Division, Brigadier General Thomas G. Stevenson's, would remain in reserve at the Old Wilderness Tavern. Grant and Meade also knew that three, fresh Confederate divisions – Major General Charles W. Field's and Brigadier General Joseph B. Kershaw's, Longstreet's Corps; and Brigadier General Richard H. Anderson's, Hill's Corps – were pushing toward the battlefield. Grant did not want Lee seizing the initiative. At 12:15 AM, Warren finished an order for his detached, division commander.

> We are ordered to make another advance...at 4:30 a.m. everywhere on the line. Set your (Wadsworth's) line of battle on a line northeast and southwest, and march directly southeast on the flank of the enemy in front of General Hancock.[32]

Shortly after midnight, Wadsworth sent an aide, Captain Robert Monteith, to secure orders and a resupply of ammunition. With two orderlies he headed due north. After stopping at Fifth Corps Headquarters, Monteith went to the division's ordnance train. The aide returned at 3:00 AM with orders and ten pack mules, each carrying two thousand rounds. Warren had attempted to offset the previous day's losses by assigning Colonel J. Howard Kitching's Independent Brigade, 6th and 15th New

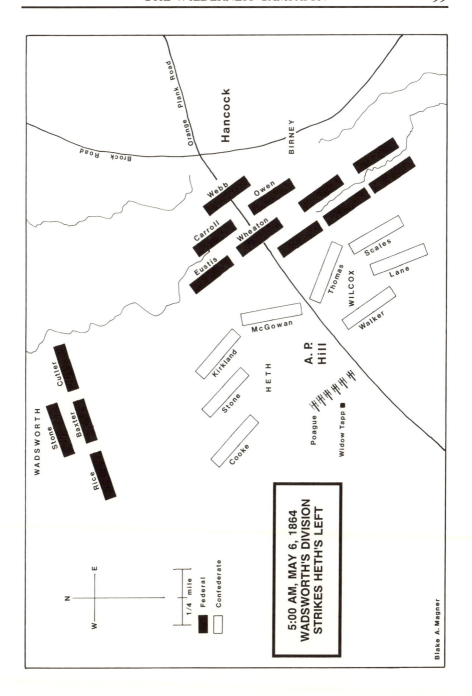

York Heavy Artillery, 2400 strong, to Wadsworth's command. There was barely enough time to distribute the ammunition.[33]

At 5:00 AM a signal gun fired, echoing off the trees. Five Federal divisions started forward in the dim light. Burnside's approaching troops were expected to close the mile long gap that now opened between Warren and Hancock. Wadsworth's three brigades struck Henry Heth's left flank, quickly overrunning Brigadier General William Kirkland's North Carolina Brigade. Driving down the Plank Road, Hancock assailed Heth and Wilcox's front. Flanked and taking fire from three directions, both Confederate divisions folded up. Survivors headed for safety at the Widow Tapp Farm, over a half mile to the rear (west). The Federals may have been too successful. Unforeseen by Warren when he issued the order, Cutler and a brigade from Brigadier General George W. Getty's Sixth Corps Division collided near the road. Rufus Dawes remembered that "the men became jammed and crowded, and there was much confusion." Valuable time was lost in straightening things out.[34]

Rice and Baxter wheeled to the right. Their brigades, now in front, faced west. A. P. Hill's men continued retreating, some already past the Tapp Farm. Finally, Wadsworth finished reforming his division into four lines, initially perpendicular to and north of the road. Cutler followed Rice and Baxter with Stone in reserve. Kitching's command advanced on the far right. Major General David Birney's and Brigadier General Gershom Mott's Divisions, with two brigades from Brigadier General John Gibbon's, all Second Corps units; plus two of Getty's Sixth Corps brigades, and Wadsworth's 5th Corps Division resumed their advance. They almost succeeded in breaking Lee's right.[35]

The Wilderness continued to take a heavy toll that morning as it had the previous day. Gaps appeared in the blue battle lines as some units wandered off and got lost. Others drifted together, intermingling the commands. Hidden in dense thickets, men from Mississippi and North Carolina opened fire and collected their own toll. Wadsworth's rear lines strayed to the left until the flank regiments were south of the road. Sent forward by George Meade, Stevenson's Ninth Corps Division approached the Brock and Orange Plank intersection. Captain Boylston Adams, 56th Massachusetts, Colonel Sumner Carruth's Brigade, "saw General Hancock ...sitting on his horse by the side of a brass 12-pounder pointing down the road (Orange Plank)." They turned right, and formed line of battle.[36]

About 6:00 AM, the leading elements of Hancock's advance reached "an old field containing thirty acres or more." Across the clearing, skirmishers from the 95th and 147th New York saw four Confederate artillery batteries positioned in a north-south line, just east of the Tapp House. James Rice's command continued toward the farm. Burnside's two divisions were not in sight. Lieutenant Colonel William T. Poague, commanding one of A. P. Hill's artillery battalions, opened a slow fire of spherical case and canister. The Federals had reached their 'high water mark' on the Plank Road.[37]

Wadsworth's advance slowed, then stopped. He ordered Rice to capture a battery to the right that was enfilading the entire line. The 56th Pennsylvania and 76th New York changed front and drove off supporting skirmishers. They moved forward but Poague pulled back his guns in time. The Ninth Corps's failure to support the drive was soon overshadowed by a greater calamity. West of the Tapp Clearing, Longstreet's men quickly wheeled into position. Hidden by a slight rise, Lee watched 'Old Pete' direct Kershaw's and Field's leading brigades to the right or south. The remainder of Field's column moved to the left. North of the Plank Road, Brigadier General John Gregg, Henry C. Benning, and Colonel William F. Perry pushed their brigades through Hill's routed men, past Poague's Batteries, and across the clearing.[38]

Poague's artillery fire struck Rice and Baxter as they advanced westward through the trees, their left resting on the road. To minimize losses, Wadsworth 'closed in mass' his four lines of infantry. Closing up the ranks, however, increased their vulnerability to Longstreet's coming attack. Massed in column, Gregg's five hundred Texans charged into the woods. Coming under heavy musketry and suffering high losses, they still managed to break through Baxter's first line. Two subsequent charges drove back Baxter's second line. Down on the road, Wadsworth lost his first horse that day to enemy fire. Close behind Gregg, came Benning's Georgians who struck Rice and what remained of Baxter. Benning's final charge and William Perry's first sent Wadsworth's two front brigades reeling rearward toward Cutler.[39]

Supported by Stone's and Kitching's commands, Lysander Cutler held the crest of a low hill, fronted by a ravine and narrow swamp. In his left rear Baxter and Rice reformed their survivors near the road. Hat off, Wadsworth led them forward, briefly taking back some of the lost ground. An enfilading fire from Kitching's men had helped stop Perry's

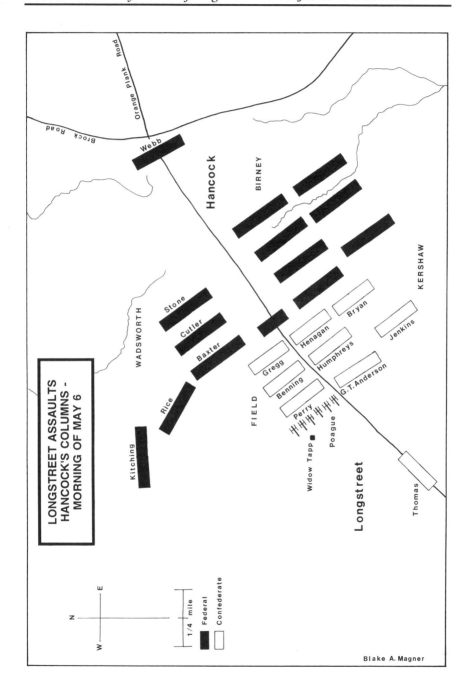

Alabamians. Across the swamp, William Perry studied the Federal line. Reaching a decision, he sent Colonel William Oates and the 15th Alabama about two hundred yards farther left. From here they launched a surprise attack that scattered Kitching's inexperienced troops. Their right flank exposed, Wadsworth and Cutler rode the lines, trying to steady the men. At first they succeeded, stopping a two prong, frontal assault by Perry and Gregg. Oates then appeared a second time on the Federal right. His enfilading volleys were too much and Wadsworth relinquished the heights. Colonel Richard Coulter, 11th Pennsylvania, Baxter's Brigade, later remembered the crisis. "Near the road the enemy had secured such a position as enabled him to deliver a most galling fire on our right flank. The regiments in front, also being hotly engaged, gave way, carrying with them those in rear."[40]

Other units from Field's Division and Hill's Corps joined William Perry's drive up the Plank Road. For the Confederates it was two steps forward and one step back. While trying to keep his front regiments in line, Henry Baxter was seriously wounded and carried off the field. Richard Coulter assumed command in time to watch his brigade collapse and be swept away. Rice's company commanders hurriedly rallied those who had not run to the rear. At first, these reformed commands held. Then they began to give way. Earlier during the advance, General Getty had shifted Brigadier General Frank Wheaton's and Henry L. Eustis's Brigades north of the road. Eustis's arrived first in column of regiments. Desperate to stop Perry, Wadsworth directed the two Sixth Corps brigades to advance but Eustis disagreed. His lead regiment, the 37th Massachusetts, however, responded to Wadsworth's urging and proceeded alone. "It was like a charge through the wildest regions of Dante's *Inferno*." Attacked on both flanks, the regiment fell back with little gained but more casualties.[41]

Trying to fill the gap left by Baxter, Eustis and Wheaton at first slowed and then finally stopped Perry's Brigade. Wheaton felt an element of luck was involved. "The enemy, on account of the dense woods, could not see the advantage gained, and his weak reconnoitering force following the Second Corps was obliged to retreat as soon as they came in view of our front." Rather than just luck, it was the timely arrival of Brigadier General Alexander S. Webb's Second Corps Brigade. Recognizing how much Baxter's collapse had stretched Wheaton's and Eustis's commands, Hancock sent Webb, his last reserve, forward just before 7:30 AM. With no skirmishers and a battle line strung out through the woods, Webb first came across stragglers from Baxter's command, then stumbled into Field's advancing brigades. Furious fighting resulted. Together, Webb, Wheaton, and Eustis held the north side of the Orange Plank Road.[42]

U. S. Grant's only success that morning was gone. For the second time in less than twenty-four hours, Wadsworth had been baldly mauled. With its commander disabled and a long casualty list from the morning's fight, Baxter's Brigade 'dropped off the broad.' Having received a severe baptism of fire from William Oates, Kitching's two, heavy-artillery regiments did not reappear until late afternoon on the Brock Road. Lysander Cutler joined other officers in trying to rally shattered units. His report effectively described the disaster.

> (The division) was furiously attacked by infantry and artillery, driven back, and badly scattered, a large portion of them taking the route over which they had marched the night before. This portion of the command was rallied and got together by me near the Old Wilderness Tavern. That portion which retired on the plank road was rallied by Generals Wadsworth and Rice....

Meade and Grant watched Cutler's men limp past the Lacy House. By 8:00 AM Fourth Division had suffered at least 2,000 casualties, and over 4,000 Federals were 'missing' from the Plank Road.[43]

Following the army's March reorganization, Captain Craig Wadsworth was assigned to the staff of General Alfred Torbert, commander First Cavalry Division. A physical problem May 5 forced Torbert to relinquish command to Brigadier General Wesley Merritt. Early the next morning, Merritt reinforced Hancock's left by shifting George Custer's Brigade toward the Brock Road. Given permission to visit his father, Craig Wadsworth accompanied Custer. Sometime between 8:00 and 9:00 AM, father and son met near the Plank Road.[44]

Hancock reestablished the Federal lines. Rice and Wadsworth pulled together about two thousand effectives and reformed north of the road. Wounded in the shoulder, General Getty left the field and Wheaton assumed division command. His former brigade took position on Wadsworth's left. Webb's and Joshua T. Owen's Second Corps Brigades extended the Federal line southward. As Stevenson's Ninth Corps Division moved forward, Captain Boylston Adams, 56th Massachusetts, saw Wadsworth "come out of the woods on the left with one or two other staff officers." He spoke briefly with Carruth then rode off. Several regiments

Brigadier General Lysander Cutler

General Cutler commanded the Fourth Division after Wadsworth was wounded. (Courtesy, Massachusetts Commandery, MOLLUS; Copy from USAMHI)

moved forward "with battalion front." After a few minutes, Carruth halted the columns. They formed line of battle perpendicular to the road and started throwing up breastworks. Assured by Meade that Burnside's divisions were ready to assault Field's right, Hancock decided at 8:40 to order another attack "to be at once pressed, especially on the right and center." In spite of the morning's heavy losses, he briefly regained the momentum.[45]

Wadsworth's and Wheaton's Divisions followed by Carruth's Brigade, which straddled the road, advanced. On their left were the remnants of Mott's and Birney's Divisions plus Samuel S. Carroll's, Webb's, and Owen's Brigades. In spite of field officers receiving conflicting orders, line officers trying to lead intermingled commands, and enlisted men confused by the Wilderness, the Federal line went forward. Coming under intense fire, the advance slowed then stopped. Attempting to revive the stalled columns, Wadsworth looked for a regiment to send forward and selected one of Webb's.[46]

Earlier Wadsworth had detached the 20th Massachusetts from Webb's Brigade and ordered it to the south of the road. Here, behind log breastworks it held a strong position facing west. In Webb's absence, Wadsworth ordered the 20th forward against Perry's Alabamians. When its Colonel, George N. Macy, protested, the general rode to the front, ignored Macy, and led the charge himself. Crashing into the woods, they received a volley from an invisible enemy. In front, Wadsworth lost his second horse. Colonel Macy and Major Henry L. Abbott were wounded, the latter mortally. The 20th ultimately suffered the same fate as the 37th Massachusetts had earlier.[47]

Unaware of the 20th Massachusetts's setback, Webb changed front twice to hold the position. Wadsworth now ordered a third advance. Alexander Webb pushed ahead his mixed command of Second and Ninth Corps regiments. Urged forward by Wadsworth, the 57th Massachusetts "lost a great many men in doing what the Twentieth Massachusetts had done before, i.e., advancing by itself to urge on the line." Hancock waited in vain for Burnside to assault the Confederate left. It never happened. In spite of this the Federal line finally stabilized on both sides of the road.[48]

During the fighting, Captain Boylston Adams was shot in the leg, abandoned on the field, and captured by the 24th Georgia, Kershaw's

Division. Field and Kershaw, reinforced by Hill, regained the ground they recently had lost. Sometime during this action, the 4th Alabama probably killed Wadsworth's second horse. The general mounted Lieutenant Colonel George B. Osborn's horse and rode into the line urging the men forward. William Perry observed that:

> the enemy had reformed also, and were evidently preparing to advance upon us. I ordered the Fourth and Forty-seventh to charge. The enemy gave way, and we again found ourselves on the advanced line of works.

Brigadier General Abner Perrin's Brigade, R. H. Anderson's Division, now came up and took position just north of the road. Perry shifted his command to the left.[49]

With both sides exhausted and no reinforcements available, fighting diminished and finally stopped about 10:00 AM. At the same time that Birney and Wadsworth began their second advance, Hancock started receiving orders from Meade to reinforce Warren, then his own left. Within an hour, four brigades were taken from Birney and sent elsewhere. Eustis's Brigade left at 9:30 for the Brock Road, later returning to Birney. First, the initiative and now the momentum had been lost to Robert E. Lee.[50]

After leading three unsuccessful charges, and having two horses killed under him, Wadsworth received word from Hancock not to make any further attempts to dislodge Longstreet's and Hill's troops. Having spent three hours with his father, Captain Craig Wadsworth departed to rejoin Merritt's Division which was preparing to move out. A brief, late morning lull provided an opportunity to rest. Alone with one of his aides, Captain Robert Monteith, Wadsworth confessed to complete mental and physical exhaustion. Considering himself unfit to command, he told Monteith that Cutler should take over the division. Recognizing, however, that there wasn't time to make this change, the general requested a cracker and returned to his own thoughts.[51]

Sometime during this lull, Wadsworth went to Second Corps Headquarters. Here he was told of being placed under Hancock's direct orders, who gave him command of two Second Corps brigades, Webb's and Brigadier General J. H. Hobart Ward's, and one Ninth Corps brigade, Sumner Carruth's. These three plus Rice's and Wheaton's remnants were all that remained north of the Plank Road. Hancock put nothing in writing and verbal notification evidently failed to reach Alexander Webb. This oversight complicated, even more, an unwieldy command situation.⁵²

Earlier that morning, Richard Anderson's Third Corps Division reached the Tapp Farm. Lee placed it under Longstreet's direct command, who held the division in reserve. The two generals searched for a way to turn Hancock's left. One of Lee's aides found an approach concealed by the forest and unobserved by the Federals. Lieutenant Colonel Moxley Sorrel, Longstreet's Chief of Staff, set out with a flanking column composed of three brigades: Brigadier General G. T. Anderson's (Field's Division), William T. Wofford's Georgians (Kershaw's), and William Mahone's Virginians (R. H. Anderson's). Heading east, Sorrel followed an unfinished railroad bed then stopped, just south of Hancock's left. Shortly after 10:00 AM they formed line of battle and then struck without warning. Mahone recalled that:

> ...In a few moments the line of attack had been formed, and the three brigades, in imposing order and with a step that meant to conquer, were now rapidly descending upon the enemy's left. The movement was a success, complete as it was brilliant. The enemy were swept from our front on the Plank Road...he (Birney) was not allowed time to "change front".⁵³

For Birney's, Mott's and Getty's Divisions, the morning lull ended abruptly. Slowly, then rapidly, Hancock's left wing collapsed. Some survivors headed east for breastworks along Brock Road, while others crossed the Plank Road and ran through Wadsworth's lines. David Birney's officers tried to rally their troops but by 11:00 AM organized resistance south of the road had ceased. Hancock later admitted that they "rolled...[him]up like a wet blanket." Sorrel's flanking column wheeled left and pushed north. At the same time Charles Field and Richard Anderson renewed the frontal attack on Hancock's right wing. After driving back Mott's Division, Mahone's Virginians began crossing the road behind Wheaton. Coming under fire from three directions, the Sixth Corps brigade broke and ran for safety.⁵⁴

South of the road, Federal units fell back in disorder. Protecting his exposed left flank became Wadsworth's first priority. He directed Webb to "go to the left to determine what was the cause of the disorder taking place there...(and) directed me (Webb) to take any four regiments I could find to replace those (Wheaton's) he had seen falling back." Before Webb

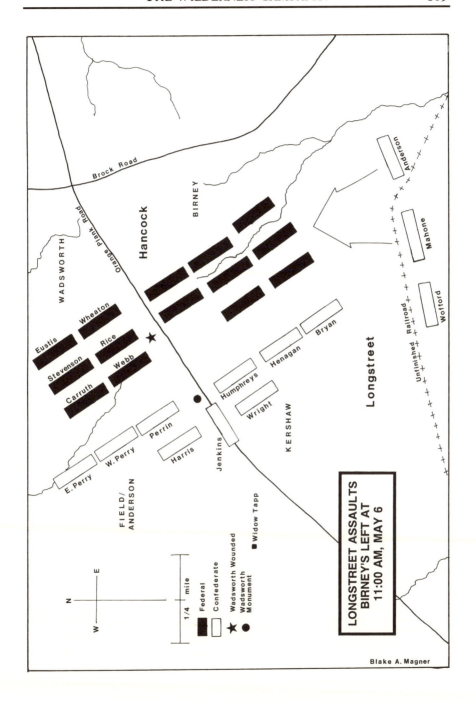

returned, Wadsworth positioned his brigade in column facing south. The general sent Robert Monteith to find and bring back what remained of Cutler's Brigade to extend his right. An aide from Hancock rode up and reported what everyone already knew. "Troops left of the road were falling back. Look out for the left flank." Wadsworth ordered James Rice's Brigade "to change front forward on the left battalion." Forming a new line, parallel to the Plank Road, they were to "take in flank the enemy as he came across." As they reformed, Rice's regiments came under heavy artillery and musket fire. This time, Perrin's Alabamians rose and fired a volley into the exposed Federal right, breaking up the 56th Pennsylvania and 76th New York. Having suffered heavy losses for over five hours, the patched-together command from Rice's, Stone's and Baxter's Brigades fell back "fleeing in wild confusion." Colonel Hofmann remembered that "an effort was made to rally the men. It was only partially successful and they retired to as far back as the Brock road and a quarter of a mile north of the plank road." It seemed that nothing could stop Sorrel's attack.[55]

For several minutes the fighting surged back and forth through the tangled and marshy forest. Then the remaining Federals retreated. Wadsworth and one of his aides, Lieutenant Earl M. Rogers, Clayton's brother, found themselves alone on the road. They could see Perrin's men approaching from the west and Mahone's from the left. Caught up in the action, the general hesitated to join the retreat. Concluding there was no alternative but to fall back, he started pulling the animal around. Shots rang out. One bullet struck Wadsworth's head, spattering his brains onto Rogers's coat. He slumped forward, then fell to the ground. Having lost his horse, Rogers hurried over and tried to remove the general's watch. The Alabamians were too close and the Lieutenant ran for his life. Fortunately, the reins of Wadsworth's horse had caught on a tree. Jumping into the saddle, Rogers managed to avoid capture and rode to Warren's headquarters. At 12:45 PM Major E. R. Platt informed Major General Andrew Humphreys, Meade's Chief of Staff that "an aide of General Wadsworth has just come in. He reports that the general is killed; that he was with him when he was struck in the head about half an hour ago. The body was left on the ground."[56]

Perrin's Alabamians advanced past Wadsworth's body. One of Webb's regiments, the 19th Maine, held their position long enough for the retreating Federals to escape eastward. Alexander Webb praised its colonel.

> (19th Maine) was halted by Colonel Connor, without orders,...
> He prevented the enemy from seeing the rout. The road was

Wadsworth's Wilderness Monument

This monument, near the Orange Plank Road, marks the area where James Wadsworth was mortally wounded. (Courtesy, Donald Pfanz, NPS)

Plaque on Wadsworth's Wilderness Monument

The plaque on Wadsworth's Wilderness Monument, was erected in 1936 by grandson and former U.S. Senator James W., Jr. (Courtesy, Donald Pfanz, NPS)

jammed with troops and the rear of the column would have suffered terribly had not Colonel Connor stopped his regiment.[57]

Later that afternoon, Benjamin Kneeland, surgeon 1st New York Dragoons, was working in a Second Corps hospital near the Brock Road. He saw General Getty come in with a serious shoulder wound. Walking over, Kneeland inquired about James Wadsworth. Just before leaving the front lines, Getty remembered seeing him.

> His (Wadsworth's) head down nearly to his horse's neck to keep clear of the branches, and in a hail of bullets that he (Getty) did not believe a humming-bird could live in a minute.

About a half hour later, Craig Wadsworth rode by the hospital. Kneeland went out and asked about his father. Craig replied, "He was mortally wounded,...probably dead already."[58]

Lysander Cutler sent two staff officers to find their missing general. They were driven back by enemy skirmishers. He then saw "horsemen and men rallying around" the division flag. Thinking that it must be Wadsworth, he quickly rode over but found only two aides and some orderlies. After talking to Captain Monteith and Lieutenant Rogers, Cutler sent word to Warren. "I just learn that General Wadsworth is killed, and that the balance of the division is scattered and gone, except what I have with me." Writing in his journal that evening, Charles Wainwright recounted hearing that Wadsworth and his men had fought superbly on the Plank Road.[59]

An Enemy Prisoner

Wadsworth whose brilliant example and fearless courage always had such an inspiring effect upon his soldiers, fell while leading them against the enemy on the morning of the 6th.
        Major General Winfield Scott Hancock[60]

Like his corps commander ten months earlier, Wadsworth was mortally wounded while leading from the front. Unlike Reynolds, he did not die immediately but fell into Confederate hands. Lying unconscious on the Plank Road, Wadsworth's body was stripped of his heirloom sword, watch, field-glasses, and map. Major John C. Haskell commanded an artillery battalion, Longstreet's Corps. Orders came the afternoon of May 6 to advance a battery. Riding eastward, the major saw:

> A large, fine-looking man in the uniform of a general, who was lying on the side of the [Orange Plank] road in the dust and heat. Noticing that he was still alive, I had two of my orderlies to move him out of the dust. They stuck some muskets up and a spread a blanket over him as an awning, then got a surgeon to examine him. The surgeon did not think that he was conscious, and gave him some water and morphine. He had been shot through the head.... He was General Wadsworth of New York and was said by some prisoners who knew him to have been a very brave man.[61]

Major General Charles Field observed the wounded brigadier propped against a tree and being provided with water. Unable to speak, Wadsworth appeared to be conscious. Field remembered that "every attention and respect [was] shown him (Wadsworth) which kindness could suggest." While carrying an order from Robert E. Lee, Colonel Charles Marshall "found General Wadsworth, whom I knew by a piece of paper which was pinned to his coat with his name on it...lying on his back...over him was extended a shelter tent, about three feet from the ground." Men from the 12th Virginia carried him to their infirmary at the Pulliam Farm, three miles west of Tapp's. Wadsworth was then taken to the field hospital for Perrin's Brigade. In a specially erected officer's tent near the road, surgeon Dr. James W. Claiborne dressed the wound and treated Wadsworth "with marked attention." He concluded that little could be done for the dying general. Meanwhile, Hancock's line along the Brock Road stopped the Confederate advance and fighting there died out as darkness approached.[62]

Late that evening, a wounded Captain Boylston Adams, 56th Massachusetts, was taken by ambulance to the same field hospital. The next morning surgeons from Mahone's Brigade discussed the injury with Adams, a doctor in civilian life. Agreeing on what needed to be done, they amputated his leg below the knee. When he regained consciousness, the captain found himself "lying on the ground beneath a tent fly, and at my side a stretcher on which lay the form of a Union general officer. His face was familiar.... Raising myself upon my elbow, I spoke to him but he made no reply." Recognizing the general who had ridden up to his regiment two days ago, he examined Wadsworth.

I lifted his eyelids, but there was "no speculation in those eyes." I felt his pulse, which was going regularly. His breathing was a little labored...no expression of pain, but occasionally a deep sigh. His mouth was drawn down at the left side...(and) his right arm was evidently paralyzed.... I found that a musket ball had entered the top of his head a little to the left of the median line. In his left hand, which lay quietly upon the breast of his buttoned coat, he held a scrap of paper, on which was written "Gen. James S. Wadsworth."[63]

Saturday afternoon the fighting became distant, moving southeast towards Spotsylvania. Confederate officers stopped by to see the dying Federal general. Adams observed that when someone took the paper from his hand to read it, Wadsworth "would frown and show restlessness, and his hand moved to and fro as if in search of something, until the paper was put into his fingers, when he would grasp it and lay his hand quietly upon his breast." Captain D. Augustus Dickert, 3rd South Carolina, Kershaw's Division, was wounded May 5 and sent to Perrin's field hospital. The next day, he walked over to a large fly-tent and went inside to see the "dying, millionaire general." Lifting Wadsworth's hat off his face, Dickert observed closed eyes, heavy breathing, and a cold, clammy face and concluded that death was imminent. The Confederate surgeons returned that evening and examined the wound "removing a piece of skull, and then probing for the ball." Except for occasional deep sighs, the night passed quietly. Sunday morning Wadsworth's breathing became erratic and he died around 2:00 PM. Adams approved releasing the general's body to a Patrick McCracken who interred it at his home.[64]

Army of the Potomac Headquarters remained unsure whether Wadsworth was dead or alive. Morning of May 7, U. S. Grant wrote General Halleck that "we have to deplore the loss of General Wadsworth." Next day, James H. Wilson reported to Major General Philip Sheridan that "a captured Rebel courier (Kershaw's Division) informs me that General Wadsworth is not yet dead, though insensible from a wound in the head, and expected to die eventually." In a May 9 update to the northern governors, Stanton announced the general's death. He later asked George Meade that every effort be made to recover the body.[65]

On May 15, Meade requested permission from Confederate command at Parker's Store for A. K. St. Clair, surgeon 1st Michigan Cavalry, to pass through their lines and "obtain the remains of the late Brig. Gen. J. S. Wadsworth, for the purpose of transferring them to his afflicted widow and relatives." Lee did not approve St. Clair's passage but instead instructed Major General Wade Hampton to make arrangements for a transfer at Wilderness Church. Before this plan could be implemented, the transfer was completed by other parties. Under a flag of truce, Captain Orlando F. Middleton, 57th New York, and Dr. Benjamin Kneeland were taken May 14 to Wadsworth's interment site at Patrick McCracken's home. They removed the black coffin, and took it in an ambulance to Fredericksburg. Meade informed Lee May 17 that the general's remains had been brought back by St. Clair. Brigadier General James S. Wadsworth returned for the third and final time to the Army of the Potomac.[66]

When confirmation of his death reached the White House, John Hay recorded:

> I have not known the President so affected by a personal loss since the death of [Colonel Edward D.] Baker, as by the death of General Wadsworth. While deeply regretting the loss of Sedgwick, he (Lincoln) added: "Sedgwick's devotion and earnestness were professional. But no man has given himself up to the war with such self-sacrificing patriotism as Gen. Wadsworth. He went into the service not wishing or expecting great success or distinction in his military career and profoundly indifferent to popular applause, actuated only by a sense of duty which he neither evaded nor sought to evade."[67]

Return to Geneseo

His death produced profound sorrow. A man of large wealth, he offered his services to the government and served without pay, nobly sacrificing his life in its defence. The Union loss by his death was equalled only by that of General Reynolds.
           O. B. Curtis, 24th Michigan[68]

Men wounded at Spotsylvania accompanied James Wadsworth on the steamer *Mary Rapley* from Belle Plain to Washington. In her book, *Reveille in Washington*, Margaret Leech described the arrival of these steamers. "At the wharves the stir of trade ceased, as out of the Potomac mist moved the white and silent transports. Thousand after thousand, men littered the landings, like spoiled freight." The morning of May 18, a crowd at the Sixth Street Wharf watched as staff members carried the black cof-

Wadsworth's Geneseo Gravesite

James Wadsworth's Gravesite in the Temple Hill Cemetery, Geneseo, New York. (Courtesy, Lawrence Turner)

fin to a waiting ambulance. The extent of decomposition ruled out embalming. Wadsworth was placed in a metallic coffin.[69]

The next day, "Wadsworth's hearse moved with ceremony to the depot, accompanied by a military guard and a delegation of New York congressmen; but no man looked again on his handsome face." Thursday evening, May 19, the general's remains arrived in New York City, lying in state at City Hall. That afternoon, a formal procession accompanied the flag draped coffin to the Erie Railroad Station. Among those officiating as pall bearers were General Irwin McDowell and Regis DeTrobriand, politician Hamilton Fish, and editor Horace Greeley. DeTrobriand later commented, "General Wadsworth, one of the bravest soldiers, one of the noblest citizens, and one of the best men whose loss the country has had to lament during this war." A detachment from the Invalid Corps escorted the body to Geneseo. After a church service, the 21st New York Infantry from Wadsworth's 'Upton's Hill' Brigade led mourners to the family cemetery.[70]

EPILOGUE

Among those who fell here (the Wilderness), none was more sincerely mourned by those who served under him, or were in any way associated with him than... "the intrepid Wadsworth." The division had other commanders whom it rightly honored, but none as it did "Pap Wadsworth."

Orville Thomson, 7th Indiana[1]

In late June 1864 George Meade received a letter from Mrs. Mary Craig Wadsworth requesting that an enclosed note be given to General R. E. Lee. In it, the widow asked for "return of certain articles found on the general's person." Meade brought the matter to U. S. Grant's attention on July 1 because "I do not feel authorized to send a flag of truce without your sanction." Grant did not think "it a fit time now to send Mrs. Wadsworth's communication through, but the first time a flag is being sent for any other purpose it can go." This was done and Lee replied July 10, 1864. "I have directed inquiries to be made for the effects of the late General Wadsworth, and if they can be found will take great pleasure in restoring them to his widow." The general's watch was returned in 1865 and his sword, field-glasses, and map several years later.[2]

Secretary of War Edwin M. Stanton sent a proposal to the President March 3, 1865, that three brigadier generals be appointed major generals: James S. Wadsworth, Alexander Hays, and Amiel W. Whipple. Lincoln agreed and added at the top of Stanton's letter:

> To the Senate of the United States,
>
> I nominate the persons named in the accompanying communication for appointment in the Volunteer force, as proposed by the Secretary of War.
>
> (signed) Abraham Lincoln

The Adjutant General prepared the formal nominations and sent them to the Senate. A week later they were returned to the President, a letter from the Senate's Secretary attached.

> Ordered, that the nomination of...having been made after the decease of the said nominees, respectively cannot, in the judg-

ment of the Senate, be properly confirmed and that they be respectfully returned....

Like Wadsworth, Confederate bullets killed Alexander Hays in the Wilderness and fatally wounded Amiel Whipple at Chancellorsville. The Senate adjourned March 11. What Lincoln started, Andrew Johnson finished. On March 27, 1867, James S. Wadsworth was appointed major general of volunteers, by brevet, to rank from May 6, 1864. The commission was issued "for gallant conduct at the battles of Gettysburg and the Wilderness." Having served to the war's end, son Craig received word of his father's brevet commission May 7.[3]

On April 27, 1865, Brigadier General Samuel W. Crawford, commanding Third Division, Fifth Corps, recommended First Lieutenant Earl M. Rogers "to be captain by brevet for remarkable gallantry on the 6th of May, 1864, while an aide-de-camp to the late Brigadier-General Wadsworth, and to be major by brevet for great personal bravery on the 18th of June, 1864, displayed during the charge on the enemy's works, when he was severely wounded." After Wadsworth's death, Rogers returned to the 6th Wisconsin and was wounded during a charge on Beauregard's lines east of Petersburg, Virginia. In a letter to his wife, Rufus Dawes described the event. "Yesterday afternoon in another hopeless assault there was enacted a horrid massacre of our corps. Our brigade charged half a mile over an open field under the musketry of the enemy." Lysander Cutler, Commanding Fourth Division, reported, "I lost in killed and wounded about one third of the men I had with me" and that no one got closer than "seventy-five yards of the enemy's works." Having suffered extremely high casualties since crossing the Rapidan, G. K. Warren proposed a reorganization of his Fifth Corps. Wadsworth's Fourth Division passed into history September 12, 1864. Survivors from the old First Corps were transferred to Crawford's Division where they served to the war's end. Meade approved Crawford's recommendations on April 28.[4]

Many individuals later claimed that they had shot James Wadsworth. William T. Lowry was one. At age sixteen, he enlisted in Company D, 8th South Carolina that later became part of Kershaw's Brigade, Kershaw's Division, Longstreet's Corps. About noon on May 6, 1864, he supposedly observed and shot a mounted, Federal general officer on the Orange Plank Road. Continuing to fight as a private, Lowry was captured in September 1864 outside Winchester, Virginia. Later released from Camp Chase, Ohio, he claimed to have recovered and kept Wadsworth's field glasses until they were destroyed in a 1917 house fire. On December 14, 1920, Private Lowry died at Cartersville, South Carolina. In another version, after the Battle of the Wilderness, an unidentified soldier gave Moxley Sorrel Wadsworth's field-glasses and map. Sorrel later returned them to Mary Craig Wadsworth.[5]

Near the end of her 1940, Pulitzer Prize winning book, Margaret Leech described the soldiers who were unable to march in the Federal Army's Grand Review.

> The decimated regiments, the youthful appearance of the general officers, the scarcity of the field officers – all had been reminders of the shadowy army of the Union dead, nearly half a million strong. In unsubstantial ranks, they seemed to form behind the ragged flags: nameless boys who had drilled and caroused in Washington; white-haired Mansfield and Edwin Sumner; Kearny, with his empty sleeve; Wadsworth, fingering his grandfather's sword.[6]

JAMES WADSWORTH REMEMBERED

In 1861 James Wadsworth volunteered to serve in any capacity deemed useful by the Federal Government. Ambition played no role in this decision and his considerable influence and power were never employed for personal advancement. At an age where retirement to Geneseo would not have been questioned and having sufficient wealth to buy a regiment of 'substitutes', Wadsworth chose the more difficult path that ultimately led to his death in the Wilderness. Today this legacy is largely forgotten and Wadsworth is 'written off' as one of Lincoln's inept, political generals. Is this verdict warranted?

Recognizing and accepting his military limitations, Wadsworth declined Governor Morgan's 1861 appointment to major general and recommended John A. Dix instead. Subsequent promotions to brigadier general and to Military Governor were politically motivated. Nothing can be found, however, to indicate that John F. Reynolds was pressured by either Lincoln or Stanton to give Wadsworth the First Division. The present-day perception of James Wadsworth is largely based on his July 1 performance at Gettysburg and Abner Doubleday's interpretation of it.[7]

The relationship between Doubleday and James Wadsworth has generally been ignored. Both were outspoken abolitionists and suffered the same consequences from their peers. Given the events of late 1862 and January 1863, it would be understandable, if not justified, that Doubleday disliked his fellow New Yorker. Whatever the case, Wadsworth moved to the 'back burner' after July 1, 1863. Doubleday never forgave George Meade for his promotion of John Newton to First Corps command. He remained convinced that Meade made this move because Oliver Howard 'reported' the morning of July 1 "that the First Corps had fled from the field at the first contact with the enemy." Neither Meade nor Howard ever mentioned this dispatch. From Doubleday's perspective, however, the incident created a wound that never healed. His lingering dislike of both generals was captured in a January 13, 1878, letter to Rufus R. Dawes, Colonel 6th Wisconsin. After complimenting Dawes for suggesting that he (Doubleday) "should write up the campaign of Gettysburg," the major general went on to say that:

> neither Howard nor Meade in my opinion are entitled to any great credit for their share of that battle....

> It was an infamous thing in Howard by the way, to state as he did at the close of the first day's battle to Genl Hancock that the First Corps had run away from the battle and had no possible foundation in truth.[8]

No evidence was found that Doubleday set out to damage James Wadsworth's reputation. Steps were taken, however, to enlarge and enhance the major general's July 1 role at the expense of Wadsworth. In *Chancellorsville and Gettysburg,* Doubleday claimed that "Cutler's brigade had been withdrawn by order of General Wadsworth, without my knowledge to the suburbs of Gettysburg." In his personal *Journal,* Abner Doubleday elaborated on what had happened the morning of July 1.

> Although I had sent notice to General Wadsworth of my arrival and that I was taking measures to remedy the disaster that occurred, he seemed to imagine that everything done to relieve him was occasioned by the spontaneous action of the troops, and that I was not on the field. He therefore gave orders, without my knowledge, for the whole line to retreat to Cemetery Hill and Hall's battery was actually sent there. He subsequently ordered it to return, advance through the woods, and drive the enemy back.

True and false. Three out of five regiments, the 76th and 147th New York and 56th Pennsylvania, were pulled back to the eastern slope of Oak Ridge. Aware of John Reynolds's earlier message to Meade, Wadsworth prepared to make a fighting retreat through Gettysburg. From his viewpoint, Cutler's Brigade had been overwhelmed and Meredith's could easily be cut off. When Cutler and Hall received this order, Doubleday was just arriving on Seminary Ridge. In spite of a veteran's efforts to set the Gettysburg record straight (see Appendix B), Doubleday's version of events is widely accepted. Wadsworth failed to leave one behind.[9]

The best measure of Wadsworth's military competence was receiving a divisional command in March 1864 when other general officers were either being shelved or given smaller commands. U. S. Grant had a free hand to reorganize the Army of the Potomac as he saw fit and Grant approved Wadsworth's posting to the Fourth Division. Winfield Scott Hancock later stated that it was based on merit and not politics. Like Gettysburg, James Wadsworth's performance in the Wilderness was controversial. Given his assignments of May 5 and 6, it is unlikely that anyone could have succeeded. In trying to achieve victory on the Plank Road, he irritated brigade and regimental commanders from other corps. At the same time, there were those who praised his efforts. Andrew A. Humphreys, Meade's Chief of Staff, remembered Wadsworth in the Wilderness.

> In the two days of desperate fighting that followed our crossing of the Rapidan, he was conspicuous beyond all others for his gallantry – prompter than all others in leading his troops again and again into action. In all these combats he literally led his men, who, inspired by his heroic bearing, continually renewed the contest, which, but for him, they would have yielded.[10]

When studying the units that served under Wadsworth, one common theme runs through all the regimental histories, articles, and speeches; officers and enlisted men alike willingly accepted him as their commander. Some claimed that Wadsworth was a 'natural soldier'. Whatever that means, he was very successful in gaining the troops' loyalty and affection. This did not result from either lax discipline or a tendency to shirk difficult assignments. They respected his desire to do what was right and appreciated Wadsworth's ongoing concern for their comfort. He was 'cool under fire,' possibly to a fault. George Meade described this aspect of Wadsworth's character.

> The moral effect of his example, his years and high social position, his distinguished personal gallantry, and daring bravery, all tended to place him in a most conspicuous position and to give him an influence over the soldiers which few men possess.[11]

Possibly the greatest tribute James Wadsworth ever received was the respect and honor shown him by his captors. In spite of being an outspoken abolitionist, Confederate officers treated him with every kindness and consideration. Given his dedication, integrity, and courage, Wadsworth proved to be the best political general that Lincoln appointed. An intelligent, well-educated individual, he readily accepted authority and responsibility. Having become acclimated to the military, Wadsworth ended his life as an effective divisional commander in the Army of the Potomac.

APPENDIX A

Commands of Brigadier General James S. Wadsworth

Upton's Hill — November, 1861[1]

Department of the Potomac
McDowell's Division
Brig. Gen. Irvin McDowell

Second Brigade
Brig. Gen. James S. Wadsworth

12th New York	21st New York
Col. George W. Snyder	*Col. William Findlay Rogers*
23rd New York	35th New York
Col. Henry C. Hoffman	*Col. William C. Brown*

80th New York (20th NYSM)
Col. George W. Pratt

Chancellorsville — May, 1863[2]

Army of the Potomac
First Army Corps
Maj. Gen. John F. Reynolds

First Division
Brig. Gen. James S. Wadsworth

First Brigade
Col. Walter Phelps, Jr.

22nd New York	24th New York
Maj. Thomas J. Strong	*Col. Samuel R. Beardsley*
30th New York	84th New York (14th NYSM)
Col. William M. Searing	*Col. Edward B. Fowler*

Second Brigade
Brig. Gen. Lysander Cutler

7th Indiana
Lieut. Col. Ira G. Grover

76th New York
Col. William P. Wainwright

95th New York
Col. George H. Biddle

147th New York
Col. John G. Butler

56th Pennsylvania
Col. J. William Hofmann

Third Brigade
Brig. Gen. Gabriel R. Paul

22nd New Jersey
Col. Abraham G. Demarest

29th New Jersey
Col. William R. Taylor

30th New Jersey
Col. John J. Cladek

31st New Jersey
Lieut. Col. Robert R. Honeyman

137th Pennsylvania
Col. Joseph B. Kiddoo

Fourth Brigade
Brig. Gen. Solomon Meredith

19th Indiana
Col. Samuel J. Williams

24th Michigan
Col. Henry A. Morrow

2nd Wisconsin
Col. Lucius Fairchild

6th Wisconsin
Col. Edward S. Bragg

7th Wisconsin
Col. William W. Robinson

Artillery
Capt. John A. Reynolds

New Hampshire Light
1st Battery
Capt. Frederick M. Edgell

1st New York Light
Battery L
Capt. John A. Reynolds

4th United States
Battery B
Lieut. James Stewart

Gettysburg — July, 1863[3]

Army of the Potomac
First Army Corps
Maj. Gen. John F. Reynolds

First Division
Brig. Gen. James S. Wadsworth

First Brigade
Brig. Gen. Solomon Meredith
Col. William W. Robinson

19th Indiana
Col. Samuel J. Williams

24th Michigan
Col. Henry A. Morrow
Capt. Albert M. Edwards

2nd Wisconsin
Col. Lucius Fairchild
Maj. John Mansfield
Capt. George H. Otis

6th Wisconsin
Lieut. Col. Rufus R. Dawes

7th Wisconsin
Col. William W. Robinson
Maj. Mark Finnicum

Second Brigade
Brig. Gen. Lysander Cutler

7th Indiana
Col. Ira G. Grover

84th New York (14th NYSM)
Col. Edward B. Fowler

147th New York
Lieut. Col. Francis C. Miller
Maj. George Harney

76th New York
Maj. Andrew J. Grover
Capt. John E. Cook

95th New York
Col. George H. Biddle
Maj. Edward Pye

56th Pennsylvania (9 cos.)
Col. J. William Hofmann

Wadsworth's Staff at Gettysburg[4]

Capt. Timothy E. Ellsworth .... Acting Assistant Adjutant General
Lieut. Col. John A. Kress .... Assistant Inspector General
Maj. Clinton H. Meneely .... Aide-de-Camp
Surg. George W. New (7th IN) .... Surgeon
Capt. Myron H. Manderville .... Assistant Quartermaster
Capt. Charles McClure .... Assistant Commissary Sergeant
First Lieut. Clayton E. Rodgers (6th WI) .... Assistant Aide-de-Camp
Second Lieut. Edward Carrington (143rd NY) .... Assistant Aide-de-Camp
First Lieut. Charles Robe (147th NY) ...... Assistant Commissary of Musters
Second Lieut. Earl M. Rogers (6th WI) .... Ordinance Officer

Wilderness — May, 1864[5]

Army of the Potomac
Fifth Army Corps
Maj. Gen. Gouverneur K. Warren

Fourth Division
Brig. Gen. James S. Wadsworth

First Brigade
Brig. Gen. Lysander Cutler

7th Indiana
Col. Ira G. Grover

19th Indiana
Col. Samuel J. Williams

24th Michigan
Col. Henry A. Morrow

1st New York Battalion Sharpshooters
Capt. Volney J. Shipman

2nd Wisconsin
Lieut. Col. John Mansfield

6th Wisconsin
Col. Edward S. Bragg

7th Wisconsin
Col. William W. Robinson

Second Brigade
Brig. Gen. James C. Rice

76th New York
Lieut. Col. John E. Cook

84th New York (14th NYSM)
Col. Edward B. Fowler

95th New York
Col. Edward Pye

147th New York
Col. Francis C. Miller

56th Pennsylvania
Col. J. William Hofmann

Third Brigade
Col. Roy Stone

121st Pennsylvania
Capt. Samuel T. Lloyd

142nd Pennsylvania
Maj. Horatio N. Warren

143rd Pennsylvania
Col. Edmund L. Dana

149th Pennsylvania
Lieut. Col. John Irvin

150th Pennsylvania
Capt. George W. Jones

APPENDIX B

Wadsworth and Doubleday at the Railroad Cut

In September 1942 Count Galeazzoi Ciano, Mussolini's son-in-law and Foreign Minister, observed, "As always, victory finds a hundred fathers, defeat is an orphan." This observation can be applied to the Gettysburg Campaign.

The Army of the Potomac's First Corps could claim few successes during the July 1 fighting northwest of Gettysburg. Possibly the most auspicious was the timely arrival of Lieutenant Colonel Rufus R. Dawes's 6th Wisconsin at the Middle Railroad Cut. The subsequent Dawes-Pye-Fowler charge not only saved Wadsworth's Division that morning but ultimately presented Winfield Scott Hancock the option of holding Cemetery Ridge. Two critical decisions were responsible for the 6th Wisconsin being in the right place at the right time; first, detaching the regiment as a divisional reserve, and second, ordering Dawes to support Cutler. Who was responsible: Doubleday, Wadsworth, or Solomon Meredith?[1]

On several occasions, during and after the war, Abner Doubleday took full credit. Probably the first was his July 1, 1863, *Journal* entry:

> ...I detached the Sixth Wisconsin and the Brigade Guard...and directed them to remain in front of the Seminary as a reserve.

and,

> To release Cutler's Brigade, which had fallen back to the woods (as I was informed), I resolved to attack the enemy (Joseph Davis's Brigade) which was advancing against him by throwing a force upon their flank. Colonel Dawes was sent forward for this purpose with my reserve force, the 6th Wisconsin and Brigade Guard.[2]

The woods referred to were on Oak Ridge.

The General's Gettysburg report, sent to George Meade December 14, 1863, stated:

> The Sixth Wisconsin, together with the brigade guard, under Lieutenants Harris, of the Sixth Wisconsin, and Showalter, of the Second Wisconsin, had been detached by my order, to remain with me as a reserve.

and,

> The whole of these events had occurred on the right so soon after my arrival, that there was no opportunity for me to interpose, issue orders, or regulate the retreat. ...The moment was a critical one, involving the defeat, perhaps the utter rout, of our forces. I immediately sent for one of Meredith's regiments (the Sixth Wisconsin), a gallant body of men, whom I knew could be relied upon. Forming them rapidly perpendicular to the line of battle on the enemy's flank, I directed them to attack immediately.[3]

Published in 1882, Doubleday's *Chancellorsville and Gettysburg*, described the July 1 action.

> The command now devolved upon me, with its great responsibilities. The disaster on the right required immediate attention for the enemy, with loud yells, were pursuing Cutler's brigade toward the town. I at once ordered my reserve...to advance against their flank.[4]

It was implied here that Wadsworth had left the field and joined Cutler somewhere on Oak Ridge, leaving Doubleday to straighten out the mess north of the Chambersburg Pike.

James Wadsworth said little about the events that morning. A brief report, submitted to Major General John Newton on July 4, recounted:

> The right encountered a heavy force, were outnumbered, outflanked, and after a resolute contest, bravely conducted by Brigadier-General Cutler, fell back in good order to Seminary Ridge, near the town, and a portion of the command to a point still nearer the town. As they fell back, followed by the enemy, the Fourteenth New York State Militia, Colonel Fowler, Sixth Wisconsin Volunteers, Lieutenant-Colonel Dawes, and Ninety-fifth New York Volunteers, Colonel Biddle, gallantly charged on the advance of the enemy, and captured a large

number of prisoners, including two entire regiments with their flags.[5]

Ten months later Wadsworth was dead. By 1883 the public accepted Doubleday's description of events. One Gettysburg survivor did not:

In May 1861 Clayton E. Rogers, a sawmill operator, enlisted as a private in the 6th Wisconsin Volunteer Infantry. Six months later he was commissioned First Lieutenant and subsequently served in the Engineer Corps and on General Irwin McDowell's staff. Abner Doubleday appointed Rogers Aide-de-camp. Later transferring to James Wadsworth's staff, he served as an Assistant Aide-de-camp during the Gettysburg Campaign. Henry Hunt, once the Army of the Potomac's Chief of Artillery, wrote an account of the First Day's fighting which appeared in the November 1886 issue of *Century* magazine. Rogers's response, which appeared in the February 13, 1887, issue of the ***Milwaukee Sunday Telegraph***, must have come as a complete surprise to Hunt.[6]

In his first paragraph Clayton Rogers fired an 'opening salvo'.

> It is but natural that some errors should be made, such as giving the credit of certain orders to General Abner Doubleday instead of to General James Wadsworth.

and later,

> The article [Hunt's]...gives General Doubleday the credit of all orders to the brigades under command of General Wadsworth, except one to fall back. General Doubleday was a wise and brave officer; from the honor due him let nothing be taken; but all the orders executed by the First Division, on that day, emanated from Wadsworth....[7]

Given this difference of opinion between Rogers and Doubleday, turning to Rufus Dawes for clarification seems prudent.

Initially, the problem appears to be solved. The October 4, 1884, issue of the ***Chippewa Herald*** contained Dawes's tribute to Rogers.

> Lieutenant Rogers had carried orders for General Wadsworth throughout the battle [Gettysburg]. For four hours of the most deadly fighting of the war, he had traversed the battle line with

Colonel Rufus R. Dawes, 6th Wisconsin

A hero at the Railroad Cut, Colonel Dawes was a firm supporter of James Wadsworth after the war. (Courtesy, State Historical Society of Wisconsin)

important orders. He gave to me, as commander of a regiment, every order I received throughout the day.[8]

Unfortunately, clarity was later replaced by confusion.

In January 1890 Dawes completed "With the Sixth Wisconsin at Gettysburg" that appeared in the Ohio MOLLUS's *Sketches of War History.* The narrative discloses that immediately after reaching the crest of Seminary Ridge:

> an aide of General Meredith came on a gallop with the order, "Colonel form your line, and prepare for action at once." ...Another aide, Lieutenant Martin [Benjamin T. Marten], came up and said, "Colonel, General Doubleday is now in command of the corps and he directs that you halt your regiment."

Several minutes later,

> Lieutenant Martin came again with orders from General Doubleday. He said, "General Doubleday directs that you move at once to the right." ...Other staff officers came urging me to move at the utmost speed, saying that the rebels were "driving Cutler's men."[9]

The key sentence may be "Other staff officers came...."

Later in 1890, Dawes published his classic regimental history, *Service with the Sixth Wisconsin Volunteers.* The July 1 discussion repeated Lieutenant Marten's arrival with Doubleday's order to halt followed by an order to advance.

> Lieutenant Meredith Jones [Murdith L.] came with orders from General Doubleday. He said: "General Doubleday directs that you move your regiment at once to the right." ...Captain J. D. Wood [James Day] came and rode beside me repeating the order from General Meredith and saying the rebels were "driving Cutler's men."[10]

Accompanied by at least three aides, Jones, Wood, and Clayton Rogers, Dawes led his regiment toward the Chambersburg Pike.

In trying to determine what happened the morning of July 1, 1863, the key issue to consider is timing; i.e., when did Doubleday reach the battlefield? Colonel Charles Wainwright recorded in his diary that General Doubleday and he were riding north at the head of Brigadier General John Robinson's Division, about three miles behind Cutler. Captain Craig Wadsworth brought news of John Reynolds's death and Doubleday hurried off. It is a reasonable assumption that before he reached the Seminary, Meredith's and Cutler's brigades were fully engaged.[11]

Returning to the two key decisions, this explanation is offered. The first order to keep Dawes's command out of the Iron Brigade's battle line that advanced into Herbst Woods came from Meredith. Wadsworth, who watched Cutler's advance, did not participate. In a few minutes Doubleday arrived, took command, and selected the 6th Wisconsin and the brigade guard to be a divisional reserve. Fearful of an enemy advance from the southwest, he positioned Dawes's Regiment near the Fairfield Road.

From the Seminary, Wadsworth watched Joseph Davis's Brigade destroy three of Cutler's Regiments. Unaware that Doubleday was on the field, he sent Clayton Rogers to Meredith for help. Davis had to be stopped. Doubleday and Meredith reached the same conclusion and ordered Dawes to march north and support Cutler's left. Three aides from three generals carried similar orders to Dawes who advanced toward the Chambersburg Pike Credit for what happened next belongs to the regimental commanders: Dawes, Major Edward Pye, and Colonel E. B. Fowler. Victory does have many fathers.[12]

APPENDIX C

Burial in the Wilderness

As is usually the case for any public figure killed on a battlefield, stories (or myths) have developed regarding James Wadsworth. One of the more interesting concerns his temporary burial in the Wilderness. During the 1914 Dedication Ceremonies, Albert M. Mills gave this version of what had happened in May 1864, claiming that "the truth of it is vouched for from an authentic source."[1]

One of Wadsworth's most troublesome duties while serving as Military Governor was finding and arresting Confederate spies. In 1862 a "humble farmer" was arrested by the Provost Guard. While in jail the individual continually pleaded his innocence. When this case ultimately came to the general's attention, Wadsworth determined that the man was what he claimed to be, a "humble farmer," similar to himself. Not only was the individual quickly released but the Military Governor gave him money to buy supplies.[2]

On May 6, 1864, James Wadsworth was mortally wounded in the Wilderness, taken prisoner, and died two days later in a Confederate field hospital. The hospital adjoined land owned by the same man whom the general had befriended two years earlier in Washington. This "humble farmer" found "his wounded friend," carried the general's body home, and, "nursed him as best he could." Following Wadsworth's death, the body was buried in the home's "door yard." After the armies moved on to Spotsylvania, the farmer informed Mrs. Mary Wadsworth of the general's internment. She then called for action by the War Department. The body was subsequently exhumed and brought back to Geneseo.[3]

Mills's version does not agree with either eyewitness reports or the *Official Records*. A letter, supposedly written by Patrick McCracken, was its basis.

Spotsylvania Court House, VA
May 9, 1864

Mrs. General Wadsworth, New York:

Dear Madam,

You have heard, before this reaches you, of the death of your husband. General Wadsworth. I saw him in the hospital, near the battle-field, on Saturday last [May 7], about ten o'clock; he could not speak or take any notice to anything; he held a paper in his hand with his name and address written on it; he was surrounded with the most eminent surgeons in the Confederacy, who done everything for him that could be done; one of them took the paper out of his hand and when he laid the paper back against his hand, he [Wadsworth] opened his hand and took it back again; he did not seem to suffer much, the ball had entered the top, or rather the back of his head. I saw him again on Sunday [May 8], about nine o'clock. I had carried some sweet milk to the hospital, and wet his lips several times, and let a little go down his mouth. But when the surgeon raised him up, he could not get him [Wadsworth] to let any go down. When I returned to the hospital about three o'clock, he was dead and in a box, ready for interment. I told the surgeon in charge that I was a prisoner nine weeks in the Old Capital, while the General was Military Governor of Washington, and that I would have a coffin made for him, and bury him in a family burying ground; he cheerfully consented. After much trouble, I had a coffin made for him, a good as any could be made in the country. When I went for his remains with the coffin, General Lee had given special orders, (not knowing I was going to take charge of his remains) that he should be buried by a large tree, the tree to be cut low, and his name marked on it. I had given the surgeon satisfactory evidence that I would take care of the body, and with the advice of Captain Z. B. Adams, Co. F., 56th Mass. Regt., they gave me the body. I removed it from the box to the coffin and brought it home last night, and buried it this morning [May 9] in the family burying ground at my house; he is buried with all his clothing, as he fell on the battlefield. The grave is dug with a vault or chamber, the coffin covered with plank, and then dirt. When arrangements are made by our government [CSA] for his removal I will take pleasure in having him moved through our lines to his friends. I live about a mile to

> the left of the plank road, as you go from Fredericksburg to Orange Court House, near New Hope Meeting House, on the plank road, twenty miles from Fredericksburg and eighteen from Orange Court House.
>
> I had a large plank planed and marked for a headstone, and placed it at the head of the grave. He received all the attention and kindness at the hands of the Confederate authorities that could be bestowed upon him as will be attested by Captain Z. B. Adams, Co. F., 56th Mass. Regiment.
>
> With great respect, I remain yours,
>
> Patrick McCracken[4]

This letter eliminates most of the conflicts between Mills's story and other sources. It is difficult to understand, however, how Robert E. Lee found the time to determine where Wadsworth should be buried. An important, collaborating witness, Captain Z. Boylston Adams, does exist. In his 1900 MOLLUS paper, Adams stated that he first met Patrick McCracken the evening of May 7, 1864. A civilian entered the Confederate field hospital and walked up to the shelter tent containing Wadsworth and Adams. He asked, "Was it really General Wadsworth?" After introducing himself, McCracken described an earlier encounter with the general.

> He (McCracken) then related how the general had saved him from long imprisonment at the time that Wadsworth was in command of the city of Washington. He...was arrested and confined in the old Capital prison as a rebel spy and had been released by the general's order on the representation that his family in the Wilderness neighborhood were suffering from his absence and on his promise, that, if allowed to return home, he would not assist in any way the cause of the Confederacy.[5]

McCracken inquired if the general desired anything to eat or drink. Wadsworth could not swallow but Adams gladly accepted the milk and food. Next afternoon Adams "gave the body of General Wadsworth into his (McCracken's) care for burial." For a few days McCracken continued to smuggle provisions into the field hospital then stopped coming. Several years later Adams received some letters from McCracken asking for assistance but he never responded.[6]

Newspaper articles describing the return of Wadsworth's body mentioned that a "Patrick Griffin," "an Irishman named Griffin," "an Irishman named McCracken," or a "Striker" had buried the general "in a neat coffin painted black." Independent sources confirm that Patrick McCracken did intern the general near his home. His role regarding the return of Wadsworth's body, however, is not clear.[7]

Eric Mink, NPS Richmond, has thoroughly researched this aspect. His current position was summarized in a letter to the author.

> I personally believe that Patrick McCracken was instrumental in making sure that Wadsworth was not buried at the hospital and therefore kept the general from possibly being placed in an unmarked grave. I do not believe however that McCracken notified Federal authorities as to the death of Wadsworth and where his body may be found. The opportunity of a civilian getting word through the lines would have been extremely difficult.[8]

The fog of war has lifted somewhat.

APPENDIX D

Wadsworth, NV 89442

Visitors to South Lake Tahoe, California take advantage of the night life offered by nearby casinos. They usually spend one or two days driving around the lake. A typical excursion begins on Route 50 which follows the Nevada shoreline north, then heads east through Spooner Summit. After descending into the Great Basin, the highway enters Carson City, the state capital. This is the best time for a short side trip to Virginia City and the Comstock. Route 395 is taken north to Reno, then I-80 West. The interstate follows the Truckee River into California toward Donner Pass. Route 89 runs south from Truckee, California, down Lake Tahoe's western shore, past Emerald Bay, and back to the city. The Sierra Nevada's mountains, forests, lakes, and foot hills make the trip a unique experience. Now, what has this to do with James Wadsworth?

Return to Reno and drive east on I-80. Leaving the "Biggest Little City in the World" behind, the highway meets the Truckee River. Dry, barren hills dominate the landscape except for a green slash marking the river's course. Just before the Truckee swings north, a highway sign announces: Wadsworth, Exit 43. Is there a connection with the general? The answer is found in Nevada history.

Prior to 1845, few individuals chose to cross Northern Nevada. That year the number of emigrants heading for California increased substantially. Lansford Hasting, an author and adventurer, began encouraging wagon trains to use his new cutoff. The Donner Party was one of the few who did in 1846. They left the Oregon Trail at Fort Bridger, headed west past the Great Salt Lake and across Utah. Hasting's route followed the Humboldt River, "a lifeline for travelers," through Nevada until it disappeared into the ground. Beyond the 'Sinks' lay nothing but stark and barren desert. Reaching the Truckee River's Big Bend now became the key to survival.[1]

Here, where the river turns north toward Pyramid Lake, was the first, plentiful supply of good drinking water west of the Humboldt Sink. Depending on recent weather, the desert trek could range from forty to seventy miles. The Donners reached the Truckee in good spirits. About seventy miles west of the Big Bend, fall snows trapped them in the Sierra

Nevada. The next spring, as news spread of the Donner Party's fate, interest in Hasting's Cutoff quickly ended. A year later, however, the discovery of gold at Sutter's Mill reversed the trend. The availability of water, fish and lush grass from the river and its meadows made the area a major landmark for California-bound wagon trains. The point where most forded the river was named Lower Emigrant Crossing, the future site of Wadsworth, Nevada. In 1859, the Federal Government set aside over 300,000 acres around Pyramid Lake as a reservation for the Paiute Tribe. Lower Emigrant Crossing fell within the land supposedly withdrawn from future settlement.[2]

The Central Pacific Railroad began building a line from Sacramento to points east in 1863. Four years would elapse before its grading crews entered Nevada. One of the first acts passed by that state's Territorial Legislature granted the CP a non-exclusive franchise to build along the Truckee River to Big Bend. Two years later, Congress gave the railroad authorization to lay tracks across Nevada and connect with the Union Pacific. The Secretary of the Interior also approved the surveyed route to Humboldt Wells. Since the railroad's right-of-way passed through the southern tip of the Pyramid Lake Reservation, he ordered that a ten mile tract within its boundaries be reserved for railroad use.[3]

Fifteen miles east of the California/Nevada stateline, a crude bridge spanned the Truckee at Fuller's Crossing. In 1861 Myron Lake bought and improved the structure. He then added a toll road, hotel, and general store. After watching survey parties pass through the region, he established a "strong claim to a large section of land directly in the path of the oncoming railroad." Lake struck a bargain with Charles Crocker, CP's Construction Superintendent. About thirty-five acres north of the river was 'donated' to the railroad for a new townsite. Crocker, in turn, promised to build a station and deed back alternate lots to Lake. The rails reached Fuller's Crossing May 4, 1868. Five days later the CP auctioned lots before a crowd of fifteen hundred anxious buyers. Charles Crocker christened the new community Reno in honor of Major General Jesse L. Reno, killed in 1862 at South Mountain. As designed, the town became a major supply center for Virginia City and the Comstock.[4]

The railroad pushed east thirty-five miles to the Truckee's Big Bend. Here the CP established a "division point" at Lower Emigrant Crossing. Joseph M. Graham, engineer in charge of construction, described what happened.

> After measuring and staking out the new town of Reno on the first day of April 1868, we went on to Wadsworth. We had a number of miles of rather difficult construction. ...I might add right here, I set the stakes where the town of Wadsworth is on the first day of July 1868. ...Charles Crocker came to this townsite...with him we walked over the ground and after about one-half hour located the site of the engine house and station buildings. I then made a detailed location of this yard and townsite and it was rapidly built.

General James S. Wadsworth, the town's namesake, would probably have disagreed with what followed. The CP took over 773 acres of Paiute land for its use and the state confiscated another 120 for a townsite. It had taken construction crews five and a half years to reach the Big Bend. Less than ten months would be required to lay the remaining five hundred miles of track to Promontory Point, Utah. Ten miles east of Wadsworth, Crocker established another station. He named it in honor of Major General William Babcock Hazen, the last station named for a Union general officer.[5]

Grass meadows that followed the Truckee east stopped at Big Bend and the Great Desert began. For almost one hundred miles there was nothing but "a vast waste of sand and sagebrush, and white alkali deposits with high mountain ranges to the south and bleak hills to the north." Out of necessity Wadsworth became a base of supply as the tracks moved eastward. Providing sufficient drinking water to the construction crews became a major challenge. Special trains hauled water in "huge, semi-conical wooden vats on flatcars" to the end of track or rail head. Tank wagons then carried it in wooden barrels to graders working in advance of the track layers. At one point water was hauled by rail over eighty-four miles. The Humboldt River soon became the primary water source. Forests surrounding Lake Tahoe supplied the CP with lumber and fuel for years to come.[6]

The summer of '68 saw rapid development on the Truckee's east bank. Beginning July 6, 1868, a train departed Sacramento daily, except Sunday, at 6:30 AM reaching Wadsworth's new terminal at 5:42 PM, a 188 mile trip. The westbound train left at 1:47 AM and arrived in the state capital at 1:00 PM. In August construction was finished on the new post office. A continuous stream of wagons brought in refined products from mines to the south and east, returning with necessary supplies. "20-Mule

Teams" hauled refined borax and soda from Columbus, Sodaville, and Rhodes 150 miles to Wadsworth.[7]

Railroad management located the Truckee Division's headquarters in Wadsworth. Given the wide expanses of desert and mountainous terrain, locomotives operating in this division carried additional water and wood. Subsequent construction of car shops, a roundhouse with twenty engine stalls, and machine shops for rebuilding engines created many new jobs. By 1871 Wadsworth's population approached seven hundred. Three years later, President Grant decided to restore the Pyramid Lake Reservation's original boundaries but nothing changed in Nevada. The Interior Department finally ruled in 1878 that the CP was entitled to the right of way only through Paiute land. Too little, too late! Non-Indians already controlled over 80% of the Reservation's arable lands and within a few years 'owned' all of it. "The tribe was shut out of what should have been its farmland."[8]

During the early 1880's the town boasted of having "two hotels, three grocery stores, two general merchandise stores, one variety store, and saloons, markets, shops, etc.," and about five hundred busy and prosperous residents. A new bridge was constructed over the Truckee River. The continued absence of a railroad in southern Nevada kept the freight wagons rolling into and out of Wadsworth.[9]

Like most frontier communities, Wadsworth experienced its share of financial setbacks. The Carson and Colorado Railroad reached Sodaville and Hawthorne in 1881, ending the long wagon hauls. In spite of lost business, the CP went ahead with a major upgrading of its facilities. Construction started on a new yard site across the Truckee. The following year saw a new round house and repair shops completed. On April 15, 1884, fire broke out in the old freight depot. Fanned by heavy winds, the flames quickly spread to the original railroad buildings and then into town. Handicapped by an inadequate water supply, efforts to contain the fire failed and by morning Wadsworth was gone. Residents rebuilt the town west of the river and close to the new railroad yard. That fall, Charles Crocker oversaw consolidation of the Central and Southern Pacific Railroads. Prosperity returned to the Truckee. A fenced park with trees, a fountain, and mowed lawn welcomed visitors to the new freight depot. In 1902 a second fire repeated the destruction wreaked by the first. While restoring essential services, the SP started looking for a new site. Wadsworth's days as a transportation center were numbered.[10]

Within a year economic calamity struck the town. To avoid upgrading facilities either fire damaged or outmoded, the Southern Pacific decided to relocate the divisional headquarters, repair shops and engine roundhouse. The site selected, just east of Reno, was Sparks, a new town named for Nevada's governor. Transfer of shop equipment began in 1904 followed by stores and homes. Trees planted in front of the 1883 depot were moved west. The *Wadsworth Dispatch* became the *Sparks Dispatch*. As a final blow, approximately three hundred houses belonging to SP employees were sawed in half, loaded on flatcars, and hauled to Sparks "leaving only lawns and trees behind."[11]

Wadsworth declined to a scattered village dependent on tourists and local ranchers. In the 1920's, Route 40 passed through the community and business picked up. After World War II, the local economy slowed again and the high school closed in 1951. Tourism and shopping ended when I-80 bypassed the town in the 1960's. Downtown buildings have either been closed up or destroyed by fire. Today, the center of town is the Natchez Elementary School, named for a Paiute Chief. Enrollment is about 140, mostly Paiutes from the reservation and some non-Indians from town. The Post Office remains open.[12]

Justice for the Pyramid Lake Paiutes came in 1990. Congress passed the Truckee River Negotiated Settlement Act to settle conflicting claims for its water. This Act also authorized "the Interior Department to exchange Federal land for privately held parcels in the reservation." Since then, several exchanges have taken place, but no one is being forced to sell or move. Ultimately, the entire town will be owned and controlled by the tribe. Economically, it will probably cease to exist. But for the luck of the draw, Wadsworth, Nevada could have been "The Biggest Little City in the World" and Reno, a Historic Marker along State Highway 34.[13]

ENDNOTES

Prologue
1. *The Gettysburg Times*, Oct. 5 & 6, 1914, p. 1; New York Monuments Commission for the Battlefields of Gettysburg, Chattanooga, and Antietam, *In Memoriam, James Samuel Wadsworth, 1807-1864*, Albany: J. B. Lyon Co., 1916, p. 16.
2. *In Memoriam*, pp. 14-15; Lewis R. Stegman, Letter to John P. Nicholson, Feb. 2, 1914, Gettysburg National Military Park (hereafter GNMP) Library; A. J. Zabriskie, Letters to Nicholson, Nov. 16, 1911 & Dec. 12, 1913, GNMP Library; Daniel Sickles, Letter to Nicholson, Jan. 21, 1911, GNMP Library.
3. *The Gettysburg Times*, Oct. 5, 1914; *In Memoriam*, pp. 18-19, 22, 63.
4. *In Memoriam*, pp. 12, 47.

Chapter 1
1. *In Memoriam*, p. 48.
2. Lewis F. Allen, "Memorial of the late James S. Wadsworth," Delivered Before the New York State Agricultural Society at the Close of Its Annual Exhibition at Rochester, Sept. 23, 1864, Buffalo: Franklin Steam Printing House, 1864; Albany: Van Benthuysen's Steam Printing House, 1865, pp. 7-8.
3. Allen, "Memorial of Wadsworth," pp. 16, 34; pp. 8-9; Henry Greenleaf Pearson, *James S. Wadsworth of Geneseo*, New York: Charles Scribner's Sons, 1913, Ann Arbor: UMI, 1997, p. 22.
4. Pearson, *Wadsworth*, pp. 16, 34; pp. 22-23; *In Memoriam*, p. 50; Horace Andrew Wadsworth, *Two Hundred and Fifty Years of the Wadsworth Family in America*, Lawrence: Eagle Steam Job Printing Rooms, 1883, p. 200; Allen, "Memorial of Wadsworth," pp. 10-11, 13-14.
5. Allen, "Memorial of Wadsworth," pp. 16, 34; *In Memoriam*, p. 50.
6. *In Memoriam*, pp. 50-51; *Proceedings of the Century Association in Honor of the Memory of Brig-Gen, James S. Wadsworth and Colonel Peter A. Porter*, New York: D. Van Nostrand, 1864, p. 26; *Dictionary of American History*, 2nd Rev. Ed., James T. Adams ed., New York: Charles Scribner's Sons, 1961, p. 164; Pearson, *Wadsworth*, pp. 40-41, 43-44.
7. Pearson, *Wadsworth*, pp. 44, 46-49; *In Memoriam*, pp. 50-51.
8. *In Memoriam*, p. 51; Pearson, *Wadsworth*, pp. 51-52.

9. U.S. War Department, *The War of the Rebellion: A Compilation of the Official Records of the Union and Confederate Armies*, Washington: Govt. Printing Office, 1880-1901, (hereafter cited as *OR*, unless otherwise noted, all subsequent references are from Series 1) Guild Press of Indiana, Series 3, Vol. 1, p. 99, 241.
10. Pearson, *Wadsworth*, pp. 55-57; Allen, "Memorial of Wadsworth," pp. 19-20; *OR*, Series 3, Vol. 1, p. 99.
11. *OR*, Series 3, Vol. 1, pp. 212, 241, 246-247; Ezra J. Warner, *Generals in Blue*, Baton Rouge: Louisiana State Univ. Press, 1994, pp. 17-18, 60-61; Mark M. Boatner III, *The Civil War Dictionary*, New York: Random House Reprint, 1991, pp. 42, 108.
12. *OR*, Vol. 51, Part 1, p. 413; Vol. 2, p. 322; Margaret Leech, *Reveille in Washington, 1860-1865*, New York: Harper & Brothers, 1941, p. 167; Pearson, *Wadsworth*, pp. 65-66.
13. *OR*, Vol. 2, p. 322.
14. Pearson, *Wadsworth*, pp. 64-66; Allan Nevins, *War for the Union*, New York: Konecky & Konecky, 1971, Vol. 1, pp. 214-216.
15. Nevins, *War for the Union*, Vol. 1, p. 160; Pearson, *Wadsworth*, p. 69; Warner, *Generals in Blue*, p. 514.
16. Pearson, *Wadsworth*, p. 70; James Longstreet, *From Manassas to Appomattox*, New York: William S. Konecky Reprint, 1992, pp. 38-39.
17. George A. Custer, "War Memoirs," *The Galaxy*, Vol. XXI, Apr. 1876, pp. 459-460.
18. Pearson, *Wadsworth*, pp. 70-72; *OR*, Vol. 2, pp. 317-318.
19. *OR*, Vol. 2, pp. 318-320, 368-369; *Historical Times Encyclopedia of the Civil War*, P. L. Faust ed., New York: Harper & Row, 1986, pp. 90-92.
20. Pearson, *Wadsworth*, p. 72; George H. Otis, *The Second Wisconsin Infantry*, Alan D. Gaff ed., Dayton: Morningside, 1984, p. 34; *OR*, Vol. 2, pp. 369, 384-385, 387-388.
21. *OR*, Vol. 2, pp. 320, 369; Nevins, *War for the Union*, Vol. 1, p. 217; Otis, *The Second Wisconsin Infantry*, p. 35.
22. *OR*, Vol. 2, pp. 320-322; 385; Pearson, *Wadsworth*, pp. 73-74.
23. Pearson, *Wadsworth*, pp. 76-78; *OR*, Vol. 2, p. 322.
24. John Harrison Mills, *Chronicles of the 21st New York Volunteers*, Buffalo: 21st Reg. Veteran Assoc. of Buffalo, 1887, Univ. Publications of America, p. 170.
25. Pearson, *Wadsworth*, pp. 81-82; *OR*, Vol. 51, Part 1, p. 455; Vol. 15, p. 112; Major General F. C. Ainsworth, Letter to Daniel E. Sickles, RG 094, Box 532, NA; Frederick H. Dyer, *A Compendium of the*

War of the Rebellion, Des Moines: Dyer Publishing Co., 1908, Part 1, pp. 274-275, Guild Press of Indiana, 1996; A.G.O. W17 CB 1863, National Archives (hereafter NA).

26. Major George B. Davis, et. al., *The Official Military Atlas of the Civil War*, Washington: GPO, 1891-1895; New York: Gramercy Books, 1983, Plate 1, 7; Mills, *21st New York Volunteers*, p. 120; Pearson, *Wadsworth*, pp. 83, 90-91.
27. Pearson, *Wadsworth*, pp. 92-93; *OR*, Vol. 51, Part 2, p. 379.
28. *OR*, Vol. 51, Part 2, Vol. 5, p. 53; Pearson, *Wadsworth*, p. 98.
29. Pearson, *Wadsworth*, pp. 109-110; *OR*, Vol. 5, pp. 708, 718; Mills, *21st New York Volunteers*, pp. 146, 150; Dyer, *A Compendium*, Part 1, pp. 274, 283.

Chapter 2

1. William P. Maxon, *Camp Fires of the 23rd New York Volunteers*, New York: Davies & Kent, 1863, p. 45.
2. *OR*, Vol. 5, p. 18; Vol. 51, Part 1, p. 550; Pearson, *Wadsworth*, pp. 98, 102-103, 107-109; Leech, *Reveille in Washington*, p. 167.
3. *OR*, Vol. 5, p. 18, Warner, *Generals in Blue*, pp. 230-231; Special Orders AOP Mar. 12, 1862, James Wadsworth, Generals Papers, NA.
4. Pearson, *Wadsworth*, p. 109; *OR*, Vol. 14, Part 3, p. 13; Vol. 15, Part 1, p. 162.
5. *OR*, Vol. 5, p. 56; Warner, *Generals in Blue*, p. 16.
6. Warner, *Generals in Blue*, pp. 489-490; *OR*, Series 2, Vol. 11, pp. 269, 577; Vol. 14, pp. 54, 60.
7. *OR*, Series 2, Vol. 14, pp. 57, 60.
8. **Ibid.**, pp. 53, 60-61; Fletcher Pratt, *Stanton, Lincoln's Secretary of War*, New York: Norton & Co., 1953, p. 180.
9. *OR*, Series 2, Vol. 14, pp. 61-62, 67-68, 73; Vol. 5, p. 61.
10. Stephen W. Sears, *To the Gates of Richmond*, New York: Houghton Mifflin, 1992, pp. 34, 39, 41.
11. Maxon, *Camp Fires*, pp. 37, 45; Theodore B. Gates, *The 'Ulster Guard' (20th N. Y. State Militia) and the War of the Rebellion*, New York: B. H. Tyrrel, 1879, p. 223; Mills, *21st New York Volunteers*, pp. 169-170.
12. *OR*, Vol. 14, p. 68; Vol. 15, p. 231; Vol. 12, Part 3, p. 408; Vol. 19, Part 2, p. 264; Series 3, Vol. 11, p. 185; Pearson, *Wadsworth*, pp. 127-128; Warner, *Generals in Blue*, pp. 486-487; Stephen W. Sears, *Landscape Turned Red*, New York: Ticknor and Fields, 1983, pp. 3-4, 12.
13. Pearson, *Wadsworth*, pp. 132, 134-135.

14. **Ibid.**, pp. 136-138.
15. **Ibid.**, p. 138; *Proceedings of the Century Association*, p. 26; *Lincoln Day by Day, A Chronology 1809-1865*, Earl S. Miers Ed-in-Chief, Dayton: Morningside, 1991, Vol. 3, pp. 113, 120.
16. David H. Donald, *Lincoln*, New York: Simon & Schuster, 1995, p. 548; Pearson, *Wadsworth*, p. 141.
17. Pearson, *Wadsworth*, pp. 150-153; Donald, *Lincoln*, p. 381; Leech, *Reveille in Washington*, pp. 25, 44.
18. *Proceedings of the Century Association*, p. 27; Pearson, *Wadsworth*, pp. 154-155; Benjamin P. Thomas and Harold M. Hyman, *Stanton, The Life and Times of Lincoln's Secretary of War*, New York: Alfred A. Knopf, 1962, p. 247.
19. Sears, *Landscape Turned Red*, p. 332.
20. **Ibid.**; *Proceedings of the Century Association*, p. 27; Pearson, *Wadsworth*, p. 157.
21. Pearson, *Wadsworth*, pp. 156-158; Sears, *Landscape Turned Red*, p. 339; Charles S. Wainwright, *A Diary of Battle The Personal Journals of Colonel Charles S. Wainwright*, Allan Nevins ed., Gettysburg: Stan Clark Military Books, 1992, pp. 125-126.
22. Pearson, *Wadsworth*, pp. 166-167; Warner, *Generals in Blue*, pp. 312-313; *OR*, Vol. 21, pp. 1, 777.

<u>Chapter 3</u>
1. John J. Hennessy, *Return to Bull Run*, New York: Simon & Schuster, 1993, pp. 466-467; Darwin L. Flaherty, "The Naming of Reno, Nevada: A Century-Old Mystery," *Nevada Historical Society Quarterly*, Vol. XXVII, Fall, 1984, pp. 176, 181.
2. *OR*, Vol. 21, pp. 1, 777, 860, 876, 965; Wainwright, *A Diary of Battle*, p. 149; Allen, "Memorial of Wadsworth," p. 21; Kalina K. Anderson, Letter to J. F. Krumwiede, Apr. 7, 1998.
3. *OR*, Vol. 21, p. 2; Vol. 51, Part I, pp. 943-944, 951, 965, 974, 991; Vol. 19, Part 2, pp. 542, 550, 569; Dyer, *A Compendium*, Part 1, pp. 284-286.
4. Dyer, *A Compendium*, Part 3, pp. 1363-1364, 1413-1414.
5. Nevins, *War for the Union*, Vol. 2, p. 366; Alan D. Gaff, *On Many a Bloody Field*, Bloomington: Indiana Univ. Press, 1996, p. 217; Orville Thomson, *Narrative of the Service of the Seventh Indiana Infantry in the War for the Union*, Published by Author, 1905, Reprint, Baltimore: Butternut & Blue, 1993, p. 147.

6. Thomson, *Service of the Seventh Indiana*, p. 148; Gaff, *On Many a Bloody Field*, p. 218.
7. *OR*, Vol. 25, Part 1, pp. 16, 18, 73; Part 2, p. 175; Vol. 51, Part 1, p. 995; Pearson, *Wadsworth*, p. 176.
8. Wainwright, *A Diary of Battle*, p. 166.
9. Rufus R. Dawes, *Service with the Sixth Wisconsin Volunteers*, Dayton: Morningside, 1996, p. 129.
10. Henry H. Lyman, "Historical Sketch," New York Monuments Commission, *Final Report on the Battle of Gettysburg* (hereafter *New York at Gettysburg*), Vol. 3, Albany, New York: J. B. Lyon Co., 1900, p. 1001.
11. Stephen W. Sears, *Chancellorsville*, Boston: Houghton Mifflin, 1996, pp. 32.
12. **Ibid.**, pp. 36, 48-49, 92.
13. **Ibid.**, pp. 63-65, 70-72, 81-82.
14. **Ibid.**, pp. 104-106; A. P. Smith, *History of the Seventy-sixth Regiment, New York Volunteers*, Cortland, New York: Truair, Smith & Miles, 1867, Reprinted 1988, Ron R. Van Sickle Military Books, p. 255.
15. Smith, *76th New York*, p. 255.
16. James S. Wadsworth, Note to General Thomas, Feb. 27, 1863; Note Mar. 24, 1863, A.G.O. W17 CB 1863, NA.
17. Sears, *Chancellorsville*, pp. 117-119.
18. **Ibid.**, pp. 131-132, 137-138.
19. *OR*, Vol. 25, Part 2, p. 234; Part 1, pp. 137, 256; Vol. 51, Part 1, p. 235; C. V. Tevis, and D. R. Marquis, *The History of the Fighting Fourteenth (Brooklyn Regiment)*, New York: Brooklyn Eagle Press, 1911, Butternut & Blue Reprint 1994, pp. 64-65; Pearson, *Wadsworth*, p. 175.
20. Pearson, *Wadsworth*, p. 176; Dyer, *A Compendium*, Part 3, p. 1414; Charles McCool Snyder, "Robert Oliver, Jr. and the Oswego County Regiment," *New York History*, Vol. XXXVIII, July 1957, pp. 291-292.
21. John T. Davidson, "General James S. Wadsworth," *Elmira Telegram*, Aug. 24, 1890.
22. Snyder, "Robert Oliver, Jr. and the Oswego County Regiment," pp. 292-293; Pearson, *Wadsworth*, p. 177; *OR*, Vol. 25, Part 1, pp. 257, 266; Dawes, *Sixth Wisconsin*, p. 135; John A. Kress, *Memoirs of Brigadier General John Alexander Kress*, 1925, pp. 15, 18; Sears, *Chancellorsville*, p. 136.
23. Sears, *Chancellorsville*, pp. 131-132, 140-141; *OR*, Vol. 25, Part 1, p.

205; Pearson, *Wadsworth*, pp. 177-178.
24. Nevins, *War for the Union*, Vol. 2, p. 347; Longstreet, *From Manassas to Appomattox*, pp. 302-303.
25. *OR*, Vol. 25, Part 1, p. 205.
26. Davidson, "General James S. Wadsworth;" Wainwright, *A Diary of Battle*, p. 172.
27. Wainwright, *A Diary of Battle*, p. 179; Theron W. Haight, "Among the Pontoons at Fitzhugh Crossing," Wisconsin Commandry MOLLUS, Vol. 1, Milwaukee: Burdick, Armitage & Allen, 1891, pp. 418-422, State Historical Society of Wis. (hereafter SHSW); Tevis and Marquis, *Fighting Fourteenth*, p. 67; O. B. Curtis, *History of the 24th Michigan of the Iron Brigade, Known as the Detroit & Wayne County Regiment*, Detroit: Winn & Hammond, 1891, Butternut Press Edition 1984, p. 125; *OR* , Vol. 25, Part 1, pp. 208, 253, 262.
28. *OR* , Vol. 25, Part 1, p. 208; Kress, *Memoirs of,* pp. 9-10; James S. Wadsworth, Letter to President Lincoln, Dec. 14, 1863, *Military Record of Brevet Brigadier General John William Hofmann*, Philadelphia: A. W. Auner, 1884, pp. 18-19, GNMP Library.
29. *OR* , Vol. 25, Part 1, pp. 253, 256, 262, 270, 273; Haight, "Among the Pontoons," pp. 421-422; Davidson, "General James S. Wadsworth;" *New York at Gettysburg*, Vol. 3, p. 1000; Dawes, *Sixth Wisconsin*, p. 135; Kress, *Memoirs of,* p. 10; Curtis, *24th Michigan*, p. 126.
30. Curtis, *24th Michigan*, p. 127; Pearson, *Wadsworth*, pp. 183, 187; *OR*, Vol. 25, Part 1, pp. 253-254, 257, 270.
31. *OR*, Vol. 25, Part 1, pp. 254, 257, 263, 270, 275; William J. K. Beaudot and Lance J. Herdegen, *An Irishman in the Iron Brigade*, New York: Fordham Univ. Press, 1993, p. 79; Pearson, *Wadsworth*, pp. 187-188.
32. Pearson, *Wadsworth*, pp. 190-191; Sears, *Chancellorsville*, p. 460; Edgar Haviland, Letter to Mother, Aug. 1863, NA Pension File; Beaudot and Herdegen, *An Irishman in the Iron Brigade*, p. 79; John Bigelow, Jr., *The Campaign of Chancellorsville*, New Haven: Yale Univ. Press, 1910, Morningside reprint, Map #36.
33. *OR*, Vol. 25, Part 1 pp. 256-257, 263-264, 271.
34. James Wadsworth, Generals Papers, NA; Richard Wheeler, *Witness to Gettysburg*, New York: Harper & Row, 1987, pp. 1-3; Longstreet, *From Manassas to Appomattox*, p. 334.

Chapter 4

1. Kress, *Memoirs of,* p. 16.
2. Longstreet, *From Manassas to Appomattox,* pp. 334-338; Wheeler, *Witness to Gettysburg,* pp. 19, 33.
3. *OR,* Vol. 27, Part 3, p. 81; Stephen M. Weld, *War Diary and Letters of Stephen Minot Weld 1861-1865,* Boston: Riverside Press, 1912, p. 213.
4. Weld, *War Diary,* p. 214; Clayton E. Rogers, "Woods, The Deserter," *Milwaukee Sunday Telegraph* (hereafter *Telegraph*), May 24, 1885, p. 3, SHSW; Dawes, *Sixth Wisconsin,* p. 150; Curtis, *24th Michigan,* pp. 143-144, 147; Gaff, *On Many a Bloody Field,* pp. 248-250; Tevis and Marquis, *Fighting Fourteenth,* pp. 77-78.
5. Tevis and Marquis, *Fighting Fourteenth,*, pp. 77-78; *OR,* Vol. 27, Part 3, pp. 89, 91; Pearson, *Wadsworth,* p. 195; J. W. Hofmann, "The 56th Regiment Pennsylvania Volunteers in the Gettysburg Campaign," *Philadelphia Weekly Press,* Jan. 13, 1886; Samuel Healy, "The Civil War Journal of Samuel Healy, 1862-3," p. 4, GNMP Library.
6. Healy, "Civil War Journal," p. 5; Pearson, *Wadsworth,* p. 196; Dawes, *Sixth Wisconsin,* pp. 151-152; Tevis and Marquis, *Fighting Fourteenth,* pp. 77-78; John Calef, "Gettysburg Notes: The Opening Gun," *Journal of the Military Service Institution of the United States,* Vol. 40, 1907, p. 41; George H. Otis, 2nd Wisconsin Infantry, Diary, SHSW, copy GNMP Library; Curtis, *24th Michigan,* pp. 147-149.
7. Curtis, *24th Michigan,* p. 142; Pearson, *Wadsworth,* p. 196; Hofmann, "The 56th Pa.;" Weld, *War Diary,* p. 215; Boatner, *Civil War Dictionary,* p. 650; *OR,* Vol. 27, Part 3, pp. 148-149, 151.
8. *OR,* Vol. 27, Part 3, p. 194; Curtis, *24th Michigan,* pp. 147-149; Tevis and Marquis, *Fighting Fourteenth,* pp. 77-78; Dawes, *Sixth Wisconsin.* p. 153; Healy, "Civil War Journal," p. 6; Weld, *War Diary,* p. 217; *Official Military Atlas,* Plate 7, Sheet 1; Pearson, *Wadsworth,* p. 198.
9. Pearson, *Wadsworth,* 198; Healy, "Civil War Journal," p. 7; *OR,* Vol. 27, Part 3, pp. 308, 329, 333-334.
10. *OR,* Vol. 27, Part 3, p. 373; Curtis, *24th Michigan,* pp. 150-152; Tevis and Marquis, *Fighting Fourteenth,* pp. 78-80; Smith, *76th New York,* p. 229; Weld, *War Diary,* p. 224; George Otis Diary; Healy, "Civil War Journal," p. 8.
11. Healy, "Civil War Journal," p. 8; William Henry Locke, *The Story of the Regiment,* New York: James Miller, 1872, p. 221; Weld, *War*

Diary, p. 226; *OR*, Vol. 27, Part 3, pp. 373, 376; George Otis Diary.
12. Lyman, "Historical Sketch," pp. 1000-1001; RG 393, Part 2, #3685, p. 209, NA.
13. Kress, *Memoirs of*, p. 16; George Otis Diary.
14. *New York at Gettysburg*, Vol. 3, p. 990; Tevis and Marquis, *Fighting Fourteenth*, p. 80; Locke, *Story of the Regiment*, p. 222; Kress, *Memoirs of*, p. 16; *OR*, Vol. 27, Part 3, pp. 376, 418-419.
15. *OR*, Vol. 27, Part I, p. 354; Smith, *76th New York*, p. 233; William W. Dudley, "Report of the Operations of the 19th Regiment Indiana Volunteers in the Battle of Gettysburg," *The Bachelder Papers*, ed. David L. & Audrey J. Ladd, Dayton: Morningside, 1994, p. 939; Dawes, *Sixth Wisconsin*, p. 158; Wainwright, *A Diary of Battle*, p. 229; John A. Kress, "Tales of the War. Thrilling Description of Scenes and Incidents at Gettysburg," *Missouri Republican*, Dec. 4, 1886; Curtis, *24th Michigan*, pp. 151-152; George Otis Diary.
16. *OR*, Vol. 27, Part 3, pp. 415-417; Part I, pp. 243-244.
17. Longstreet, *From Manassas to Appomattox*, pp. 333, 347-348.
18. *OR*, Vol. 27, Part I, pp. 243-244; Part 3, pp. 415-417.
19. *1858 Map of Adams County*, Adams County Historical Society, Drawn G. M. Hopkins, Traced J. R. Hershey May 5, 1980; Tevis and Marquis, *Fighting Fourteenth*, p. 80; Sidney G. Cooke, "The First Day of Gettysburg," Kansas Commandry MOLLUS, Nov. 4, 1897, War Paper #17, Kansas State Historical Society, p. 4; J. W. Hofmann, "Remarks on the Battle of Gettysburg," Presentation to the Historical Society of Pennsylvania (hereafter HSP), Mar. 8, 1880, Philadelphia: A. W. Auner, 1880, p. 3, Manuscript Collection, Gettysburg College; Henry C. Marsh, *The Nineteenth Indiana at Gettysburg*, n. p., n. d., p. 1, Copy GNMP Library; *OR*, Vol. 27, Part 1, p. 354; Part 3, pp. 334-336, 417.
20. Edwin B. Coddington, *The Gettysburg Campaign*, New York: Charles Scribner's Sons, 1984, pp. 266-267, 272-273.
21. Gates, *The 'Ulster Guard,'* p. 421.
22. Augustus Buell, *The Cannoneer*, Washington: The National Tribune, 1890, Ann Arbor: UMI, 1997, pp. 63-64.
23. Coddington, *The Gettysburg Campaign*, fn #7, p. 681; David G. Martin, *Gettysburg July 1*, Conshohocken: Combined Books, rev. ed. 1995, p. 91.
24. Tevis and Marquis, *Fighting Fourteenth*, p. 81; Pearson, *Wadsworth*, p. 204; Charles McCool Snyder, "The One Hundred Forty-Seventh Infantry; Immortality at Gettysburg," *Oswego County, New York in*

the Civil War, Oswego: Oswego County Historical Society (hereafter OCHS), 1962, p. 59; *New York at Gettysburg*, Vol. 3, p. 990; Wainwright, *A Diary of Battle*, p. 222; Testimony of Brigadier General James S. Wadsworth, Washington, Mar. 23, 1864, Joint Congressional Committee on the Conduct of the War, *Report of 1865*, Vol. I, p. 413, GNMP Library; Earl M. Rogers, "The Second or Fifty-Sixth— Which?", *Telegraph*, June 22, 1884, SHSW; Buell, *The Cannoneer*, p. 64.

25. Richard S. Shue, *Morning at Willoughby Run*, Gettysburg: Thomas Publications, 1995, p. 53; Abner Doubleday, *Chancellorsville and Gettysburg*, New York: Da Capo Press, 1994, pp. 124-125; Martin, *Gettysburg July 1*, p. 92.

26. Dudley, "Report of 19th Indiana," p. 939; Cooke, "First Day of Gettysburg," p. 4; *OR*, Vol. 27, Part 1, p. 284; Hofmann, "The 56th Pa."

27. Hofmann, "The 56th Pa.;" Kress, "Tales of the War;" Hofmann, "Remarks on Gettysburg," p. 4; Kress, *Memoirs of*, p. 16; Peter F. Rothermel, "Dress of the Troops of the Second Brigade, First Division, First Army Corps at the Battle of Gettysburg, July 1, 1863," Rothermel Papers, Pennsylvania State Archives, Wayne Motts Collection.

28. Hofmann, "The 56th Pa;" A. S. Coe, "Address at the Dedication of Monument, 147th New York Regiment Infantry," July 1, 1888, Gettysburg, Pa., Copy with H. H. Lyman's comments, p. 19, OCHS; Testimony of James S. Wadsworth, p. 413; Smith, *76th New York*, p. 236.

29. Weld, *War Diary*, pp. 229-230, 231-232.

30. Snyder, "The One Hundred Forty-Seventh Infantry," pp. 59, 63; J. W. Hofmann, "Gettysburg Again. Gen. Hofmann on the Action of the 147th New York at the Opening of the Battle," *National Tribune*, June 5, 1884, GNMP Library; H. H. Lyman, Statement as to Location of 147th Regiment, NY at the Beginning of the Infantry Fighting at the Battle of Gettysburg, July 1, 1863, circa 1889, p. 1, OCHS; J. V. Pierce, Statement as to Location of 147th Regiment, N. Y. V. at the Beginning of the Infantry Fighting at the Battle of Gettysburg, July 1, 1863, Nov. 25, 1897, p. 2, OCHS; J. V. Pierce, Letter to John B. Bachelder, Nov. 1, 1882, *The Bachelder Papers*, pp. 910; John Bartlett, Sworn Statement Concerning Events of July 1, 1863, n. d., p. 1, OCHS; James L. McLean, Jr., *Cutler's Brigade at Gettysburg*, Rev. 2nd Ed., Baltimore: Butternut & Blue, 1994, map p. 55; James P. Sullivan, "Gettysburg. Member of 6th Wisconsin Takes Is-

sue with Carleton," *National Tribune*, May 14, 1885, GNMP Library; Earl M. Rogers, "The Second or Fifty-Sixth;" Hofmann, "The 56th Pa."

31. Hofmann, "The 56th Pa.;" Curtis, *24th Michigan*, p. 156; Rufus R. Dawes, "Reminiscences of the Battle of Gettysburg," *The Star and Sentinel*, Mar. 8, 1872; Dudley, "Report of 19th Indiana," p. 939.

32. Hofmann, "Gettysburg Again;" Kress, *Memoirs of*, pp. 17-18; *New York at Gettysburg*, Vol. 3, p. 1006; James A. Hall, Letter to John B. Bachelder, Dec. 29, 1869, J. B. Bachelder Papers, New Hampshire Historical Society (Hereafter NHHS), copy GNMP Library, pp. 333-334.

33. Hall, Letter to Bachelder, Dec. 29, 1869, p. 334; *Maine at Gettysburg: Report of the Maine Commissioners Prepared by the Executive Committee*, Portland: Lakeside Press, 1898, p. 16; James A. Hall, Letter to John B. Bachelder, Feb. 27, 1868, J. B. Bachelder Papers, p. 342, NHHS, Copy GNMP Library; James A. Hall, Letter to H. H. Lyman, July 19, 1888, p. 1, OCHS; Kress, "Tales of the War;" Kress, *Memoirs of*, pp. 17-18; T. E. Ellsworth, Letter to H. H. Lyman, Sept. 3, 1888, p. 3, OCHS; Testimony of James S. Wadsworth, p. 413; Gates, *The 'Ulster Guard,'* p. 426.

34. Cooke, "First Day of Gettysburg," p. 4; Coe, "Address at the Dedication," p. 19; Hofmann, "The 56th Pa;" McLean, *Cutler's Brigade*, map p. 56; Smith, *76th New York*, p. 237.

35. *OR*, Vol. 27, Part. 1, pp. 330, 355; James K. P. Scott, *The Story of the Battle of Gettysburg*, Harrisburg: The Telegraph Press, 1927, p. 144; Kathleen Georg Harrison, *Edward McPherson Farm: Historical Study*, GNMP, Oct. 14, 1977, p. 37; A. S. Coe, Letter to J. B. Bachelder, Dec. 28, 1888, *The Bachelder Papers*, p. 1564.

36. Coe, Letter to Bachelder, Dec. 28, 1888, *The Bachelder Papers*, p. 1564; Bartlett, Sworn Statement, n. d., p. 1; OCHS; *New York at Gettysburg*, Vol. 1, p. 733; John L. Beveridge, "The First Gun at Gettysburg," Illinois Commandery MOLLUS, *The Gettysburg Papers*, Comp. by Ken Brandy & Florence Freeland, Dayton: Morningside, 1986, p. 175; E. B. Fowler, Letter to J. V. Pierce, Mar. 31, 1888, OCHS; Cooke, "First Day of Gettysburg," p. 5; H. H. Lyman, Letter to J. P. Bachelder, n. d., p. 1, OCHS; Lyman, Statement Location of 147th, p. 3; Marc & Beth Storch, "'What a Deadly Trap We Were In' Archer's Brigade on July 1, 1863," *Gettysburg Magazine*, Issue No. 6, pp. 21-22; E. M. Sperry, Letter to H. H. Lyman, June 8, 1889, OCHS.

37. William N. Ulmer, Letter to H. H. Lyman, Aug. 6, 1888, p. 1, OCHS; Hall, Letters to Bachelder, Feb. 27, 1868, p. 341-342 and Dec. 29, 1869.
38. John B. Bachelder, "Notes from a Conversation with Colonel Lucius Fairchild, 2nd Wis. Vol's.," *The Bachelder Papers*, pp. 335-336; Hofmann, "Remarks on Gettysburg," p. 5; Kress, "Tales of the War;" Kress, *Memoirs of*, pp. 18, 33; *OR*, Vol. 27, Part 1, pp. 273, 267.
39. *OR*, Vol. 27, Part 1, p. 284; Pierce, Statement Location of 147th, p. 2; D. E. Parkhurst, "At Gettysburg. Heroism of the 147th New York," *National Tribune*, Nov. 1, 1888, GNMP Library; Lyman, Letter to Bachelder, n. d., p. 2; Lyman, Statement Location of 147th, p. 2; Coe, Letter to Bachelder, *The Bachelder Papers*, p. 1564; James Coey, "Cutler's Brigade. The 147th New York's Magnificent Fight on the First Day at Gettysburg," *National Tribune*, July 15, 1915, GNMP Library; Amos Allport, "Memory of the First Engagement of the Battle of Gettysburg," n. d., p. 1, OCHS; Ellsworth, Letter to Lyman, p. 2, OCHS; Gates, *The 'Ulster Guard,'* p. 427.
40. Gates, *The 'Ulster Guard,'* p. 430; Martin, *Gettysburg July 1*, pp. 86-87; T. P. Williams, *The Mississippi Brigade of Brig. Gen. Joseph R. Davis*, Dayton: Morningside, 1999, pp. 84-85.
41. Gates, *The 'Ulster Guard,'* pp. 425, 430; Cooke, "First Day of Gettysburg," p. 5; Lysander Cutler, et. al., "Gettysburg. The Great Battle of July 1, 2, and 3, 1863," *The Star and Sentinel*, May 5, 1885; Hofmann, "Remarks on Gettysburg," p. 4; Hofmann, "The 56th Pa;" H. H. Lyman, Letter to J. V. Pierce, Nov. 16, 1897, p. 4, OCHS; John A. Kellogg, Letter to J. B. Bachelder, Nov. 1, 1865, *The Bachelder Papers*, pp. 204; *Histories of the Several Regiments & Battalions from North Carolina*, Walter Clark ed., Goldsboro: Nash Brothers, 1901, Reprinted Wendell: Broadfoot, 1982, p. 297; Sperry, Letter to Lyman, p. 1; *OR*, Vol. 27, Part 1, pp. 281, 285; McLean, *Cutler's Brigade*, pp. 64, 69.
42. Haviland, Letter to Mother, NA.
43. McLean, *Cutler's Brigade*, map p. 73; Lyman, Letter to Bachelder, p. 2, OCHS; Lyman, Typed Excerpt from Diary, OCHS; Lyman, Statement Location of 147th, p. 2, OCHS; Coey, "Cutler's Brigade," OCHS; Bartlett, Sworn Statement, p. 1, OCHS; Parkhurst, "At Gettysburg;" *New York at Gettysburg*, Vol. 3, pp. 991, 1001, 1003.
44. Hofmann, "Remarks on Gettysburg," p. 5; Kress, "Tales of the War;" Ellsworth, Letter to Lyman, p. 4, OCHS; Hofmann, "Gettys-

burg Again."
45. Hofmann, "Gettysburg Again;" Coey, "Cutler's Brigade," OCHS; N. A. Wright, Letter to H. H. Lyman, Nov. 18 1897, OCHS; N. A. Wright, Statement as to Location of 147th Regiment, N. Y. V., at the Beginning of the Infantry Fighting at the Battle of Gettysburg, July 1, 1863, (n. d.), p. 2, OCHS; H. H. Lyman, Letter to J. P. Bachelder (n. d.), *The Bachelder Papers*, p. 331.
46. Lyman, Letter to Bachelder, *The Bachelder Papers*, p. 331; Ellsworth, Letter to Lyman, pp. 3-4, OCHS; Pierce, Letter to Bachelder, *The Bachelder Papers*, p. 911; George G. Meade, *The Life and Letters of General George Gordon Meade*, Baltimore: Butternut & Blue, 1994, Vol. 2, pp. 35-36; Doubleday, *Chancellorsville and Gettysburg*, p. 132; *OR*, Vol. 27, Part 1, p. 282; Kellogg, Letter to Bachelder, *The Bachelder Papers*, p. 204.
47. Hall, Letters to Bachelder, Dec. 29, 1869, pp. 334-335, and Feb. 27, 1868, pp. 342-344; H. H. Lyman, Letter to James A. Coey, Nov. 19, 1897, p. 2, OCHS.
48. Hall, Letter to Bachelder, Dec. 29, 1869, pp. 335-336; *OR*, Vol. 27, Part 1, p. 359.
49. *Histories of the Several Regiments*, p. 289; Ellsworth, Letter to Lyman, p. 4, OCHS; Lyman, Letter to Coey, p. 2, OCHS; Sperry, Letter to Lyman, June 15, 1889, p. 1, OCHS; Sperry, Letter to Lyman, June 8, 1889, OCHS; Earl M. Rogers, Statement to J. A. Watrous n. d, typescript draft Watrous Collection, SHSW; *New York at Gettysburg*, Vol. 3, pp. 992-994, 1001-1004; Pierce, Letter to Bachelder, *The Bachelder Papers*, p. 911; (See Appendix B).
50. Wainwright, *A Diary of Battle*, p. 233; Samuel P. Bates, *History of Pennsylvania Volunteers, 1861-5*, Harrisburg: D. Singerly, 1870, Vol. I, p. 211; Locke, *Story of the Regiment*, p. 226; Doubleday, *Chancellorsville and Gettysburg*, p. 130.
51. Doubleday, *Chancellorsville and Gettysburg*, p. 131; Dawes, *Sixth Wisconsin*, pp. 160-161, 164-166; Rufus R. Dawes, "A Gallant Officer," *Telegraph*, Feb. 3, 1884, SHSW; Albert V. Young, "A Pilgrimage," *Telegraph*, Apr. 22, 1888, SHSW; *Histories of the Several Regiments*, p. 298; A. H. Belo, "Battle of Gettysburg," *Confederate Veteran*, Apr. 1900, p. 165; Clayton E. Rogers, "Gettysburg Scenes," *Telegraph*, Feb. 13, 1887, SHSW; Rogers, Statement to Watrous, p. 1, SHSW; Rufus R. Dawes, "With the Sixth Wisconsin at Gettysburg," Ohio Commandery MOLLUS, *The Gettysburg Papers*, pp. 215-216 (See Appendix B).

52. Dawes, "6th Wis. at Gettysburg," *The Gettysburg Papers*, pp. 215-216; James P. Sullivan, "The Charge of the Iron Brigade at Gettysburg by Mickey of Company K," *Mauston Star*, 1883, p. 2, SHSW; Tevis and Marquis, *Fighting Fourteenth*, p. 83; Gates, *The 'Ulster Guard,'* p. 427; Fowler, Letter to Pierce, OCHS; *OR*, Vol. 27, Part 1, p. 286.
53. J. V. Pierce, "Address at the Dedication of Monument, 147th New York Regiment Infantry," July 1, 1888, Gettysburg, Pa., Copy with H. H. Lyman's comments, p. 9, OCHS; Pierce, Letter to Bachelder, *The Bachelder Papers*, p. 912; Lyman, Letter to Bachelder, p. 2, OCHS; Lyman, Statement Location of 147th, p. 3, OCHS; Coey, "Cutler's Brigade," OCHS; Kellogg, Letter to Bachelder, Mar. 31, 1868, *The Bachelder Papers*, p. 337; *New York at Gettysburg*, Vol. 3, pp. 992-993, 1001-1002.
54. *New York at Gettysburg*, Vol. 3, pp. 993, 1005-1006; Pierce, Statement Location of 147th, p. 4, OCHS; Sullivan, "Gettysburg. Member Takes Issue;" J. A. Blair, Letter to H. H. Lyman, Sept. 6, 1888, p. 1, OCHS; *OR*, Vol. 27, Part 1, p. 276; Williams, *The Mississippi Brigade*, p. 87; Dawes, *Sixth Wisconsin*, pp. 161, 167.
55. Dawes, *Sixth Wisconsin*, pp. 161, 167-168, 170; Tevis and Marquis, *Fighting Fourteenth*, pp. 83-84; Rogers, Statement to Watrous, p. 1; Young, "A Pilgrimage;" Sullivan, "Gettysburg. Member Takes Issue;" Williams, *The Mississippi Brigade*, p. 87.
56. Sullivan, "Charge of the Iron Brigade," p. 3; Lance J. Herdegen and J. K. Beaudot, *In the Bloody Railroad Cut at Gettysburg*, Dayton: Morningside, 1991, pp. 197, 206, fn. #39, p. 192; Lance J. Herdegen, "The Lieutenant who Arrested a General", *Gettysburg Magazine*, Issue No. 4, p. 26; Earl M. Rogers, Letter to Jerome A. Watrous, n. d., Original Watrous Collection, SHSW.
57. Blair, Letter to Lyman, Sept. 6, 1888, OCHS; Curtis, *24th Michigan*, p. 157; Pearson, *Wadsworth*, p. 211.
58. Hall, Letter to Bachelder, Dec. 29, 1869, p. 336; James A. Hall, Letter to J. V. Pierce, Aug. 8, 1888, OCHS; Kellogg, Letter to Bachelder, Nov. 1, 1865, *The Bachelder Papers*, p. 204; E. T. Boland, "Beginning of the Battle of Gettysburg," *Confederate Veteran*, July 1906, p. 309; *OR*, Vol. 27, Part 1, pp. 359-360; *Maine at Gettysburg*, p. 20.
59. Sullivan, "Gettysburg. Member Takes Issue;" Smith, *76th New York*, p. 229; Testimony of James S. Wadsworth, p. 413; Lyman, Statement Location of 147th, p. 3, OCHS; Blair, Letter to Lyman, OCHS; Coe, "Address at the Dedication," p. 24, OCHS; *OR*, Vol. 27, Part 1, pp.

246, 266, 267, 274, 279, 282.
60. *OR*, Vol. 27, Part 1, pp. 246, 266, 355, 1028, 1031-1032; Calef, "Gettysburg Notes," p. 49; Whitelaw Reid, *A Radical View: The "Agate" Dispatches of Whitelaw Reid, 1861-1865*, Memphis: Memphis St. Univ. Press, 1976, Vol. 2, p. 28; Doubleday, *Chancellorsville and Gettysburg*, p. 140; John B. Bachelder, "Hall's Maine and Calef's U. S. Batteries at Gettysburg," *Scout and Soldiers Mail*, Dec. 26, 1885, p. 1, copy GNMP Library; Wainwright, "Three Missing Paragraphs." fn. p. 234, *A Diary of Battle*, copy GNMP Library.
61. Wainwright, "Three Missing Paragraphs." fn. p. 234, *A Diary of Battle*, copy GNMP Library; Calef, "Gettysburg Notes," p. 50; Reid, *A Radical View*, p. 28; Bachelder, "Hall's Maine and Calef's Batteries;" *OR*, Vol. 27, Part 1, p. 356, 1031.
62. *OR*, Vol. 27, Part 1, pp. 276, 356; Wainwright, "Three Missing Paragraphs;" Dawes, "6th Wis. at Gettysburg," *The Gettysburg Papers*, p. 226; Dawes, *Sixth Wisconsin*, p. 174.
63. Gates, *The 'Ulster Guard,'* pp. 433, 436; Chapman Biddle, "The First Day of the Battle of Gettysburg," Address Delivered before HSP, Mar. 8, 1880, Philadelphia: J. B. Lippincott & Co., 1880, p. 31; Bates, *History of Pa. Volunteers*, p. 215; Doubleday, *Chancellorsville and Gettysburg*, pp. 135, 139.
64. Dawes, "6th Wis. at Gettysburg," p. 223.
65. Coddington, *The Gettysburg Campaign*, p. 280; *OR*, Vol. 27, Part 2, p. 444.
66. Wheeler, *Witness to Gettysburg*, p. 133; Doubleday, *Chancellorsville and Gettysburg*, p 134; Bates, *History of Pa. Volunteers*, p. 214; Hofmann, "The 56th Pa;" Pearson, *Wadsworth*, p. 212.
67. Pearson, *Wadsworth*, p. 214; Gates, *The 'Ulster Guard,'* p. 437; Kress, "Tales of the War;" Kress, *Memoirs of,* p. 18; Wheeler, *Witness to Gettysburg*, pp. 140-141; *OR*, Vol. 27, Part 3, p. 463.
68. *OR*, Vol. 27, Part 1, pp. 276, 282; Gary G. Lash, "Brig. Gen. Henry Baxter's Brigade at Gettysburg, July 1," *Gettysburg Magazine*, Issue No. 10, p. 12; Hofmann, "Remarks on Gettysburg," p. 6; Gates, *The 'Ulster Guard,'* p. 435; McLean, *Cutler's Brigade*, p. 131, map p. 130; John Purifoy, "The Battle of Gettysburg, July 1, 1863," *Confederate Veteran*, Apr. 1923, p. 141.
69. Tevis and Marquis, *Fighting Fourteenth*, p. 85; Wainwright, "Three Missing Paragraphs;" Calef, "Gettysburg Notes," pp. 50-51; Hall, Letter to Bachelder, Dec. 29, 1869, p. 336; *OR*, Vol. 27, Part 1, p. 360, 362, 1032.

70. Locke, *Story of the Regiment*, p. 229; Kress, *Memoirs of,* p. 18; Hall, Letter to Bachelder, Dec. 29, 1869, p. 337.
71. Oliver O. Howard, "Campaign and Battle of Gettysburg, June and July, 1863," *Atlantic Monthly,* July 1876, p. 56; Testimony of James S. Wadsworth, p. 413; Doubleday, *Chancellorsville and Gettysburg,* p. 141; Martin, *Gettysburg July 1,* p. 270; *OR,* Vol. 27, Part 1, pp. 266, 360.
72. *OR,* Vol. 27, Part 1, pp. 282; Lash, "Henry Baxter's Brigade," pp. 16, 18-19; Hofmann, "Remarks on Gettysburg," p. 6; McLean, *Cutler's Brigade,* pp. 132, 138, maps pp. 136-137; Biddle, "First Day of Gettysburg," p. 28; Purifoy, "Battle of Gettysburg," Jan. 1923, p. 24; Richard A. Sauers, "The 16th Maine Volunteer Infantry at Gettysburg," *Gettysburg Magazine,* Issue No. 13, p. 37.
73. Sauers, "16th Maine," p. 36, map 35; Doubleday, *Chancellorsville and Gettysburg,* pp. 144-145; Lyman, Letter to Bachelder, *The Bachelder Papers,* p. 331; Cooke, "First Day of Gettysburg," p. 7; Coe, "Address at the Dedication," p. 24; Martin, *Gettysburg July 1,* p. 254.
74. Biddle, "First Day of Gettysburg," pp. 26, 39; Curtis, *24th Michigan,* p. 160; Dudley, "Report of 19th Indiana," p. 940; *OR,* Vol. 27, Part 2, p. 638; Part 1, pp. 248, 268.
75. *OR,* Vol. 27, Part 2, pp. 267, 274; Curtis, *24th Michigan,* pp. 159, 162; Biddle, "First Day of Gettysburg," pp. 26, 39; Dudley, "Report of 19th Indiana," p. 942.
76. H. S. Huidekoper, Letter to J. B. Bachelder, n. d., "Memoranda of Lieutenant Colonel Huidekoper concerning the 150th Regt. Pa.," *The Bachelder Papers,* pp. 952-953; McLean, *Cutler's Brigade,* map p. 139; *OR,* Vol. 27, Part 1, pp. 248, 274, 283, 356, 362.
77. Howard, "Campaign and Battle," p. 57; Curtis, *24th Michigan,* p. 163; J. Michael Miller, "Perrin's Brigade on July 1, 1863," *Gettysburg Magazine,* Issue No. 13, p. 25; Kress, *Memoirs of,* p. 20; Martin, *Gettysburg July 1,* p. 396.
78. Martin, *Gettysburg July 1,* pp. 399, 469; Varina D. Brown, *A Colonel at Gettysburg and Spotsylvania,* Columbia: The State Co., 1931, pp. 216, 231; Pearson, *Wadsworth,* pp. 219, 221; Kress, *Memoirs of,* p. 20.
79. Kress, *Memoirs of,* p. 21; Testimony of James S. Wadsworth, p. 413; John D. S. Cook, "Personal Reminiscences of Gettysburg," Kansas Commandery MOLLUS, *The Gettysburg Papers,* p. 922; E. P. Hallstead, "The First Day of the Battle of Gettysburg," District of Co-

lumbia Commandery MOLLUS, *The Gettysburg Papers*, p. 156; *OR*, Vol. 27, Part 1, pp. 257, 259, 266, 269, 276, 280, 357, 360; Miller, "Perrin's Brigade," p. 29.

80. Miller, "Perrin's Brigade," p. 25; Lash, "Henry Baxter's Brigade," p. 24; Hofmann, "Remarks on Gettysburg," pp. 6-7; Hofmann, "56th Pa.;" Beveridge "First Gun at Gettysburg," p. 179; Locke, *Story of the Regiment*, p. 231; Tevis and Marquis, *Fighting Fourteenth*, p. 87.

81. Tevis and Marquis, *Fighting Fourteenth*, p. 87; *Maine at Gettysburg*, p. 88.

82. Brown, *A Colonel at Gettysburg and Spotsylvania*, pp. 223-224, 227-228; Transcript of the Court Martial of Brig. General Thomas A. Rowley, 1981, ed. by Kathleen Georg Harrison, pp. 2-3, copy GNMP Library; George Fairfield, Letter to J. A. Watrous, n. d., SHSW; Cooke, "First Day of Gettysburg," p. 8.

83. Cooke, "First Day of Gettysburg," p. 9; Marsh, *19th Indiana at Gettysburg*, p. 5; Tevis and Marquis, *Fighting Fourteenth*, p. 88; Dawes, "A Gallant Officer."

84. Charles H. Morgan, "Report of Lieutenant Colonel Charles H. Morgan," *The Bachelder Papers*, pp. 1351-1352; Edward N. Whittier, "The Left Attack (Ewell's), Gettysburg," *The Gettysburg Papers*, p. 762; Doubleday, *Chancellorsville and Gettysburg*, pp. 147-148; Howard, "Campaign and Battle" p. 58; Winfield Scott Hancock, "Gettysburg. A Reply to General Howard," *The Galaxy*, Dec. 1876, pp. 825, 830; Winfield Scott Hancock, Letter to James Longstreet, Jan. 17, 1878, *The Southern Historical Society Papers* (Hereafter *SHSP*), Vol. 5, 1878, pp. 168-172, Broadfoot Publishing; *Maine at Gettysburg*, p. 89.

85. Thomson, *Service of the Seventh Indiana*, pp. 162-165; J. N. Hubbard, "Gettysburg, Wadsworth's Division on Culp's Hill," *National Tribune*, Apr. 15, 1915, GNMP Library; Hofmann, "Remarks on Gettysburg," pp. 6-7; *OR*, Vol. 27, Part 1, p. 284.

86. *OR*, Vol. 27, Part 1, pp. 277; Transcript Rowley Court Martial, pp. 7-8; *Maine at Gettysburg*, p. 90; Morgan, "Report of," p. 1352; Rogers, "Gettysburg Scenes;" Dawes, "With the 6th Wis.," p. 233; Hofmann, "56th Pa.;" Kellogg, Letter to Bachelder, *The Bachelder Papers*, p. 205; Dawes, *Sixth Wisconsin*, p. 179; Tevis and Marquis, *Fighting Fourteenth*, p. 137; McLean, *Cutler's Brigade*, p. 144.

87. Coe, "Address at the Dedication," p. 20; Curtis, *24th Michigan*, p. 163; Fairfield, Letter to J. A. Watrous, p. 3, Copy GNMP Library; H. H. Lyman, Letter to Daniel E. Sickles, Nov. 23, 1897, OCHS; Kress,

Memoirs of, p. 22.
88. Hubbard, "Wadsworth's Division."
89. Doubleday, *Chancellorsville and Gettysburg,* p. 154; Testimony of James S. Wadsworth, p. 413; Charles C. Fennell, "The Attack and Defense of Culp's Hill: Greene's Brigade at the Battle of Gettysburg, July 1-3, 1863," Ann Arbor: UMI, 1996, p. 116; Charles F. Morse, "The Twelfth Corps at Gettysburg," *Papers Military Historical Society of Mass.,* Vol. 14, Wilmington: Broadfoot Publishing, 1990, p. 23; Lyman, Letter to Bachelder, *The Bachelder Papers,* p. 331; *OR,* Vol. 27, Part 1, pp. 261, 283, 855-856.
90. *OR,* Vol. 27, Part 1, p. 362; Wainwright, *A Diary of Battle,* pp. 244-245; Conversation with Timothy H. Smith, Apr. 24, 1998.
91. *OR,* Vol. 27, Part 2, pp. 446-447.
92. Harry W. Pfanz, *Gettysburg - Culp's Hill and Cemetery Hill,* Chapel Hill: Univ. of North Carolina Press, 1993, pp. 194-195, 200.
93. Hubbard, "Wadsworth's Division;" Fennell, "Culp's Hill," pp. 126, 141-143; Morse, "12th Corps at Gettysburg," p. 28; Dawes, *Sixth Wis.,* p. 182; Hofmann, " 56th Pa.;" Kress, *Memoirs of,* p. 23; Lyman, Diary Excerpt, OCHS; Lyman, Letter to Bachelder, *The Bachelder Papers,* p. 331; Tevis and Marquis, *Fighting Fourteenth,* p. 91; McLean, *Cutler's Brigade,* pp. 152; *OR,* Vol. 27, Part 1, pp. 284, 287, 288, 856.
94. *OR,* Vol. 27, Part 1, p. 287; Curtis, *24th Michigan,* p. 191; Tevis and Marquis, *Fighting Fourteenth,* pp. 96. 98, 100; Lyman, Letter to Bachelder, p. 332; Morse, "12th Corps at Gettysburg," p. 33.
95. Kress, *Memoirs of,* pp. 23-24; *In Memoriam,* pp. 46-47.
96. Kress, "Tales of the War;" Hofmann, "56th Pa;" *OR,* Vol. 27, Part 1, pp. 266-267, 285; Lyman, Diary Excerpt, OCHS.
97. Lyman, Diary Excerpt, OCHS; Coe, "Address at the Dedication," p. 26; Gaff, *On Many a Bloody Field,* p. 281; Healy, "Civil War Journal," p. 9.
98. Healy, "Civil War Journal," pp. 9-10; Lyman, Diary Excerpt, OCHS; Tevis and Marquis, *Fighting Fourteenth,* p. 104; *OR,* Vol. 27, Part 1, p. 263; Pearson, *Wadsworth,* pp. 229-230.
99. Pearson, *Wadsworth,* p. 231; Tevis and Marquis, *Fighting Fourteenth,* p. 104; Healy, "Civil War Journal," p. 10.
100. Healy, "Civil War Journal," p. 10; Tevis and Marquis, *Fighting Fourteenth,* p. 105; Weld, *War Diary,* p. 241; Testimony of James S. Wadsworth, p. 415.
101. Testimony of James S. Wadsworth, p. 415; Wainwright, *A Diary of*

Battle, pp. 260-261; Meade, *Life and Letters*, Vol. 2, p. 363.
102. Testimony of James S. Wadsworth, pp. 415-416; Pearson, *Wadsworth*, p. 234; Weld, *War Diary*, p. 242.
103. Noah Brooks, *Washington in Lincoln's Time*, New York: The Century Co., 1895, pp. 93-95.
104. James S. Wadsworth, Letter to the Adjutant General, July 14, 1863, RG 094, Box 132, NA.
105. *Army Register of the Volunteer Force of the United States, 1861-5*, War Department, Washington: GPO, 1867; Reprint, Gaithersburg: Olde Soldier Books, 1987, Vol. 6, p. 170; Smith, *76th New York*, pp. 254-255; Dawes, "A Gallant Officer;" *OR*, Vol. 27, Part 3, p. 718.

Chapter 5
1. "General James S. Wadsworth," Obituary, *New York Times*, May 10, 1864.
2. Nevins, *War for the Union*, Vol. 3, p. 431; Leech, *Reveille in Washington*, p. 333; *Lincoln Day by Day*, Vol. 3, p. 168; John Hay, *Lincoln and the Civil War in the Diaries and Letters of John Hay*, Tyler Dennett ed., New York: Dodd, Mead, & Co., 1939, Da Capo Reprint, 1988, p. 67.
3. Hay, *Lincoln and the Civil War*, pp. 67-68.
4. *OR*, Series 3, Vol. 3, pp. 872-873; E. D. Townsend, "Special Order No. 452," War Dept. Oct. 9, 1863, James Wadsworth, Generals Papers, NA.
5. *Proceedings of the Century Association*, pp. 30-31.
6. E. D. Townsend, "Special Order No. 562, War Dept., Dec. 19, 1863," James Wadsworth, Generals Papers, NA; Kress, *Memoirs of*, p. 31; *OR*, Series 3, Vol. 3, p 1044.
7. Warner, *Generals in Blue*, p. 108; James S. Wadsworth, "General Orders No. 21," Mar. 27, 1864, 4th Div., 5th Army Corps, NA; W17 CB 1863, NA; Dyer, *A Compendium*, Part 1, pp. 284, 294; *OR*, Vol. 51, Part 1, pp. 1151, 1154; Vol. 30, Part 1, pp. 1142-1143, 1052; RG 393, Part 2, #3685, p. 293, NA; Pearson, *Wadsworth*, p. 245.
8. Pearson, *Wadsworth*, pp. 249-250; Warner, *Generals in Blue*, p. 533; "General Hancock on General Wadsworth," *The* (New York) *Evening Post*, Sept. 29, 1864.
9. Dyer, *A Compendium*, Part 1, pp. 302-307; *OR*, Vol. 36, Part 1, pp. 110-111.
10. *OR*, Vol. 36, Part 2, p. 360; Pearson, *Wadsworth*, p. 252.

Chapter 6

1. Gordon C. Rhea, *The Battle of the Wilderness May 5-6, 1864*, Baton Rouge: Louisiana State Univ. Press, 1994, p. 66; Bruce Catton, *A Stillness at Appomattox*, Garden City: Doubleday and Co., 1957, p. 55.
2. David M. Jordan, *Winfield Scott Hancock, A Soldier's Life*, Bloomington: Indiana Univ. Press, 1988, pp. 111-112; Longstreet, *From Manassas to Appomattox*, pp. 552-553.
3. Longstreet, *From Manassas to Appomattox*, pp. 553, 555; Jordan, *Hancock*, pp. 111-112; *OR*, Vol. 36, Part 1, p. 189.
4. *OR*, Vol. 36, Part 1, p. 189; Jordan, *Hancock*, pp. 111-112; Longstreet, *From Manassas to Appomattox*, pp. 552-553.
5. Rhea, *The Wilderness*, p. 66; Catton, *A Stillness at Appomattox*, p. 55; Theodore Lyman, *Meade's Headquarters 1863-1865, Letters of Colonel Theodore Lyman from the Wilderness to Appomattox*, George Agassiz ed., Boston: Atlantic Monthly Press, 1922, pp. 87, 180; John W. Northrop, *Chronicles from the Diary of a War Prisoner*, Wichita: Author, 1904, p. 23.
6. Northrop, *Chronicles from the Diary of a War Prisoner*, p. 24; Gaff, *On Many a Bloody Field*, p. 338; *OR*, Vol. 36, Part 1, pp. 539, 579, 610, 622.
7. Wainwright, *A Diary of Battle*, p. 348; Smith, *76th New York*, p. 283; Northrop, *Chronicles from the Diary of a War Prisoner*, p. 25.
8. Jordan, *Hancock*, p. 112.
9. John Anderson, **The *57th Regiment of Massachusetts Volunteers in the War of the Rebellion**, Boston: E. B. Stillings, 1896, p. 41.
10. **Ibid.**, p. 112.
11. *OR*, Vol. 36, Part 1, pp. 539, 575, 579, 592, 614, 622; Part 2, pp. 416, 418, 420; Northrop, *Chronicles from the Diary of a War Prisoner*, p. 25.
12. Jordan, *Hancock*, p. 114; Robert Monteith, "Battle of the Wilderness and Death of General Wadsworth," Jan. 6, 1886, *Civil War Papers*, Vol. 1, Wisconsin Commandry MOLLUS, Wilmington: Broadfoot, 1993, p. 411; Richard E. Matthews, *The 149th Penn. Vol. Infantry Unit in the Civil War*, Jefferson, NC: McFarland & Co., 1994, pp. 133-134.
13. Matthews, *The 149th*, map p. 136; Dawes, *Sixth Wisconsin*, p. 259; *OR*, Vol. 36, Part 2, p. 420.
14. *OR*, Vol. 36, Part 1, p. 614; Matthews, *The 149th*, pp. 133-134.
15. *OR*, Vol. 36, Part 2, pp. 418, 420.

16. **Ibid.**, pp. 418-420.
17. **Ibid.**, Part 1, p. 189; Lyman, *Letters of Colonel Theodore Lyman*, p. 88.
18. *OR*, Vol. 36, Part 1, p. 575; Part 2, pp. 417, 420; Matthews, *The 149th*, p. 134; Dawes, *Sixth Wisconsin*, p. 259.
19. Rhea, *The Wilderness*, map p. 158; *OR*, Vol. 36, Part 1, pp. 614, 616-617.
20. *OR*, Vol. 36, Part 1, pp. 614, 616-617, 623; Smith, *76th New York*, p. 284; Thomson, *Service of the Seventh Indiana*, pp. 184-185; Matthews, *The 149th*, map p. 136.
21. Matthews, *The 149th*, pp. 134-135, 137-138, map p. 136.
22. **Ibid.**, p. 138; *OR*, Vol. 36, Part 1, pp. 610-611, 614-615.
23. *OR*, Vol. 36, Part 1, pp. 540, 593; Jordan, *Hancock*, pp. 114, 117; Monteith, "Battle of the Wilderness," p. 412; Pearson, *Wadsworth*, p. 268; Matthews, *The 149th*, p. 144; Smith, *76th New York*, pp. 290-291.
24. *OR*, Vol. 36, Part 1, pp. 595-596, 615.
25. Matthews, *The 149th*, pp. 141, 143.
26. **Ibid.**, pp. 141, 143-144; *OR*, Vol. 36, Part 1, p. 615.
27. *OR*, Vol. 36, Part 1, pp. 596, 611.
28. John W. Busey and David G. Martin, *Regimental Strengths and Losses at Gettysburg*, Hightstown: Longstreet House, 1982; John W. Busey, *These Honored Dead*, Hightstown: Longstreet House, 1996.
29. Busey, *These Honored Dead*; Buell, *The Cannoneer*, pp. 63-64; *OR*, Vol. 27, Part 1, pp. 173-174.
30. Z. Boylston Adams, "In the Wilderness," *Civil War Papers*, Vol. II, Massachusetts Commandry MOLLUS, Boston, 1900, Wilmington: Broadfoot, Reprint 1993, p. 394.
31. "The Wilderness Campaign Against Grant," *Confederate Military History* (Hereafter *CMH*), Carmel: Indiana Guild Press, 1997, Vol. 3, p. 439; Jordan, *Hancock*, pp. 117.
32. Jordan, *Hancock*, pp. 118-119; Rhea, *The Wilderness*, Order of Battle, pp. 317-318; *OR*, Vol. 36, Part 1, pp. 190, 458; Anderson, *The 57th Regiment of Massachusetts*, p. 35.
33. Monteith, "Battle of the Wilderness," pp. 412-413.
34. Rhea, *The Wilderness*, p. 292; Dawes, *Sixth Wisconsin*, p. 262; Matthews, *The 149th*, p. 145; Williams, *The Mississippi Brigade*, p. 144; Jordan, *Hancock*, p. 118.
35. Jordan, *Hancock*, pp. 118-119; Rhea, *The Wilderness*, p 318, maps pp. 284, 296; "The Wilderness Campaign," *CMH*, p. 439.

Chapter 6   ENDNOTES

36. Thomas Chamberlin, *History of the 150th Regiment Pennsylvania Volunteers*, Philadelphia: F. McManus, 1905, Butternut and Blue Reprints, 1986, p. 210; Curtis, *24th Michigan*, pp. 234-235; Adams, "In the Wilderness," p. 376; Anderson, *The 57th Regiment of Massachusetts*, p. 36; Williams, *The Mississippi Brigade*, p. 144.
37. William F. Perry, "Reminiscences of the Campaign of 1864 in Virginia," *SHSP*, Vol. 7, p. 51; Jordan, *Hancock*, pp. 119-120; Smith, *76th New York*, p. 291.
38. Smith, *76th New York*, p. 291; "The Wilderness Campaign," *CMH*, pp. 439-440; Longstreet, *From Manassas to Appomattox*, p. 560; *OR*, Vol. 36, Part 1, pp. 190, 614, 622; Matthews, *The 149th*, p. 146; Perry, "Reminiscences," pp. 51-52; Rhea, *The Wilderness*, Order of Battle, p. 299.
39. Rhea, *The Wilderness*, pp. 302-305; Longstreet, *From Manassas to Appomattox*, p. 560; Perry, "Reminiscences," pp. 51, 53.
40. Perry, "Reminiscences," pp. 53-54; *OR*, Vol. 36, Part 1, p. 596; Pearson, *Wadsworth*, p. 278; Chamberlin, *History of the 150th*, p. 216; Edward Steere, *The Wilderness Campaign*, Harrisburg: Stackpole, 1960, p. 348; Rhea, *The Wilderness*, pp. 305-306.
41. Rhea, *The Wilderness*, pp. 306-307; James L. Bowen, *History of the Thirty-Seventh Regiment Massachusetts Volunteers*, Holyoke, MA: Clark W. Bryan Co., 1884, p. 278; *OR*, Vol. 36, Part 1, pp. 596, 677-678.
42. *OR*, Vol. 36, Part 1, p. 682; Morris Schaff, *The Battle of the Wilderness*, New York: Houghton Mifflin, 1910, pp. 256-258; Rhea, *The Wilderness*, p. 336.
43. Rhea, *The Wilderness*, pp. 308, 334, 390, 436; *OR*, Vol. 36, Part 1, pp. 506, 611, 614.
44. Allen, "Memorial of Wadsworth," p. 26; Pearson, *Wadsworth*, p. 252; Rhea, *The Wilderness*, pp. 255, 344.
45. Rhea, *The Wilderness*, pp. 307, 310; Adams, "In the Wilderness," pp. 376-377; *OR*, Vol. 36, Part 1, pp. 320-321, 611, 615; Part 2, p. 442; Schaff, *The Battle of the Wilderness*, pp. 257-258; Steere, *The Wilderness Campaign*, p. 358; Jordan, *Hancock*, pp. 122-123.
46. Jordan, *Hancock*, pp. 122-123; Adams, "In the Wilderness," p. 377; Rhea, *The Wilderness*, pp. 338-339; *OR*, Vol. 36, Part 2, pp. 352, 442; Part 1, pp. 437-438.
47. Longstreet, *From Manassas to Appomattox*, p. 563; Rhea, *The Wilderness*, map p. 352, pp. 364-365; George A. Bruce, *The Twentieth*

Regiment of Massachusetts Volunteer Infantry 1861-1865, New York: Houghton Mifflin, 1906, pp. 352, 354; *OR*, Vol. 36, Part 1, pp. 438-439.
48. *OR*, Vol. 36, Part 1, p. 438; Schaff, *The Battle of the Wilderness*, p. 269; Steere, *The Wilderness Campaign*, p. 363.
49. Longstreet, *From Manassas to Appomattox*, p. 561; Perry, "Reminiscences," pp. 54, 57; Earl M. Rogers, "How Wadsworth Fell," *National Tribune*, Dec. 24, 1885, Eric J. Mink Collection.
50. Rhea, *The Wilderness*, pp. 338-340; *OR*, Vol. 36, Part 1, p. 352.
51. *OR*, Vol. 36, Part 1, p. 26; Monteith, "Battle of the Wilderness," p. 414; Pearson, *Wadsworth*, pp. 281-282.
52. Pearson, *Wadsworth*, pp. 278-279; *OR*, Vol. 36, Part 1, p. 438.
53. Longstreet, *From Manassas to Appomattox*, pp. 561-562; Report of General William Mahone, *SHSP*, Vol. 6, No 2, Aug. 1878, Guild Press of Indiana, 1998, pp. 84-85; Rhea, *The Wilderness*, pp. 313, 356-357, map p. 352.
54. Rhea, *The Wilderness*, pp. 361-363; Longstreet, *From Manassas to Appomattox*, pp. 562-563; Jordan, *Hancock*, p. 123; *OR*, Vol. 36, Part 1, p. 682.
55. *OR*, Vol. 36, Part 1, pp. 437-438, 624; Rhea, *The Wilderness*, pp. 362-363; Matthews, *The 149th*, pp. 147-149; Rogers, "How Wadsworth Fell;" Monteith, "Battle of the Wilderness," p. 414; Pearson, *Wadsworth*, pp. 281-282; Smith, *76th New York*, p. 292; Schaff, *The Battle of the Wilderness*, p. 271; Longstreet, *From Manassas to Appomattox*, p. 563.
56. *OR*, Vol. 36, Part 2, p. 452; Rogers, "How Wadsworth Fell."
57. *OR*, Vol. 36, Part 1, p. 439.
58. J. R. Bowen, *Regimental History of the First New York Dragoons*, Published by Author, 1900, p. 307.
59. Wainwright, *A Diary of Battle*, p. 353; *OR*, Vol. 36, Part 2, pp. 459, 506.
60. *OR*, Vol. 36, Part 1, p. 326.
61. John Haskell, *The Haskell Memoirs*, ed. Gilbert E. Govan & James W. Livingood, New York: G. P. Putnam, 1969, p. 64; Rhea, *The Wilderness*, Order of Battle.
62. George S. Bernard, Letter to John R. Turner, n. d., "The Battle of the Wilderness," *SHSP*, Vol. 20, 1892, Broadfoot Reprint, 1990, p. 77; E. M. Feild, Letter to John R. Turner, n. d., *SHSP*, Vol. 20, 1892, p. 86; William C. Smith, Letter to John R. Turner, Feb. 26, 1892, *SHSP*, Vol. 20, 1892, p. 83; *Army and Navy Journal*, Vol. 1, July 23,

1864, p. 793, NA; Pearson, *Wadsworth*, p. 285, fn #2; Eric J. Mink, "The Death, Retrieval, and Remembrance of Brigadier General James S. Wadsworth," *Civil War Regiments*, Vol. 6, No. 4, p. 96, fn #111; Adams, "In the Wilderness," p. 389.
63. Adams, "In the Wilderness," pp. 388-389.
64. **Ibid.**, pp. 390-392; Augustus Dickert, *History of Kershaw's Brigade*, Dayton: Morningside, 1973, p. 352.
65. *OR*, Vol. 36, Part 1, p. 1082; Part 2, pp. 480, 554, 654; Series 3, Vol. 4, pp. 280-281.
66. **Ibid.**, Part 2, pp. 783; 841; "General Wadsworth's Body," *The New York Times*, May 18, 1864; Mink, "Death, Retrieval, and Remembrance," p. 102; Bowen, *Regimental History*, p. 307.
67. Hay, *Lincoln and the Civil War*, p. 182.
68. Curtis, *24th Michigan*, p. 235.
69. "Arrival of the Remains of Gen. Wadsworth," *The New York Tribune*, May 19, 1864; Leech, *Reveille in Washington*, pp. 222, 322.
70. Leech, *Reveille in Washington*, p. 326; "Honors to the Remains of Gen. Wadsworth," *New York Times*, May 21, 1864; Allen, "Memorial of Wadsworth," p. 29; Regis, De Trobriand, *Four Years with the Army of the Potomac*, Boston: Ticknor & Co., 1889, Reprinted Van Sickle Military Books, 1988, p. 572.

Epilogue
1. Thomson, *Service of the Seventh Indiana*, p. 183.
2. *OR*, Vol. 40, Part 2, p. 561; Part 3, p. 125; Pearson, *Wadsworth*, p. 285, fn #1.
3. Ainsworth, Letter to Sickles, Oct. 9, 1911, RG 094, Box 532, NA; Alexander Hays Military File, Box 432, NA; *Lincoln Day by Day*, p. 319; Craig Wadsworth, Note to C. Kelton, May 7, 1867, W17 CB 1863, NA; *In Memoriam*, pp. 54-55.
4. *OR*, Vol. 46, Part 3, pp. 976-977; Dawes, *Sixth Wisconsin*, pp. 290-291; Matthews, *The 149th*, p. 193.
5. William Godfrey, William T. Lowry Obituary, *Confederate Veteran*, Vol. 29, Jan. 1921, p. 31; Pearson, *Wadsworth*, p. 285, fn #1.
6. Leech, *Reveille in Washington*, pp. 417-418.
7. Allen, "Memorial of Wadsworth," p. 29; "General Hancock on General Wadsworth," *The* **(New York)** *Evening Post*, Sept. 29, 1864.
8. Henry W. Pfanz, *Gettysburg - The First Day*, Chapel Hill: Univ. of North Carolina Press, 2001, p. 122; Coddington, *The Gettysburg Campaign*, fn #82 pp. 690-691, fn #107, pp. 693-694; Doubleday,

Chancellorsville and Gettysburg, p. 135; Abner Doubleday, Letter to Rufus R. Dawes, Jan. 13, 1878, Slack Research Collections, Dawes Memorial Library, Marietta College.
9. Doubleday, *Chancellorsville and Gettysburg*, p. 132; *Supplement to the Official Records of the Union and Confederate Armies*, J. B. Hewett, N. A. Trudeau, B. A. Suderow ed's., Wilmington, NC: Broadfoot Publishing Co., 1995, Part I, Vol. 5, Addendum, Vol. 27, Serial Nos. 43-44, p. 92.
10. *Proceedings of the Century Association*, pp. 28-29.
11. **Ibid.**, p. 28.

Appendix A
1. Dyer, *A Compendium*, Part 1, pp. 107, 274-275; *OR*, Vol. 5, p. 718.
2. *OR*, Vol. 25, Part 1, pp. 157-158.
3. **Ibid.**, Vol. 27, Part 1, p. 155.
4. *Supplement Army Official Records*, Vol. 5, Addendum, Vol. 27, Serial 43-44, p. 111.
5. *OR*, Vol. 36, Part 1, pp. 110-111.

Appendix B
1. Herdegen and Beaudot, *In the Bloody Railroad Cut at Gettysburg*, pp. 176-177 fn. #3.
2. *Supplement Army Official Records*, Part 1, Vol. 5, Serial No 5, pp. 90-91.
3. *OR*, Vol. 27, Part 1, pp. 245-246.
4. Doubleday, *Chancellorsville and Gettysburg*, p. 131-132.
5. *OR*, Vol. 27, Part 1, p. 266.
6. *Supplement Army Official Records*, Vol. 5, Addendum, Vol. 27, Serial 43-44, p. 111; A Brief Memorial Tribute to Captain Clayton E. Rogers, Hayward, Wisconsin, Apr. 30, 1900, p. 1, SHSW; Rogers, "Gettysburg Scenes."
7. Rogers, "Gettysburg Scenes."
8. *Chippewa Herald*, Jan. 4, 1884.
9. Dawes, "Sixth Wisconsin at Gettysburg," pp. 215-216; *Supplement Army Official Records*, Vol. 5, Addendum, Vol. 27, Serial 43-44, pp. 111-114.
10. *Supplement Army Official Records*, Vol. 5, Addendum, Vol. 27, Serial 43-44, pp. 111-114; Dawes, *Sixth Wisconsin*, pp. 165-166.
11. Wainwright, *A Diary of Battle*, p. 233.
12. Shue, *Morning at Willoughby Run*, pp. 150-151; Martin, *Gettysburg*

July 1, p. 122.

Appendix C
1. *In Memoriam*, p. 52.
2. **Ibid.**
3. **Ibid.**
4. Allen, "Memorial of Wadsworth," pp. 27-28.
5. Adams, "In the Wilderness," pp. 396-397.
6. **Ibid.**
7. "General Wadsworth's Body," *The New York Times*, May 18, 1864; "Arrival of the Remains of Gen. Wadsworth," *The New York Tribune*, May 19, 1864; "Arrival of the Remains of Gen. Wadsworth at Washington," *The New York Herald*, May 19, 1864; "General Wadsworth's Remains Brought to Washington," **(Washington)** *National Republican*, May 18, 1864.
8. Eric J. Mink, Letter to J. F. Krumwiede, Feb. 25 and Mar. 28, 2001.

Appendix D
1. Russell R. Elliot, *History of Nevada*, Lincoln: Univ. of Nebraska Press, 1987, pp. 43, 47.
2. Thompson and West, *History of Nevada 1881 with Illustrations*, Berkeley: Howell-North, 1958, p. 645; Helen S. Carlson, *Nevada Place Names*, Reno: Univ. of Nevada Press, 1974, pp. 195-196.
3. Elliot, *History of Nevada*, p. 112; David F. Myrick, *Railroads of Nevada and Eastern California*, Berkeley: Howell-North, 1963, pp. 12-13; Don Cox, *Stories from the Sagebrush*, Reno: Nevada Humanities Comm., p. 161; Faith Bremner, "Reservation has a long history of squatters," *Reno Gazette-Journal*, Dec. 22, 1997, p. 4A.
4. Elliot, *History of Nevada*, p. 113; Myrick, *Railroads of Nevada*, p. 13; George Kraus, "Central Pacific Construction Vignettes," *The Golden Spike*, ed. David E. Miller, Salt Lake City: Univ. of Utah Press, 1973, p. 56.
5. Elliot, *History of Nevada*, p. 113; Carlson, *Nevada Place Names*, p. 132; Kraus, "Central Pacific Construction Vignettes," *The Golden Spike*, pp. 56-57; Bremner, "Reservation has a long history," *Reno Gazette-Journal*, p. 4A.
6. Myrick, *Railroads of Nevada*, p. 18; Kraus, "Central Pacific Construction Vignettes," *The Golden Spike*, p. 57; Stephen E. Ambrose, *Nothing Like It in the World*, New York: Simon & Schuster, 2000, p. 309.

7. Thompson and West, *History of Nevada*, pp. 645-646; Don Ashbaugh, *Nevada's Turbulent Yesterday*, Westernlore Press, 1963, pp. 140-141; Elliot, *History of Nevada*, p. 113; Myrick, *Railroads of Nevada*, p. 18; Stanley W. Paher, *Nevada Ghost Towns and Mining Camps*, Las Vegas: Nevada Publications, n. d., p. 38.
8. Paher, *Nevada Ghost Towns and Mining Camps*, p. 38; Thompson and West, *History of Nevada*, p. 645; Cox, *Stories from the Sagebrush*, p. 161; Bremner, "Reservation has a long history," *Reno Gazette-Journal*, p. 4A; Eric N. Moody, Letter to J. F. Krumwiede, June 11, 2001.
9. Thompson and West, *History of Nevada*, p. 646.
10. Ashbaugh, *Nevada's Turbulent Yesterday*, p. 141; Paher, *Nevada Ghost Towns and Mining Camps*, pp. 36, 38; Carlson, *Nevada Place Names*, pp. 131, 220-221; Nevada Historic Marker #68; Ambrose, *Nothing Like It in the World*, p. 379.
11. Carlson, *Nevada Place Names*, p. 221; Bremner, "Reservation has a long history ," *Reno Gazette-Journal*, p. 4A.
12. Paher, *Nevada Ghost Towns and Mining Camps*, p. 38; Cox, *Stories from the Sagebrush*, p. 156.
13. Cox, *Stories from the Sagebrush*, pp. 160-161; Faith Bremner, "Purchases assist Paiutes toward goal," *Reno Gazette-Journal*, Dec. 22, 1997, p. 4A.

BIBLIOGRAPHY

Books and Pamphlets

Allen, Lewis F., *"Memorial of the Late James S. Wadsworth," Delivered Before the New York State Agricultural Society at the Close of Its Annual Exhibition at Rochester, September 23, 1864*, Buffalo: Franklin Steam Printing House, 1864; Albany, NY: Van Benthuysen's Steam Printing House, 1865.

Army Register of the Volunteer Force of the United States, 1861-5, 9 vols., U.S. War Department, Washington, D.C.: GPO, 1867; Reprint, Gaithersburg, MD: Olde Soldier Books, 1987.

Anderson, John, *The 57th Regiment of Massachusetts Volunteers in the War of the Rebellion*, Boston, MA: E. B. Stillings, 1896.

The Bachelder Papers, 3 vols., David L. & Audrey J. Ladd eds., Dayton, OH: Morningside, 1994.

Bates, Samuel P., *History of Pennsylvania Volunteers, 1861-5*, 5 vols., Harrisburg, PA: D. Singerly, 1870.

Beaudot, William J. K., and Herdegen, Lance J., *An Irishman in the Iron Brigade*, New York, NY: Fordham University Press, 1993.

Biddle, Chapman, *"The First Day of the Battle of Gettysburg," An Address Delivered Before the Historical Society of Pennsylvania, March 8, 1880*, Philadelphia, PA: J. B. Lippincott & Co., 1880.

Bigelow, John, Jr., *The Campaign of Chancellorsville*, New Haven, CT: Yale University Press, 1910, Morningside reprint.

Boatner, Mark M. III, *The Civil War Dictionary*, New York, NY: Random House Reprint, 1991.

Bowen, J. R., *Regimental History of the First New York Dragoons*, Published by Author, 1900, Eric J. Mink Collection.

Bowen, James L., *History of the Thirty-Seventh Regiment Massachusetts Volunteers*, Holyoke, MA: Clark W. Bryan Co., 1884.

Brooks, Noah, *Washington in Lincoln's Time*, New York, NY: The Century Co., 1895.

Brown, Varina D., *A Colonel at Gettysburg and Spotsylvania*, Columbia, SC: The State Co., 1931.

Bruce, George A., *The Twentieth Regiment of Massachusetts Volunteer Infantry, 1861-1865*, New York, NY: Houghton Mifflin, 1906.

Buell, Augustus, *The Cannoneer*, Washington, D.C.: The National Tribune, 1890; Reprint, Ann Arbor, MI: University of Michigan Press, 1997.

Busey, John W., *These Honored Dead*, Hightstown, NJ: Longstreet House, 1996.

Busey, John W., and Martin, David G., *Regimental Strengths and Losses at Gettysburg*, Hightstown, NJ: Longstreet House, 1982.

Catton, Bruce, *A Stillness at Appomattox*, Garden City, NY: Doubleday and Co., 1957.

Proceedings of the Century Association in Honor of the Memory of Brig-Gen. James S. Wadsworth and Colonel Peter A. Porter, New York, NY: D. Van Nostrand, 1864.

Chamberlin, Thomas, *History of the 150th Regiment Pennsylvania Volunteers*, Philadelphia, PA: F. McManus, 1905; Reprint, Baltimore, MD: Butternut and Blue, 1986.

Confederate Military History, Carmel, IN: Guild Press of Indiana, 1997.

Curtis, O. B., *History of the 24th Michigan of the Iron Brigade, Known as the Detroit & Wayne County Regiment*, Detroit, MI: Winn & Hammond, 1891; Reprint, Gaithersburg, MD: Butternut Press, 1984.

The Civil War Day by Day, John S. Bowman ed., New York, NY: Barnes and Noble, 1993.

Coddington, Edwin B., *The Gettysburg Campaign*, New York, NY: Charles Scribner's Sons, 1984.

Davis, Major George B., Perry, Leslie J., and Kirkley, Joseph W., *The Official Military Atlas of the Civil War*, Washington, D.C.: GPO, 1891-95; Reprint, Gramercy Books, 1983.

Dawes, Rufus R., *Service with the Sixth Wisconsin Volunteers*, Dayton, OH: Morningside House Inc., Reprint No. 79, 1996.

DeTrobriand, Regis, *Four Years with the Army of the Potomac*, Boston, MA: Ticknor & Co., 1889; Reprint, Van Sickle Military Books, 1988.

Dickert, D. Augustus, *History of Kershaw's Brigade*, Dayton, OH: Morningside Bookshop, 1973.

Dictionary of American History, 2nd Rev. Ed., James T. Adams ed., New York, NY: Charles Scribner's Sons, 1961.

Donald, David H., *Lincoln*, New York, NY: Simon & Schuster, 1995.

Doubleday, Abner, *Chancellorsville and Gettysburg*, New York, NY: Da Capo Press, 1994.

Dyer, Frederick H., *A Compendium of the War of the Rebellion*, Des Moines, IA: The Dyer Publishing Co., 1908; Reprint, Carmel, IN: Guild Press of Indiana, 1996.

Fennell, Charles C., "The Attack and Defense of Culp's Hill: Greene's Brigade at the Battle of Gettysburg, July 1-3, 1863," Dissertation Submitted to West Virginia University, 1992; Ann Arbor, MI: University of Michigan Press, 1996.

Gaff, Alan D., *On Many a Bloody Field*, Bloomington, IN: Indiana University Press, 1996.

Gates, Theodore B., *The 'Ulster Guard' (20th N. Y. State Militia) and the War of the Rebellion*, New York, NY: B. H. Tyrrel, 1879.

The Gettysburg Papers, Comp. by Ken Brandy and Florence Freeland, Dayton, OH: Morningside, 1986.

Harrison, Kathleen Georg, "Edward McPherson Farm: Historical Study," Unpublished, GNMP.

Harrison, Kathleen Georg, "Transcript of the Court Martial of Brig. General Thomas A. Rowley;" Unpublished, GNMP Library.

Haskell, John, *The Haskell Memoirs*, Gilbert E. Govan & James W. Livingood ed., New York, NY: G. P. Putnam, 1969.

Hay, John, *Lincoln and the Civil War in the Diaries and Letters of John Hay*, Tyler Dennett ed., New York, NY: Dodd, Mead, & Co., 1939; Reprint, New York, NY: Da Capo Press, 1988.

Heitman, Francis B., *Historical Register and Dictionary of the United States Army*, Washington, D.C.: GPO, 1903.

Hennessy, John J., *Return to Bull Run*, New York, NY: Simon & Schuster, 1993.

Herdegen, Lance J., and Beaudot, J. K., *In the Bloody Railroad Cut at Gettysburg*, Dayton, OH: Morningside House Inc., 1991.

Historical Times Encyclopedia of the Civil War, P. L. Faust ed., New York, NY: Harper & Row, 1986.

Histories of the Several Regiments and Battalions from North Carolina, Walter Clark ed., Goldsboro, NC: Nash Brothers, 1901; Reprint, Wendell, NC: Broadfoot's Bookmark, 1982.

Hofmann, John W., *Military Record of Brevet Brigadier General John William Hofmann*, Philadelphia, PA: A. W. Auner, 1884, Philadelphia Civil War Library and Museum, copy GNMP Library.

Hofmann, J. W., "Remarks on the Battle of Gettysburg," Presentation to the Historical Society of Pennsylvania, March 8, 1880, Manuscript Collection, Gettysburg College.

Howard, Oliver O., *Autobiography of Oliver O. Howard*, New York, NY:

The Baker & Taylor Co., 1907.

Jordan, David M., *Winfield Scott Hancock, A Soldier's Life*, Bloomington, IN: Indiana University Press, 1988.

Kress, John A., *Memoirs of Brigadier General John Alexander Kress*, Philadelphia, PA: Author, 1925.

Leech, Margaret, *Reveille in Washington, 1860-1865*, New York, NY: Harper & Brothers, 1941.

Lincoln Day by Day, A Chronology 1809-1865, 3 vols., Earl S. Miers Editor-in-Chief, Dayton, OH: Morningside, 1991.

Locke, William Henry, *The Story of the Regiment*, New York, NY: James Miller, 1872.

Longstreet, James, *From Manassas to Appomattox*, New York, NY: William S. Konecky Reprint, 1992.

Lyman, Theodore, *Meade's Headquarters, 1863-1865: Letters of Colonel Theodore Lyman from the Wilderness to Appomattox*, George Agassiz ed., Boston, MA: Atlantic Monthly Press, 1922.

Maine at Gettysburg: Report of the Maine Commissioners, Portland, ME: Lakeside Press, 1898.

Martin, David G., *Gettysburg July 1*, Rev. Ed., Conshohocken, PA: Combined Books, 1995.

Matthews, Richard E., *The 149th Pennsylvania Volunteer Infantry Unit in the Civil War,* Jefferson, NC: McFarland & Co., 1994.

Maxon, William P., *Camp Fires of the 23rd New York Volunteers*, New York, NY: Davies and Kent, 1863.

McLean, James L., Jr., *Cutler's Brigade at Gettysburg*, Rev. 2nd Ed., Baltimore, MD: Butternut and Blue, 1994.

Meade, George, *The Life and Letters of General George Gordon Meade*, 2 vols., George Gordon Meade ed., Baltimore, MD: Butternut and Blue, 1994.

Mills, John Harrison, *Chronicles of the 21st New York Volunteers*, Buffalo, NY: 21st Reg. Veteran Assoc. of Buffalo, 1887, University Publications of America.

Nevins, Allan, *War for the Union*, 5 vols., New York, NY: Konecky & Konecky, 1971.

New York Monuments Commission for the Battlefields of Gettysburg, Chattanooga, and Antietam, *Final Report on the Battle of Gettysburg*, 3 vols., Albany, NY: J. B. Lyon Co., 1900.

New York Monuments Commission for the Battlefields of Gettysburg, Chattanooga, and Antietam, *In Memoriam, James Samuel Wadsworth, 1807-1864*, Albany, NY: J. B. Lyon Company, Printers, 1916, Copy D. Lorello, New York State Archives.

Nolan, Alan T., *The Iron Brigade*, Indianapolis, IN: Indiana University Press Edition, 1994.

Northrop, John W., *Chronicles from the Diary of a War Prisoner*, Wichita, KS: Author, 1904.

Otis, George H., *The Second Wisconsin Infantry*, Alan D. Gaff ed., Dayton, OH: Morningside, 1984.

Pearson, Henry Greenleaf, *James S. Wadsworth of Geneseo*, New York, NY: Charles Scriber's Sons, 1913; Reprint, Ann Arbor, MI: University of Michigan Press, 1997.

Pennsylvania at Gettysburg, 3 vols., John P. Nicholson ed., Harrisburg, PA: State Printer, 1904.

Pfanz, Henry W., *Gettysburg–Culp's Hill and Cemetery Hill*, Chapel Hill, NC: University of North Carolina Press, 1993.

Pfanz, Henry W., *Gettysburg–The First Day*, Chapel Hill, NC: University of North Carolina Press, 2001.

Pitzer, John E., *The Three Days Battle at Gettysburg*, Gettysburg, PA: News Press, circa 1913, GNMP.

Pratt, Fletcher, *Stanton, Lincoln's Secretary of War*, New York, NY: Norton & Co., 1953.

Rhea, Gordon C., *The Battle of the Wilderness, May 5-6, 1864*, Baton Rouge, LA: Louisiana State University Press, 1994.

Reid, Whitelaw, *A Radical View: The "Agate," Dispatches of Whitelaw Reid, 1861-1865*, 2 vols., Memphis: Memphis State University Press, 1976.

Schaff, Morris, *The Battle of the Wilderness*, New York, NY: Houghton Mifflin, 1910.

Scott, James K. P., *The Story of the Battle of Gettysburg*, Harrisburg, PA: The Telegraph Press, 1927.

Sears, Stephen W., *Chancellorsville*, Boston, MA: Houghton Mifflin, 1996.

Sears, Stephen W., *Landscape Turned Red*, New York, NY: Ticknor and Fields, 1983.

Sears, Stephen W., *To the Gates of Richmond*, New York, NY: Houghton Mifflin, 1992.

Shue, Richard S., *Morning at Willoughby Run*, Gettysburg, PA: Thomas Publications, 1995.

Smith, A. P., *History of the Seventy-sixth Regiment, New York Volunteers*, Cortland, NY: Truair, Smith & Miles, 1867; Reprint, Ron R. Van Sickle Military Books, 1988.

Snyder, Charles McCool, *Oswego County, New York in the Civil War*, Oswego, NY: The OCHS and the Oswego County Civil War Centennial Commission, 1962.

The Southern Historical Society Papers, 52 vols., 1876-1959, Carmel, IN: Guild Press of Indiana.

Steere, Edward, *The Wilderness Campaign*, Harrisburg, PA: Stackpole,

1960.

Supplement to the Official Records of the Union and Confederate Armies, J. B. Hewett, N. A. Trudeau, and B. A. Suderow ed., Wilmington, NC: Broadfoot Publishing Co., 1995.

Tevis, C. V. and D. R. Marquis, *The History of the Fighting Fourteenth (Brooklyn Regiment)*, New York, NY: Brooklyn Eagle Press, 1911; Reprint, Baltimore, MD: Butternut and Blue, 1994.

Thomas, Benjamin P., and Hyman, Harold M., *Stanton, The Life and Times of Lincoln's Secretary of War*, New York, NY: Alfred A. Knopf, 1962.

Thomson, Orville, *Narrative of the Service of the Seventh Indiana Infantry in the War for the Union*, Published by the Author, 1905; Reprint, Baltimore, MD: Butternut and Blue, 1993.

Wadsworth, Horace Andrew, *Two Hundred and Fifty Years of the Wadsworth Family in America*, Lawrence, MA: Eagle Steam Job Printing Rooms, 1883.

Wainwright, Charles S., *A Diary of Battle The Personal Journals of Colonel Charles S. Wainwright*, Allan Nevins ed., Gettysburg, PA: Stan Clark Military Books, 1992.

Warner, Ezra J., *Generals in Blue*, Baton Rouge, LA: Louisiana State University Press, 1994.

Warner, Ezra J., *Generals in Gray*, Baton Rouge, LA: Louisiana State University Press, 1994.

Weld, Stephen M., *War Diary and Letters of Stephen Minot Weld, 1861-1865*, Boston, MA: Riverside Press, 1912.

Wheeler, Richard, *Witness to Gettysburg*, New York, NY: Harper & Row, 1987.

Williams, T. P., *The Mississippi Brigade of Brig. Gen. Joseph R. Davis*, Dayton, OH: Morningside, 1999.

BIBLIOGRAPHY

Manuscript Collections and Newspaper Sources

Gettysburg College Library and Manuscript Collection
   New York Times, The Gettysburg Star and Sentinel, and *The Gettysburg Times.*

Gettysburg National Military Park Library and Vertical Files
   General Officers, 1st Corps, AOP; Infantry Regiments and Artillery Batteries, 1st Div., 1st Corps, AOP; James Wadsworth Monument; J. B. Bachelder Papers Transcripts; *National Tribune* and *Scout and Soldiers Mail.*

Oswego County Historical Society, Henry Harrison Lyman Collection

National Archives
   General's Papers: James Wadsworth; Pension File: John Newton; Staff Officer File: Lysander Cutler, John Newton, and Alexander Hays; Box #448, W17 CB 1863; RG 94, Correspondence; RG 393, Part 1, 1st and 2nd Brigades, 1st Div., 1st Corps, and 4th Div., 5th Corps AOP.

Nevada Historical Society
   Reno and Wadsworth, Nevada Files; *Reno Gazette-Journal.*

Slack Research Collections, Dawes Memorial Library, Marietta College
   Rufus Dawes Papers.

State Historical Society of Wisconsin, Library and Archives
   Rufus Dawes and Jerome A. Watrous Papers; *Milwaukee Sunday Telegraph* and *Mauston Star.*

U. S. Army Military History Institute, Library, Manuscript and Photo Archives, Carlisle, PA
   General Officers, 1st and 5th Corps, AOP; Infantry Regiments and Artillery Batteries, 1st Div., 1st Corps, AOP; Infantry Regiments, 4th Div., 5th Corps, AOP; Robert Blake Collection; *Civil War Times Illustrated* Collection; Civil War Miscellaneous Collection.

Vernon County Historical Society, Viroqua, WI, Files and Collections

Magazine and Journal Articles

Belo, A. H. "Battle of Gettysburg," *Confederate Veteran*, Vol. VIII, April 1900, pp. 165-168.

Bernard, George S., Letter to John R. Turner, n. d., "The Battle of the Wilderness," *Southern Historical Society Papers* (Hereafter *SHSP*), Vol. 20, 1892, pp. 68-87, Broadfoot Publishing Co., Reprint, 1990.

Boland, E. T., "Beginning of the Battle of Gettysburg," *Confederate Veteran*, Vol. XIV, July 1906, pp. 308-309.

Calef, John, "Gettysburg Notes: The Opening Gun," *Journal of the Military Service Institution of the United States*, Vol. 40, 1907, pp. 40-58.

Custer, George A. , "War Memoirs," *Galaxy*, Vol. XXI, April 1876

Feild, E. M., Letter to John R. Turner, n. d., "The Battle of the Wilderness," *SHSP*, Vol. 20, 1892, pp. 68-87, Broadfoot Reprint, 1990.

Flaherty, Darwin L., "The Naming of Reno, Nevada: A Century-Old Mystery," *Nevada Historical Society Quarterly*, Vol. XXVII, Fall 1984.

Godfrey, William, "William T. Lowry Obituary," *Confederate Veteran*, Vol. 29, January 1921, p. 31.

Hancock, Winfield Scott, "Gettysburg. A Reply to General Howard," *Galaxy*, December 1876, pp. 821-831.

Hancock, Winfield Scott, Letter to James Longstreet, January 17, 1878, *SHSP*, Vol. 5, 1878, pp. 168-172, Broadfoot Reprint, 1990.

Herdegen, Lance J., "The Lieutenant who Arrested a General," *Gettysburg Magazine*, Issue No. 4, January 1991, pp. 25-32.

Howard, Oliver O., "Campaign and Battle of Gettysburg, June and July, 1863," *Atlantic Monthly*, July 1876.

Lash, Gary G., "Brig. Gen. Henry Baxter's Brigade at Gettysburg, July 1," *Gettysburg Magazine*, Issue No. 10, January 1994, pp. 7-27.

Lyman, Henry H., "Historical Sketch," New York Monuments Commission for the Battlefields of Gettysburg, Chattanooga, and Antietam, *Final Report on the Battle of Gettysburg,* Vol. 3, Albany: J. B. Lyon Co., 1900, p. 1001.

Miller, J. Michael, "Perrin's Brigade on July 1, 1863," *Gettysburg Magazine,* Issue No. 13, July 1995, pp. 22-32.

Mink, Eric J., "The Death, Retrieval, and Remembrance of Brigadier General James S. Wadsworth," *Civil War Regiments,* Vol. 6, No. 4, pp. 77-119.

Morse, Charles F., "The Twelfth Corps at Gettysburg," *Papers of the Military Historical Society of Massachusetts,* Vol. 14, Wilmington, NC: Broadfoot, 1990, pp. 19-42.

Purifoy, John, "The Battle of Gettysburg, July 1, 1863," *Confederate Veteran,* Vol. XXXI, January and April 1923, pp. 22-25 and 138-141.

Rockwell, Joseph E., Letter to John R. Turner, n. d., "The Battle of the Wilderness," *SHSP,* Vol. 20, 1892, pp. 68-87, Broadfoot Reprint, 1990.

Sauers, Richard A., "The 16th Maine Volunteer Infantry at Gettysburg," *Gettysburg Magazine,* Issue No. 13, July 1995, pp. 33-42.

Smith, William C., Letter to John R. Turner, February 26, 1892, "The Battle of the Wilderness," *SHSP,* Vol. 20, 1892, pp. 68-87, Broadfoot Reprint, 1990.

Snyder, Charles McCool, "Robert Oliver, Jr. and the Oswego County Regiment," *New York History,* Vol. XXXVIII, July 1957, pp. 276-293.

Storch, Marc and Beth, ""What a Deadly Trap We Were In" Archer's Brigade on July 1, 1863," *Gettysburg Magazine,* Issue No. 6, January 1992, pp. 13-27.

Newspaper Articles

"Arrival of the Remains of Gen. Wadsworth," *The New York Tribune*, May 19, 1864, Eric J. Mink Collection.

"Arrival of the Remains of Gen. Wadsworth at Washington," *The New York Herald*, May 19, 1864, Eric J. Mink Collection.

Bachelder, John B., "Hall's Maine and Calef's U. S. Batteries at Gettysburg," *Scout and Soldiers Mail*, December 26, 1885.

Coey, James, "Cutler's Brigade. The 147th New York's Magnificent Fight on the First Day at Gettysburg," *National Tribune*, July 15, 1915.

Cutler, Lysander, et. al., "Gettysburg: The Great Battle of July 1, 2, and 3, 1863," *The Gettysburg Star and Sentinel*, May 5, 1885, p. 1.

Davidson, John T., "General James S. Wadsworth," *Elmira Telegram*, August 24, 1890.

Dawes, Rufus R., "Reminiscences of the Battle of Gettysburg," *The Gettysburg Star and Sentinel*, March 8, 1872, p. 1.

Dawes, Rufus R., "A Gallant Officer," *Milwaukee Sunday Telegraph*, February 3, 1884, p. 3.

"General Hancock on General Wadsworth," *The (New York) Evening Post*, September 29, 1864.

"General Wadsworth's Body," *The New York Times*, May 18, 1864, Eric J. Mink Collection.

"General Wadsworth's Remains Brought to Washington," *(Washington) National Republican*, May 18, 1864, Eric J. Mink Collection.

Hofmann, J. W., "The 56th Regiment Pennsylvania Volunteers in the Gettysburg Campaign," *Philadelphia Weekly Press*, January 13, 1886.

Hofmann, J. W., "Gettysburg Again. Gen. Hofmann on the Action of the 147th New York at the Opening of the Battle," *National Tribune*, June 5, 1884.

Hubbard, J. N., "Gettysburg, Wadsworth's Division on Culp's Hill," *National Tribune*, April 15, 1915.

Kress, John A., "Tales of the War. Thrilling Description of Scenes and Incidents at Gettysburg," *Missouri Republican*, December 4, 1886.

Parkhurst, D. E., "At Gettysburg. Heroism of the 147th New York," *National Tribune*, November 1, 1888.

Rogers, Clayton E., "Woods, The Deserter," *Milwaukee Sunday Telegraph*, May 24, 1885, p. 3.

Rogers, Clayton E., "Gettysburg Scenes," *Milwaukee Sunday Telegraph*, February 13, 1887, p. 3.

Rogers, Earl M., "The Second or Fifty-Sixth—Which?", *Milwaukee Sunday Telegraph*, June 22, 1884.

Rogers, Earl M., "How Wadsworth Fell," *National Tribune*, December 24, 1885, Eric J. Mink Collection.

Sullivan, James P., "Gettysburg: Member of 6th Wisconsin Takes Issue with Carleton," *National Tribune*, May 14, 1885.

Sullivan, James P., "The Charge of the Iron Brigade at Gettysburg by Mickey of Company K," *Mauston Star*, 1883.

Whitney, M. M., "The 76th New York: How It Opened the Fight on the First Day at Gettysburg," *National Tribune*, July 21, 1887.

Young, Albert V., "A Pilgrimage," *Milwaukee Sunday Telegraph*, April 22, 1888.

Photographs, Paintings, etc.

1858 Map of Adams County, Adams County Historical Society, Drawn from Actual Survey by G. M. Hopkins, Traced by J. R. Hershey, May 5, 1980.

Gallon, Dale, *Men of Iron*, Released Summer 1994.

Gallon, Dale, *Reynolds at Gettysburg*, Released Summer 1996, Commentary by Wayne E. Motts.

INDEX

— A —

Adams, Capt. Z. Boylston, 98, 100, 104, 106, 114-115, 137-139
Alabama regiments:
  4th Infantry, 107
  15th Infantry, 103
  47th Infantry, 107
Arlington, VA, 3, 8, 10, 12, 15
Armies, Confederate:
  Army of Northern Virginia (Lee), 21, 23-26, 31, 33-37, 39-40, 79-80, 88, 91
    Longstreet's Corps (First), 23, 33-34, 37, 40, 75, 88, 98, 101, 114, 120
      (R. H.) Anderson's Division, 23
      Field's Division, 98, 101, 103-104, 106
        (G. T.) Anderson's Brigade, 108
        Benning's Brigade, 101
        Gregg's Brigade, 101, 103
        Perry's Brigade, 101-103, 106-107
      Kershaw's Division, 98, 101, 106-107, 115, 120
        Wofford's Brigade, 108
      McLaws's Division, 23
        Barksdale's Brigade, 27
    Jackson's Corps (Second), 23, 30-31
      Early's Division, 30
    Ewell's Corps (Second), 33-37, 40-41, 60, 62, 65, 75, 88, 90-91, 94-95, 98,
      Early's Division, 39, 73
        Gordon's Brigade, 95
      Johnson's Division, 75, 94
        Jones's Brigade, 75, 94
        Steuart's Brigade, 75
        Williams's Brigade, 75
      Rodes's Division, 39, 62-63, 67, 71
        Daniel's Brigade, 65, 95
        Doles's Brigade, 72
        Iverson's Brigade, 65
        Carter's Artillery Battalion, 62-64, 67
    Hill's Corps (Third), 33-34, 37-38, 40, 60, 75, 88, 91-92, 95-96, 98, 100-101, 103
      (R. H.) Anderson's Division, 98, 107-108
        Mahone's Brigade, 108, 110, 114
        Perrin's Brigade, 107, 110, 114-115
      Heth's Division, 40, 46, 48, 59, 67, 92, 95, 98
        Archer's Brigade, 46, 48, 59, 62
        Brockenbrough's Brigade, 62, 67, 69
        Davis's Brigade, 48, 55-56, 59, 62, 130, 135
        Kirkland's Brigade, 100
        Pettigrew's Brigade, 40, 62, 67, 69
      Pender's Division, 62, 67, 69, 71-72
        Perrin's Brigade, 69, 72
        Scales's Brigade, 69
      Wilcox's Division, 95-96, 100
        Poague's Artillery Battalion, 101
  Army of the Valley (Jackson), 15
Armies, Federal:
  Army of Northeastern Virginia (McDowell), 3-4, 6-8

Hunter's Division, 6-8
Tyler's Division, 6-7
  Keyes's Brigade, 6-7
  Sherman's Brigade, 6-7
Heintzelman's Division, 6-7
Army of the Potomac (McClellan, Burnside, Hooker, Meade), 8, 11, 13-14, 19, 21, 23-25, 34-37, 40, 79, 81, 85, 88, 95-96, 115-116, 124, 130, 132
  McDowell's Division, 8, 10, 125
    Keyes's Brigade, 10
    Wadsworth's Brigade, 8, 10-11, 15, 118, 125
  McDowell's Corps (First) 11, 14

Chancellorsville/Gettysburg

Reynolds's Corps (First), 19, 21-22, 25-27, 30, 35-41, 65, 67, 71-72, 74, 85, 107, 120, 122-123, 125-128, 130
  Doubleday's (Rowley's) Division, 21, 30-31, 39, 40-42, 59, 61, 97
    Rowley's (Chapman Biddle's) Brigade, 39-41, 61, 63, 67, 71, 97
    Stone's Brigade, 40, 61, 63, 65, 69, 97
  Robinson's Division, 30-31, 36, 37, 39, 41-42, 55, 59, 65, 67, 69, 135
    Baxter's Brigade, 37, 65, 67
    Paul's Brigade, 67, 97, 126
  Wadsworth's Division, 19-22, 25-27, 30-31, 34-42, 56, 59, 77, 79, 81, 97, 122, 125-128, 130, 132
    Cutler's Brigade, 31, 36, 39, 41-46, 48, 56, 60-61, 63, 65, 67, 71-74, 77, 79, 81, 97, 123, 126, 128, 130-131, 134-135
    Meredith's Brigade (Iron), 21-22, 26, 28, 30, 36, 39-44, 46, 52, 55-56, 60-61, 69, 73-74, 77, 81, 97, 123, 126-127, 135
    Paul's Brigade, 21, 36
    Phelps Brigade, 21, 28, 36, 125
  Wainwright's Artillery, 39
    Cooper's Battery (B, 1st PA.), 61, 63, 71
    Hall's Battery (2nd ME), 39, 42, 44, 46, 51-52, 55, 60, 65, 123
    Reynolds's Battery (L, 1st NY), iv, 31, 61, 63, 69, 74, 127
    Steven's Battery (5th ME), 69, 71-73
    Stewart's Battery (B, 4th US), 63, 65, 69, 127
Couch's/Hancock's Corps (Second), 25
  Gibbon's Division, 31
Sickles's Corps (Third), 24-25, 35, 37, 39, 75, 85
Meade's/Sykes's Corps (Fifth), 25-26, 31, 35, 79
  Sykes's Division, 31
    Ayres's Brigade, 31
Sedgwick's Corps (Sixth), 25, 27-28, 31, 40, 79
Burnside's Corps (Ninth), 23
Howard's Corps (Eleventh), 24-26, 30-31, 35, 37-39, 63, 67, 69, 71-72, 74
  Smith's Brigade, 72-73
Slocum's Corps (Twelfth), 25-26, 74-75
  Geary's Division, 74-75, 77
    Greene's Brigade, 74-75, 77
Pleasonton's Cavalry Corps, 34-35
  Buford's Division, v, 40-41,

INDEX

46
Devin's Brigade, 40, 44, 63
Gamble's Brigade, v, 40, 71
Calef's Battery (A, 2nd US), 60-61, 63
Benham's Engineering Brigade, 27
Wilderness
Hancock's Corps (Second), 85, 90-92, 95-96, 98, 100, 103, 106-107, 113
  Birney's Division, 100, 106, 108
    Ward's Brigade, 107
  Gibbon's Division, 100
    Owen's Brigade, 104, 106
    Webb's Brigade, 103-104, 106-107, 110
  Mott's Division, 100, 106, 108
Warren's Corps (Fifth), 85-86, 89-92, 95, 98, 100, 120, 128
  Crawford's Division, 86, 90-91, 94, 120
  Griffin's Division, 86, 90-92, 94-96
  Robinson's Division, 86, 90, 96
    Baxter's Brigade, 96-97, 100-101, 103-104, 110
  Wadsworth's Division, 85-86, 89-91, 94-97, 100, 103-104, 106, 108, 120, 124, 128-129
    Cutler's Brigade, 86, 91, 94-97, 100-101, 104, 108, 120, 129
    Kitching's Brigade, 98, 100-101, 103-104
    Rice's Brigade, 86, 91, 94-97, 100-101, 103, 107, 110, 129
    Stone's Brigade, 86, 91, 94-97, 100-101, 110, 129

Wainwright's Artillery
  Breck's Battery (L, 1st NY), 89, 94
  Stewart's Battery (B, 4th US), 89, 94
Sedgwick's Corps (Sixth), 90-91, 98
  Getty's/Wheaton's Division, 92, 100, 103, 106-108
    Eustis's Brigade, 103, 107
    Wheaton's Brigade, 103, 107-108
Burnside's Corps (Ninth), 88, 98, 100-101, 106
  Stevenson's Division, 98, 100, 104
    Carruth's Brigade, 100, 104, 106-107
Sheridan's Cavalry Corps, 104, 107, 115
  Wilson's Division, 89-90, 92
Army of the Shenandoah (Banks), 13-14, 21

— B —

Banks, Maj. Gen. Nathaniel P., 3, 13, 15
Banks Ford, 21, 23-25
Baxter, Brig. Gen. Henry, 65, 103
Bealeton Station, VA, 34-35
Beauregard, Gen. Pierre G. T., 4, 120
Belle Plain, VA, 21-22, 26, 116
Benham, Brig. Gen. Henry W., 27, 28
Biddle, Col. Chapman, 39, 69, 71
Birney, Maj. Gen. David B., 107-108
Blackburn's Ford, 6, 36
Brandy Station, battle of, 34-35
Brock Road, 92, 95, 100, 104, 107-108, 110, 113-114
Buford, Brig. Gen. John, v, 39-43,

48, 61, 63
Bull Run
 first battle of, 6-8, 10
 second battle of, 17, 19
Burnside, Maj. Gen. Ambrose E., 17, 19, 21-23, 27, 101, 106

— C —

Calef, Lieut. John H., 60-61
Carruth, Col. Sumner, 104, 106
Catoctin Mountains, 37, 79
Cemetery Hill, 60, 65, 69, 71-72, 75, 77, 79, 123
Central Pacific Railroad, 19, 141-143
Centreville, VA, 4, 8, 10-11, 35-36
Chambersburg, PA, 37, 39
Chambersburg Pike, 40, 44-46, 48, 52, 55-56, 59, 65, 69, 71, 73, 131, 134-135
Chancellorsville, battle of, 26-28, 30-31, 83, 88, 90, 120, 125-127
Chewing Farm, 91, 94
Committee on the Conduct of the War, 12
Coulter, Col. Richard, 103
Crawford, Brig. Gen Samuel W., 86, 91-92, 94, 120
Culp's Hill, 72-75, 77
Custer, Lieut. George A., 6, 104
Cutler, Brig. Gen. Lysander, 39, 41-45, 48, 52, 60, 63, 65, 69, 71, 73, 81, 86, 94-95, 101, 103-105, 107, 113, 120, 123, 126, 128-131, 135

— D —

Dana, Col. Edmund L., 96, 129
Dawes, Lieut. Col. Rufus R., 22, 55-56, 59, 61, 71-73, 100, 120, 122, 127, 130, 132-135
Dickert, Capt. D. Augustus, 115
Dix, Maj. Gen. John A., 13, 16, 122

Doubleday, Maj. Gen. Abner, 19, 21, 35, 38-42, 52, 55, 59-63, 65, 69, 71-74, 122-123, 130-132, 134-135

— E —

Edward's Ferry, 37
Ellsworth, Capt. Timothy E., 44, 52, 55-56, 85, 128
Emancipation, 16-17
Emmitsburg, MD, 38, 40-41, 73, 79
Emmitsburg Road (Gettysburg Pike), 39-42, 97
Eustis, Brig. Gen., Henry L., 103-104
Ewell, Lieut., Gen., Richard S., 33, 37, 62, 95, 97

— F —

Fairchild, Col. Lucius, 22, 46, 126-127
Fairfield, PA, 39-41
Fairfield Road, 44, 55, 67, 69, 71, 135
Falmouth, VA, 15, 21
Field, Maj. Gen. Charles. A., 107-108, 114
Fitzhugh's Crossing, 26-27
Fowler, Col. Edward B., 26, 42, 45-46, 56, 59, 125, 128-131, 135
Franklin, Maj. Gen. William B., 12, 19
Franklin's Crossing, 27
Frederick, MD, 26, 37
Fredericksburg, VA, 21, 25-27, 33-34, 88-89, 116, 138
 battle of, 18, 21, 25, 27, 88
Fugitive Slave Law, 16
Fugitive Slaves, contraband, 10, 16, 22

INDEX

— G —

Gates, Col. Theodore B., 41, 61
Georgia regiments:
  13th Infantry, 30
  24th Infantry, 106
Germanna Ford, 89
Germanna Plank Road, 90, 92
Getty, Brig. Gen. George W., 103-104, 113
Gettysburg, PA, 39-43, 45, 62, 71
  battle of, 34-81, 97, 120, 122-123, 127-128, 130-132, 134-135
Grant, Lieut. Gen. Ulysses S., 86, 88-92, 95-96, 98, 104, 115, 119, 124
Greeley, Horace, 2, 16, 118
Greene, Brig. Gen., George S., 74-75
Griffin, Brig. Gen. Charles, 86, 91, 94
Grover, Maj. Andrew J., 42, 48, 50-51, 128

— H —

Hall, Capt. James A., 44, 46, 52, 55, 60, 65, 123
Halleck, Maj. Gen. Henry, 24, 115
Hancock, Maj. Gen. Winfield S., 72-74, 80, 86, 91, 98, 100-101, 103-104, 106-108, 113-114, 123-124, 130
Harmon house/farm, 61
Harney, Maj. George, 52, 54, 56, 59, 128
Haskell, Maj. John C., 113
Haviland, Sgt. Edgar, 48, 51
Hay, John, 83, 116
Hays, Brig. Gen. Alexander, 119-120
Henry House Hill, 7
Herbst woodlot/Woods, 45-46, 55, 59-60, 67, 69, 135
Herr Ridge, 44, 48, 62
Heth, Maj. Gen. Henry, 62, 67

Hill, Lieut. Gen. Ambrose P., 33-34, 59, 62, 67, 92, 98, 107
Hitchcock, Maj. Gen. Ethan A., 12, 14
Hofmann, Col. J. William, 42, 48, 77, 110, 126, 128-129
Hooker, Maj. Gen. Joseph, 22-27, 30, 34-38, 40, 80
Howard, Maj. Gen. Oliver O., 24, 38-39, 61, 63, 65, 69, 71, 73-75, 80, 122-123
Humphreys, Maj. Gen. Andrew A., 110, 124
Hunt, Brig. Gen. Henry J., 132
Hunter, Col./Maj. Gen. David, 6-8, 80

— I —

Illinois regiments:
  8th Cavalry, 45
Indiana regiments:
  7th Infantry, 21, 39, 42, 73-74, 77, 86, 94, 119, 126, 128-129
  19th Infantry, 28, 35, 39-40, 42, 44, 67, 72, 86, 97, 126-127, 129
Iron Brigade, *see Meredith's Brigade*

— J —

Jackson, Lieut. Gen. Thomas J., 7, 15, 31, 33, 83
Johnston, Gen. Joseph E., 4, 7-8
Jones's Farm 91, 94

— K —

Kill von Kull, 3
Kneeland, Dr. Benjamin, 113, 116
Kress, Lieut. Col. John A., 9, 16, 28, 39, 42-44, 46, 52, 60, 63, 65, 77, 128

— L —

Lacy House, 90, 95-96, 104
Lamon, Ward Hill, 16
Lee, Gen. Robert E., 23, 25, 27, 33-34, 36-37, 40, 42, 62, 67, 75, 79, 83, 88, 90, 92, 98, 100-101, 107-108, 114, 116, 119, 137-138
Lincoln, Abraham, 2, 12, 14-17, 21, 24, 37, 83, 116, 119-120, 122, 124
Longstreet, Lieut. Gen. James, 6, 23, 31, 34, 39-40, 75, 98, 101, 107-108
Louisiana regiments:
  6th Infantry, 30
Lowry, Pvt. William T., 120
Lyman, Col. Theodore, 89

— Mc —

McClellan, Maj. Gen. George B., 8, 10, 12-15, 17, 19, 22
McCracken, Patrick, 115-116, 136-139
McDowell, Maj. Gen. Irvin, 3-4, 6-8, 10, 14, 19, 118, 125, 132
McPherson farm, 44-46, 56, 63, 69, 97,
McPherson Ridge, 44-46, 48, 51-52, 60-61, 63, 74

— M —

Mahone, Brig. Gen. William, 108
Maine regiments:
  19th Infantry, 110, 112
Manassas, VA, 4, 10, 13-14, 36
Marsh Creek, 39, 41-42
Marshall, Col. Charles, 114
Massachusetts regiments:
  19th Infantry, 27
  20th Infantry, 27, 106
  37th Infantry, 103, 106
  56th Infantry, 98, 104, 114, 137-138
  57th Infantry, 90, 106
Meade, Maj. Gen., George G., 21, 25, 37, 39-40, 42-43, 52, 72, 74-75, 77, 79-81, 83, 85, 88-92, 95, 98, 100, 104, 106-107, 115-116, 119-120, 122-124, 130
Meredith, Brig. Gen. Solomon, 21, 28, 41, 46, 51, 55-56, 60, 67, 74, 126-127, 130-131, 134-135
Michigan regiments:
  1st Cavalry, 115
  7th Infantry, 27
  19th Infantry, 27
  24th Infantry, 21, 25-26, 28, 30, 44, 67, 69, 73, 86, 97, 116, 126-127, 129
Middle Ridge, 45-46, 48, 52, 60, 63, 65, 69
Middletown, MD, 37, 79
Miller, Lieut. Col. Francis C., 42, 46, 52, 54, 126, 128-129
Mills, Capt. Albert M., v, 1, 136
Mississippi regiments:
  2nd Infantry, 48, 51, 59
  42nd Infantry, 51-52, 55-56, 59
Monteith, Capt. Robert, 98, 107-108, 113
Morgan, Gov. Edwin D., 3, 16, 122
Moritz Tavern, 40, 42
Morrow, Col. Henry A., 26, 30, 44, 67, 126-127, 129
Mount St. Mary's College, 38, 41
Mud March, 21-23
Mummasburg Road, 63, 67

— N —

New York regiments:
  1st Dragoons, 113
  8th Cavalry, v, 46
  50th Engineers, 26-27, 30
  6th Heavy Artillery, 98, 100

15th Heavy Artillery, 98, 100
8th Infantry, 7
12th Infantry, 7, 125
14th Brooklyn (84th Infantry), 21, 25, 28, 42, 44-46, 48, 53, 56, 59-61, 63, 65, 69, 71, 75, 77, 86, 97, 125, 128-129, 131
20th Militia (80th Infantry), 8, 41, 61
21st Infantry, 8, 118, 125
22nd Infantry, 28, 125
23rd Infantry, 8, 12, 125
24th Infantry, 26, 28, 125
30th Infantry, 28, 125
35th Infantry, 8
57th Infantry, 116
60th Infantry, 75
76th Infantry, 21, 31, 42-45, 48-49, 52, 60, 65, 69, 81, 89, 101, 110, 123, 126, 128-129
78th Infantry, 74
94th Infantry, 67
95th Infantry, 21, 42, 44-46, 48, 56, 59-60, 77, 86, 101, 126, 128-129, 131
97th Infantry, 65
102nd Infantry, iv, 77
104th Infantry, iv
147th Infantry, iv, 23, 42, 44-46, 51-53, 54-56, 59-60, 65, 69, 73, 75, 77, 86, 97, 101, 123, 126, 128-129
Newton, Maj. Gen. John, 74, 77-80, 122, 131
North Carolina regiments:
  26th Infantry, 69
  55th Infantry, 48, 51

— O —

Oak Hill, 45, 63
Oak Ridge, 45, 51, 56, 60-61, 63, 65, 67, 71, 123, 130-131
Oates, Col. William, 103-104

Orange and Alexandria Railroad, 35
Orange Court House, VA, 88-89, 138
Orange Plank Road, 90-92, 95-97, 100-101, 103-104, 106-108, 110, 113-114, 120, 124, 138
Orange Turnpike, 89-92, 95-96

— P —

Parker's Store, 89-91, 94, 98, 115
Patrick, Brig. Gen. Marsena R., 11, 15
Paul, Brig. Gen. Gabriel, 36, 126
Pennsylvania regiments:
  11th Infantry, 37, 65
  56th Infantry, 21, 28, 35, 38, 42, 44-45, 48, 52, 60, 65, 77, 86, 101, 110, 123, 126, 128-129
  121st Infantry, 39, 86, 97, 129
  142nd Infantry, 86, 129
  143rd Infantry, 86, 96, 129
  149th Infantry, 86, 97, 129
  150th Infantry, 69, 86, 94, 97, 129
  151st Infantry, 67
Perry, Col. William F., 103, 107
Pleasonton, Maj. Gen. Alfred, 34, 80
Poague, Lieut. Col. William T., 101
Port Royal, VA, 23, 25-26
Pye, Col. Edward Pye, 128-130, 135

— R —

Railroad, unfinished, 45, 56, 60, 71
Railroad Cuts
  East, 45, 52, 63, 67, 69
  Middle, 45, 52, 56, 59, 63, 130
  West, 45-46, 52, 56
Rapidan River, 25, 30, 88-89, 120, 124

Rappahannock River, 21, 25, 27-28, 30-31, 34-35, 39

Reynolds, Maj. Gen. John F., 18-19, 21-22, 25, 27-28, 30-31, 33, 35-46, 52, 55, 63, 80, 113, 122-123, 125, 127, 135

Rice, Brig. Gen. John C., 94-95, 101, 104, 129

Robinson, Brig. Gen., John C., 41, 54, 56, 67, 86

Robinson, Col. William W., 67, 73-74, 126-127, 129

Roebling, Col. George W., 92

Rogers, Lieut. Clayton E., 35, 42-43, 55, 59, 71, 73, 81-82, 110, 128, 132, 134-135

Rogers, Lieut. Earl M., 110, 113, 120, 128

Rowley, Brig. Gen. Thomas A., 39-40, 56, 69, 73

— S —

Schurz, Maj. Gen. Carl, 62-63, 71, 74

Scott, Gen. Winfield, 3-4, 6, 12

Sedgwick, Maj. Gen. John, 27, 80, 86, 98, 116

Seminary, Lutheran, 40, 43, 55, 60, 69, 71-72, 130, 135

Seminary Ridge, 40, 44-46, 52, 55, 59, 62, 65, 69, 71, 77, 123, 131, 134

Seward, William H., 2, 16

Seymour, Horatio, 16-17

Sickles, Maj. Gen. Daniel E., 24, 39

Sisters of Charity, 38

Slocum, Maj. Gen. Henry W., 25, 75, 80

Sorrel, Lieut. Col. Moxley L., 108, 110, 121

South Carolina regiments:
1st Infantry, 72
3rd Infantry, 115
8th Infantry, 120
14th Infantry, 72

South Mountain, 37, 42, 79

Spotsylvania Court House, VA, 90, 115-116, 136

Stanton, Edward M., 10, 12-14, 16-18, 24, 81, 83, 85, 115, 119, 122

Steven's Run, 44, 60

Stevens, Capt. Greenleaf T., 72

Stone, Col. Roy, 94-97, 129

Stuart, Maj. Gen. James E. B., 10, 34

Sturgis, Brig. Gen. Samuel D., 15

Sumner, Brig. Gen. Edwin "Bull", 13

— T —

Taneytown, PA, 39

Tapp clearing/farm/house, 100-101, 108, 114

Tennessee regiments:
7th Infantry, 48

Thomas, Adj. Gen. Lorenzo, 14, 24, 83, 85

Tyler, Brig. Gen. Daniel, 4, 6, 12

— U —

Ulster Guard, see 20th NY Militia

Union Defense Committee, 3

United States Ford, 30-31

Upton's Hill, 8, 10, 125

— V —

Virginia regiments:
12th Infantry, 114
42nd Infantry, 73
50th Infantry, 94

INDEX

— W —

Wadsworth, NV, 140-144
Wadsworth, Lieut. Charles F., 24
Wadsworth, Lieut./Capt. Craig W., 8-9, 18, 55, 73, 86-87, 104, 107, 113, 120, 135
Wadsworth, James S.
  Gettysburg monument, iv-v
  education, 1
  marriage and children, 1
  opposition to slavery, 2, 10, 15, 22, 122
  joins Republican Party, 2
  aide to McDowell, 3-8
  action at First Bull Run, 6-8
  commissioned brigadier, 8
  brigade on Upton's Hill, 8-11
  foraging parties, 10, 22
  as seen by officers and enlisted men, 11, 14-15, 19, 21-22, 27-28, 30, 38-39, 52, 55, 63, 73-77, 86, 89, 96, 106, 113-116, 118-119
  Military Governor of Washington, 12-16, 136-139
  problems with McClellan, 10, 12-14, 17
  enforcement of Fugitive Slave Law, 15-16
  relationship with Stanton, 12-13, 16, 18, 24, 81, 85
  with Lincoln, 15-16, 24, 83
  1862 governor's campaign, 16-18
  rejoins Army of the Potomac, 19
  assumes First Division command, 19
  stops mutiny, 26-27
  crossing at Fitzhugh's, 26-30
  at Chancellorsville, 30-31
  march to Gettysburg, 34-36, 40-43
  concern for his men, 14-15, 21-24, 31, 36-38, 42, 73, 79, 81, 85, 89
  First Corps reorganization, 36
  fighting at Gettysburg
    July 1, 1863, 41-74, 130-135
    July 2, 1863, 74-77
    July 3, 1863, 77
  pursuit of Lee, 79-80
  resignation, 81
  new assignment, 83-85
  rejoins Army of the Potomac, 85
  Fifth Corps divisional command, 85-86
  enters the Wilderness, 88-90
  fighting in the Wilderness
    May 5, 1864, 90-97
    May 6, 1864, 98-110
  mortally wounded and captured, 110-114, 137
  death in Confederate hospital, 114-115, 136-138
  recovery of body, 115-116
  mourning in Washington and New York, 116-118, 139
  burial, 118, 136
  major general 119
  effectiveness as a general officer, 86, 122-124
Wadsworth, James W., iv, vi, 1, 87
Wadsworth, James W. Jr., iv, vi, 112
Wadsworth, Mary Craig (Wharton), 1, 86, 119, 121, 136
Wainwright, Col. Charles S., 18-19, 22, 28, 55, 60-61, 65, 69, 74-76, 86, 89, 113, 135
Warren, Maj. Gen. Gouverneur K., 80, 85-86, 89, 91-92, 94-98, 100, 107, 110, 113, 120, 128
Warrenton Turnpike, 6-7
Washington, DC, 12, 18, 35, 37, 83, 85, 116
  Military District of, 12-15
Webb, Brig. Gen. Alexander S., 103-104, 106, 108, 110, 112
Weld, Capt. Stephen M., 35, 43
Wheaton, Brig. Gen. Frank, 103-104

INDEX

Whipple, Brig. Gen. Amiel W., 119-120
Wilderness, battle of, 88-118, 120-121, 124, 128-129, 136, 138
Wilderness, region of, 88-90, 94-95, 97, 100-101, 104, 106, 136, 138
Wilderness Tavern (Old), 89-90, 98, 104
Willoughby Run, 48, 60-61
Wisconsin regiments:
  2nd Infantry, 7, 22, 28, 30, 44, 46, 69, 97, 126-127, 129, 131
  6th Infantry, 22, 26, 28, 30, 35, 44, 55-56, 59, 61, 63, 69, 73, 75, 77, 120, 122, 126-127, 129-132, 134-135
  7th Infantry, 26, 28, 30, 35, 44, 67, 71, 126-127, 129
Woods, Pvt. John P., 35